MW01027610

MAIMONIDES

PIRKEI AVOT

with a commentary and introduction by the Rambam

MAIMONIDES
PIRKEI AVOT

with the Rambam's commentary

including
Shemoneh Perakim
the Rambam's classic work of ethics
and Maimonides' introduction to *Perek Chelek*
which contains his 13 Principles of Faith

A new translation with notes

by
Rabbi Eliyahu Touger

MOZNAIM PUBLISHING CORPORATION
NEW YORK / JERUSALEM

רמב"ם
פרקי אבות
עם פרוש המשניות של הרמב"ם

הכולל

שמונה פרקים
שהם חיבורו הנודע על מדות
הקדמת הרמב"ם לפרק חלק

תורגם מחדש לאנגלית
עם מקורות והערות

מאת
הרב אליהו תגר

בית הוצאת ספרים
מאזנים
ירושלים – ניו יארק
תשנ"ד

For information write:
Moznaim Publishing Corporation
4304 12th Avenue
Brooklyn, New York 11219
Tel. (718) 438-7680, 853-0525

ISBN: 0-940118-98-X

Printed and bound in Jerusalem, Israel
by Vagshal Ltd.
Typesetting by Vagshal Ltd.
Jerusalem
plates by Frank, Jerusalem

Printed in Israel

TABLE OF CONTENTS

Shemoneh Perakim - The Rambam's Introduction
to the Tractate of *Avot*

Pirkei Avot - The Ethics of Our Fathers

Appendices

Introduction

This volume contains the very fundamentals of Jewish faith and ethics, including the Rambam's Thirteen Principles of Faith, *Shemoneh Perakim* - his classic work of ethics, and his commentary to *Pirkei Avot*. In these works, the Rambam outlines his fundamental set of beliefs and his guidelines for purpose-oriented life in clear and succinct terms. Conscious that his ideas are unique, and unabashed by the criticism they might draw, the Rambam challenges his readers to think objectively, and to have their thoughts control their deeds.

* * *

Originally, this project was conceived as a translation of the Rambam's Commentary to *Pirkei Avot*. *Avot* is studied by many in the summer months, and the Rambam's approach of balanced, thoughtful life provides a valuable asset to a reader who seriously considers the concepts of personal development mentioned in this tractate.

Together with *Pirkei Avot*, we included *Shemoneh Perakim*, the Rambam's introduction to his commentary in which he crystallizes his conception of character growth, explaining in a systematic way, the nature of our personal makeup, and how we can control our conduct, and make it more productive.

Since *Avot* is studied primarily as is customary on Sabbath afternoons during summer, we appended three additional elements to the text that enable this text to be used in observance of this custom:

a) the sixth chapter of *Pirkei Avot* as printed in the *Siddurim*. This chapter is not part of the *Mishnah*, but rather a collection of *bereitot* added by our Rabbis to allow one chapter to be studied on each of the six Sabbaths between Pesach and Shavuot. There is no commentary by the Rambam to this chapter.

b) the Rambam's introduction to the Tenth Chapter of *Sanhedrin, Perek Chelek*. This introduction is based on the *mishnah*, "All Israel have a share in the World to Come," which according to custom is studied as a preface to each chapter of *Pirkei Avot* during the summer.

c) the *mishnah*, "Rabbi Chananiah ben Akasha says..." and the Rambam's commentary to this teaching from the tractate of *Makkot*, for this *mishnah* is customarily studied after each chapter of *Pirkei Avot.*

We have not included the Hebrew texts of the Rambam's commentary or introductions, only that of *Pirkei Avot.* Our rationale is that, in contrast to the *Mishneh Torah,* the Rambam did not compose his Commentary on the Mishnah in Hebrew, but rather in Arabic. The Hebrew versions that exist are translations, and there are differences of opinion regarding which translation is more accurate. We used both the translations of Ibn Tibben and Rav Kapach, but since these are not the Rambam's own words, we did not feel that it was imperative that either of these texts be included in this volume.

*   *   *

When presenting classic works of this nature, a writer feels a natural tendency to provide extensive commentary to highlight the points of relevance and compare the Rambam's approach with that of other thinkers. This tendency was, nevertheless, restrained. Partially, the reason was the justified humility one feels in coupling one's own ideas with those of the Rambam. And even more than that, our desire was to showcase the Rambam's ideas - to provide our readers with the opportunity to focus on his thoughts as he presented them without being diverted by other concepts. We have, however, added references, and brief explanations in certain places.

*   *   *

One of the fundamental ethical values is the need for a person to rise above his own personal nature, and join with others in purposeful action. For the benefits produced by such synergism far exceed the contributions which any individual can make on his own. This principle was put into practice in the composition of this text; it was a team effort, made possible by the combined efforts of many individuals.

The full list of all those involved is too long to mention. At the very least, however, recognition must be granted to the following individuals:

Rabbi Moshe Weiner for checking the sources and the accuracy of the translation;

Ira L. Jacobson for his editorial contributions;

Hinda Esther Baruch for proofreading;

Avraham Eisenbach, Dov Schwartz, Michah Witzel, and the entire staff

of Moznaim publications for the graphics and layout, which greatly enhance the text;
Finally, my publishers, Rabbis Chanoch and Menachem Wagshall, whose cooperation, support and dedication to the spread of Torah have made working with them a pleasure.

*   *   *

The ultimate expression of personal development will be in the Era of the Redemption, when to quote the conclusion of the Rambam's *Mishneh Torah*: "there will be neither envy, nor competition,... and the occupation of the entire world will be solely to know God."
We cannot, however, postpone our efforts toward personal development until the coming of that era. Moreover, the Era of the Redemption will be brought closer by our efforts to develop our characters, and join in positive relationships with others. May the publication of this work contribute to this goal, and hasten the coming of that era.

Tevet 20, the Rambam's yahrzeit,   *Rabbi Eliyahu Touger*
                                                                          5754, Jerusalem

THE RAMBAM'S INTRODUCTION TO THE TRACTATE OF AVOT

SHEMONEH PERAKIM

PREFACE

In the introduction to [the Commentary on the Mishnah], we explained the reason the redactor [of the Mishnah] chose to include this tractate in the Order [of *Nezikin*].[1] Also, on several occasions in this text, we have promised to discuss constructive matters with regard to this tractate and to elaborate upon them. Although [this tractate is short and][2] its meaning appears straightforward and easy to comprehend, the application of its teachings is not easy at all. Moreover, certain elements cannot be comprehended without adequate explanation. In addition, its [insights] bring a person to a high level of fulfillment and true happiness. Therefore, I have chosen to elaborate upon it.

[Our Sages,] may they rest in peace, state,[3] "A person who desires to be pious should apply the teachings of *Avot*." There is no attribute greater than piety except prophecy, and [indeed,] piety leads to prophecy, as [our Sages] say,[4] "Piety leads to the spirit of Divine inspiration." From their statement, it follows that conducting oneself according to the ethical teachings of this tractate will lead to prophecy. [Accordingly,] I will explain the truth of these matters, for [this tractate] embodies a large portion of the [desirable] character traits.

1. "After he completed [in the previous tractates,] the discussion of everything that a judge requires, he began *Avot*. There are two reasons why he chose [this order]: a) To make known the integrity of the Oral Tradition... so that a person should not say, 'Why should we accept the judgment rendered by so and so?'.... For the judgment was not authored by this particular judge, but by God.... And it is one law that has been passed down from person to person throughout the generations.

"b) To communicate the ethical teachings of each of our Sages so that we can ascertain eminent character traits from them. Judges are in greater need of this than are people at large. If the general public do not learn ethics, the harm is minimal, for they will injure themselves alone. When, however, a judge is neither ethical nor virtuous, he destroys the entire nation...."
2. This phrase has been placed in brackets because, although it is included in the standard published text of the Rambam's Commentary on the Mishnah, it is not found in many of the authoritative manuscripts.
3. *Bava Kama* 30a.
4. *Avodah Zarah* 20b.

Before I begin to explain each law [in the Mishnah individually], I thought it beneficial to include as a preface several chapters to help a person grasp axiomatic principles that will serve as a key to [the comprehension of] the concepts to be explained.

Take note - the concepts stated in these chapters and the forthcoming explanations are not new concepts that I have invented. They are, rather, an anthology of the words of our Sages from the *Midrashim,* the Talmud and other sources, the works of philosophers of the early and later generations, and many other texts. Accept the truth [regardless of] which person said it.[5]

There are times when I will quote an entire concept from a well known text. I mean no harm [in doing so]. I am not trying to claim as my own, insights authored by my predecessors. [On the contrary,] I admit that even when I do not mention my sources [the statements are not original].

[I have chosen not to mention my sources for two reasons:] a) because this prolongs the text without any advantage. b) By mentioning the name of an author of whom a particular reader might not approve, I might cause him [to reject the concept, thinking] that it is harmful and that it contains an undesirable intent. For this reason, I have chosen to omit the name of the author. For my intent is to benefit the reader and to explain the concepts concealed within this tractate.

I will now begin the chapters that I regard as necessary introductions to achieve the above purpose. There are eight [such] chapters.

---

5. With this statement, the Rambam appears to referring to the fact that some of the sources he used were composed by gentiles. Note his statements in the *Mishneh Torah* (*Hilchot Kiddush HaChodesh* 17:24): "Since these concepts can be proven in an unshakable manner, leaving no room for question; the identity of the author, be he a prophet or a gentile, is of no concern. When the rationale of a matter... has proven truthful in an unshakable manner, we do not rely on [the personal authority] of the person who made these statements..., but on the proofs he has presented."

CHAPTER ONE

ON THE SOUL AND ITS POWERS

Know that the soul of a person is a single entity and it has many means of expression. Some of these expressions [because they are general in scope] are referred to by certain individuals as "souls." Thus, some individuals think that there are many souls. [For example,] the most eminent physician[1] begins [his work] with the statement that there are three souls: the natural soul, the vital soul and the spiritual soul.

Some of these [expressions of the soul] are referred to as powers and others as elements - thus the term, "the elements of the soul." These terms are employed by many philosophers. By using the term "elements," their intent is not that [the soul] divides into actual parts as do material entities. Rather, they are listing the different expressions of the soul, whose relationship to the soul as a totality resembles that of a whole and its composite parts.

You surely know that the development of [our] character traits is nothing but the healing of the soul and its powers. A physician who heals a physical body must first have general knowledge about the body and must be aware of the various elements of human anatomy. He must also know the causes of illness and should distance himself from them, and know the various medications and apply them.

Similar concepts apply with regard to one who desires to heal the soul and refine its character traits. He must first know the soul in all its dimensions and its elements, what causes its maladies, and what heals it.

There are five elements of the soul: [one that governs] nutrition, [one that governs] sensation, [one that governs] imagination, [one that governs] stimulation and [one that governs] conceptualization. As mentioned previously in this chapter, we are concerned only with [the function of these elements within] the human soul. For the power that governs human nutrition differs from the powers governing the

1. I.e., Hippocrates.

nutrition of a horse or a donkey. For man's nutrition stems from the nutritive faculty in the human soul, while a donkey, by contrast, derives its nutrition from the nutritive faculty in the donkey's soul. Similarly, a palm tree[2] derives its nutrition from the nutritive faculty in its own soul.

When the term nutrition is applied to all these various forms, the intent is to employ a general term, although the subject is not, in fact, the same. Similarly, when the term sensation is used with regard to both a human being and an animal, the intent again is to employ a general term, and not to imply that sensation is the same within a man as within a horse. Nor is the power of sensation of any one species the same as another's. Rather, every life form that possesses a soul has a unique soul, different from that of every other life form. As a result, each of these types of soul will have expressions. There are those who will compare the expressions of two [different souls] and consider them the same, but this is not so.

To illustrate by means of analogy: there were three dark places. Into one the light of the sun shone and illuminated it. The second was illuminated by the moon; and in the third, a candle was lit and shone forth. In all three, light is found, but in one the light is caused by the sun, in the other by the moon, and in the third by a candle.

[In the analogy,] the factor that causes human sensation is the human soul. The factor that causes a donkey to feel sensation is the donkey's soul, and the vulture's sensation stems from the vulture's soul. These [different types of sensation] share no common factor except the term used to describe them. This concept is of fundamental importance. Many philosophers have erred regarding this matter, and accordingly have developed strange conceptions and ideas that are in error.

To return to the discussion of the elements of the soul: The element governing nutrition includes the powers of ingestion, storing food, digestion, excretion, growth, reproduction, and the power that distinguishes between the fluids necessary for nutrition and those to be excreted. A description of these seven powers, in which manner and how they function, with which organs is their function more distinct and obvious, what are their constant activities and their infrequent activities - [this knowledge] is necessary for the practice of medicine, but is not of present concern.

2. Our translation is based on Rav Kapach's text. The standard published text states "an eagle." This raises a question of more general scope: Does the Rambam describe the life force of a plant as a soul or not?

The element [governing] sensation is the source of the five senses: sight, sound, taste, smell and touch. [The latter sense is] found throughout the body and does not have specific organs [that control it], as do [the other] four senses.

The element of imagination: this power [relates to the faculty of memory and makes it possible to] recall the impression of various incidents after they are no longer perceptible by the senses. [This faculty can also] combine and separate different [recollections]. Thus, this power has the potential to develop [a notion] that was never thought of previously and that cannot be understood, based on one's previous perception. For example, one might imagine an iron ship flying through the air, or a man with his head in the heavens and his feet on the earth, a beast with one thousand eyes and the like. Many impossible things of this nature can be conceived by the power of imagination.

In this matter, the sect of *medabrim*[3] erred grossly and established a false foundation with regard to the distinctions concerning what must exist, what may exist and what cannot exist. For they thought - or imagined - that anything that could be imagined [by a person] could actually exist. They did not realize that this power has the potential of making a combination of various matters that cannot possibly exist, as explained above.

The element [that governs] stimulation is the power that attracts or repels a person from an entity. The actions this power will inspire are seeking, fleeing, the appreciation of a particular entity or the rejection of it, anger, desire, fear, courage, cruelty, mercy, love, hate and many other emotional states.

The vessels that express these [various] actions are the limbs and organs. For example, the action of the hands is motion, the action of the feet is walking, the action of the eyes is sight, and the action of the heart is either courage or fear. Similarly, the other organs and limbs of the body and their actions are vessels that express this power of stimulation.

The element [that governs] conceptualization is the power granted to man[4] that enables him to think and to contemplate. With this power, he acquires knowledge and distinguishes positive activities from

3. A sect of Arab philosophers. The root of the word *medaber* is *dabber* (speak). The name *medaber* was given to this sect because its members perfected the technique of philosophic dialogue. (See the Rambam's statements concerning them in the Guide for the Perplexed, Volume I, Chapter 73.)
4. I.e., in contrast to other creatures.

undesirable ones. The term "activities" refers to both the applied and the abstract realms.

The applied realm involves both actual and intellectual activities. The abstract realm, by contrast, involves the study of entities that are unchanging; this study is referred to as wisdom.

By actual activities, we refer to the power with which we learn vocations - e.g., carpentry, agriculture, medicine and seafaring. The intellectual activities involve the consideration of whether or not it is possible to perform a particular task that he desires when he desires; and if it is possible, whether or not it is proper to perform it. The above suffices for a description of the soul that is appropriate for this text.

Know that this one soul, whose powers and elements have been described above, can be compared to matter, for which intellect serves as form.[5] When [the soul] is not given form [through intellect], it will be as if the preparation [of the soul] to receive a form was for naught, and that its existence will lack substance.

This is implied by the verse,[6] "Even without knowledge, the soul [exists], [but] it is not good." This means that if [the soul] has not grasped its form, but it remains a soul without knowledge, it is not good. Nevertheless, a discussion of the definition of form, matter and intellect and how they are acquired is not in place here. For this text is devoted to [a study of our] character traits. The subject matter mentioned above is more appropriate for the Book of Prophecy[7] that we mentioned. This concludes this chapter and [lays the foundation for] the next.

5. In this context, it is worthwhile to refer to the Rambam's statements in *Hilchot Yesodei HaTorah* 4:8-9:

> The soul of all flesh is the form which it was given by God. The extra dimension that is found in the soul of man is the form of man that is perfect in its knowledge. Concerning this form, the Torah states [Genesis 1:26]: 'Let us make man in our image and in our likeness' - i.e., granting man a form that knows and comprehends ideas that are not material....
> [This verse] does not refer to the form of the body perceived by the eye... [or] the soul found in all living flesh that allows it to eat, drink, reproduce, feel and think, but rather to knowledge, for it is the form of the soul....
> The form of this soul is not a combination of the fundamental [elements] into which it will ultimately decompose, nor does it come from the [vital] soul.... Rather, it is from God... it knows and comprehends knowledge that is above matter, knows the Creator of all things and exists forever.

(See also *Hilchot Teshuvah* 8:5.)

. Proverbs 19:2.
. In his introduction to the tenth chapter of the tractate of *Sanhedrin*, the Rambam mentions his desire to compose a text concerning prophecy. Although he never actually composed such a text, he prepared material for it and subsequently used that material when composing the Guide for the Perplexed.

CHAPTER TWO

THE NATURE OF THE SOUL'S POWERS; DEFINING THE ELEMENTS WHERE [BOTH] POSITIVE AND UNDESIRABLE QUALITIES ARE FOUND

Know that the observance of the Torah's [directives] or the rebellion [against them] involves only two of the soul's elements: the element [that governs] sensation and the element [that governs] stimulation. All the mitzvot and all transgressions concern these two elements.

With regard to the element [that governs] nutrition and the element [that governs] imagination, there is no concept of observance or rebellion. For thought and will do not affect them at all. A person cannot willfully stop or limit these activities, as reflected by the fact that, in contrast to the soul's other potentials, these two elements - that [governing] nutrition and that [governing] imagination - are active during sleep.

With regard to the element [that governs] conceptualization, there is confusion [as to whether or not the concept of mitzvah or sin applies]. I maintain that it is possible to identify [areas where the concepts of] observance and rebellion - e.g., the belief in a defective idea or the belief in a true idea - apply. There is, however, no deed [associated with this element] that one can refer to as a mitzvah or a sin. Therefore, I have stated above that the aspects of sin and mitzvah apply only with regard to the two categories mentioned.

[Man possesses] two types of positive virtues - intellectual virtues and ethical virtues - and conversely, two types of failings. The intellectual virtues relate to the element of conceptualization. They include:

a) wisdom - i.e., the knowledge of the immediate and distant causes for an entity that we are investigating;[1]

b) intellect - i.e., abstract thought. This is an innate quality. [It refers to] the basic comprehension of an idea. Acquired knowledge stems

---

1. See also the Guide for the Perplexed, Vol. I, Chapter 54.

`rom it. This is not the place for [a detailed discussion of] this issue; and
ɔ) clarity of understanding, the ability to perceive concepts immediately, ɔr at least quickly.

The failings associated with this power are the converse [of these positive virtues].

The ethical virtues relate to the element [governing] stimulation alone. The element [governing] sensation is subsidiary to the element [governing] stimulation in this regard. There are very many positive traits associated with this quality; among them: discipline, generosity, justice, patience, humility, contentment,[2] courage and sensitivity. The undesirable qualities in this element reflect instances where these qualities are diminished or increased.[3]

It is, by contrast, malapropos to say that the elements [that govern] nutrition and imagination have virtues or failings. Rather, it is proper to say that they operate effectively, or ineffectively. For example, one might say, "so and so's digestion is good," or "it is ineffective or impaired." Similarly, one might say that a person's imagination is impaired, or that it works effectively. But in this regard, there is no concept of virtue or failing. This concludes the subject matter intended for this chapter.

2. The standard published texts of the Rambam's Commentary on the Mishnah state, "wealth, as our Sages (*Avot* 4:1) state: 'Who is rich? One who is content with his portion.'" The authoritative manuscripts of the Rambam's Commentary do not contain this elaboration.

3. This concept is further explained in Chapter 4 of this text, and the first chapter of *Hilchot De'ot*. The Rambam explains that the ideal ethical attributes are the middle path, and that deviating from the mean, to the side of increase or decrease, reflects improper conduct.

CHAPTER THREE

SPIRITUAL ILLNESS

The [philosophers of] the earlier generations declared that just a
the body has states of illness and health, so too, the soul has states o
illness and health.

The soul is healthy when its tendencies and those of its elements lead
to good, kind conduct and pleasant deeds. Illness reflects a state when
it and its elements lead to evil conduct, damage, and reproachable acts
[Here we will not discuss] the health and the illness of the body, fo
that is the domain of the science of medicine.

[Nevertheless, physical illness can serve as an analogy.[1]] When people
are ill, their senses are confused and they taste the sweet as bitter, and
the bitter as sweet. They consider things that are pleasurable to be
disagreeable, and will powerfully desire - and will derive pleasure from
- things that will not gratify the healthy at all. Moreover, [at times,]
their conduct will even be harmful - e.g., they will eat soap, charcoal,
dust, or very bitter and sour objects that a healthy person not only
would not desire, but would be disgusted by.

Similarly, [in the analogy,] those with ailments of the soul, the
wicked and the unworthy, will consider the undesirable to be good,
and the good to be undesirable. For the wicked will seek motives that
are in fact evil, and yet, because of the infirmity of his spirit, he will
deem them to be good.

When an ill person becomes aware of his illness and he does not
know the science of medicine, he seeks a physician to instruct him
with regard to the course of action to follow. [The physician] will
warn him against those things that he considers to be pleasant and
will force him to take medicines that [even though they] are bitter and
distasteful, will cure the body. This will enable him to choose the good
[in the future] and to be repelled by what is [truly] repulsive.

1. See also *Hilchot De'ot* 2:1, where the Rambam employs the same analogy to explain
the concept that follows. See also the Jerusalem Talmud, *Ta'anit* 1:1.

Similarly, in the analogy, it is proper for those who have spiritual ailments to seek out the wise, who heal souls, who will warn them against the evils that they consider to be good, and will heal them through activities that heal the character traits of the soul, as will be explained in the following chapter.

Those people who have spiritual ailments, but who do not appreciate them and consider themselves to be healthy, or who do appreciate them but will not be cured, will surely perish, as would an ill person who follows his desires without being cured.

With regard to those who are aware [of the base nature of their conduct] and yet persist, as the Torah of truth says,[2] "to add satisfaction to thirst." I.e., he intends to satisfy his thirst, but instead, he merely adds to it.

And with regard to those who are unaware of [their infirmity], King Solomon said,[3] "The way of the crooked is straight in his eyes, and he who listens to advice is wise" - i.e., one who listens to the advice of the wise becomes wise himself, for they will show him the true path and not the path that they guess is true. And he says,[4] "There is a way that appears right to a person, but ultimately its ways are death." And also with regard to those people who are spiritually ill and who do not know what will benefit them and what will harm them, it is said,[5] "The path of the wicked is like darkness; they do not know over what they will stumble."

The craft of curing souls will be described in the fourth chapter.

2. Deuteronomy 29:18.
3. Proverbs 12:15.
4. *Ibid.* 14:12.
5. *Ibid.* 4:19.

CHAPTER FOUR

HEALING THE SPIRITUALLY ILL

Good conduct is conduct that is balanced between two extremes, each of which is unfavorable: one is excess and the other restriction. [Personal] virtue refers to tendencies and habits that are equally balanced between the bad tendencies of excess and restriction. For from one's character traits comes one's conduct.

For example, restraint is the intermediate quality between indulgence and the lack of any feelings of desire. Thus, restraint is a positive activity. The character trait that leads to restraint is a positive character trait.

Gluttonous desire, by contrast, is one extreme, and the lack of desire is another extreme, both of which are utterly undesirable. They stem from the character traits of excess and restriction, respectively, and represent two of the inferior qualities.

Similarly, generosity is the median between stinginess and profligacy. Assurance is the median between rashness and timidity. Good-naturedness is the median between aggressiveness and shyness.[1] Humility is the median between pride and lowliness. Modesty is the median between ostentatiousness and ignobility. Self-content is the median between greed and indolence. Patience is the median between anger and insensitivity. Reservation is the median between impudence and reticence. Similar concepts apply with regard to other emotional traits. The names we have used for these traits are not significant; what is important is for the concept as a whole to be understood.[2]

1. Our translation follows Rav Kapach's version of the text. The standard published text follows a different order and contains explanations that are not found in the authoritative manuscripts.
2. The Rambam is referring to the fact that he has translated terms used by Greek philosophers into Arabic, and in doing so, found difficulty in finding precise synonyms. It must be added that his translators encountered similar difficulties in rendering the Arabic terms into Hebrew (and this translator in rendering the Hebrew into English). What he - and his translators - were concerned with was not to focus on

Many people err with regard to these forms of conduct, thinking that either of the extremes is desirable. For example, when they see a rash individual who is willing to risk danger, who enters perilous situations on the chance that he will be able to escape, they praise him and call this courage. And there are others who designate the insensitive as patient and the indolent as self-content. Similarly, they might refer to a person who is frigid and passionless by nature as restrained. Also, this mistaken approach might consider lavishness and boastfulness as praiseworthy conduct.

This is all an error. The intermediate path is what is praiseworthy; it should be the path to which a person should aspire and according to which he should direct his conduct.

Know that positive and negative character traits are acquired and reinforced solely through the repetition of the types of conduct that stem from these traits, [repeating these deeds] numerous times over an extended period of time. When a person habituates himself to positive conduct, he will acquire the virtues [that motivate] it. And when he habituates himself to undesirable conduct, he will acquire these faults. For, as will be explained in Chapter 8, at the outset a person's nature is neither virtuous nor faulty. But as he matures, he develops habits according to those of his family and those of the people around him.

At times, [these habits train] him to conduct himself according to the median. And at times, he may conduct himself according to the extremes, as we mentioned. And then his soul will develop an infirmity. [To heal himself,] he should emulate the example followed when healing the body; i.e., when the balance of the body deviates to one extreme, one should [intentionally compel] it to the other until an equilibrium is established. Once he reaches equilibrium, he should turn away from the other extreme and return to persistently follow the path that will enable him to maintain his equilibrium. This approach should be followed with regard to all the emotional traits.

For example, we see a person who has already developed miserly qualities. This is one of the undesirable character traits that leads to improper conduct, as explained previously in this chapter. If we want to heal this person, we should not instruct him to conduct himself with generosity. This would be like trying to use a balanced [remedy] to heal someone whose nature has been overcome with warmth. This would not

the terminology, but to show the importance of moderation and of balancing one's conduct between extremes.

cure his affliction. Rather, we should instruct him to spend freely time after time, repeating free-spending conduct until he has driven from his soul the character traits that led him to miserly conduct. [Indeed, he should continue] almost to the point that he has acquired the nature of a free spender. At that point, he should abandon free spending, and we should instruct him to follow [the median of] generosity consistently, showing neither excess nor deficiency.

Similarly, if we see him behaving like a spendthrift, we should instruct him to conduct himself frequently as a miser. But there is no need to repeat miserly conduct as frequently as mentioned above with regard to free-spending. This point is a fundamental principle of healing and is its secret: it is easier for a person to return to [the median,] generosity, from free-spending than for him to return to generosity from miserliness.

Similarly, it is easier to return from a lack of desire to [the median of] restraint than to return from overindulgence to restraint. Therefore, we will instruct the overindulgent to repeat acts that show a lack of desire more frequently than is necessary for a person who lacks desire, to perform acts of indulgence. Similarly, we will instruct the timid to act rashly more frequently than the rash to act timidly, and the ignoble to display ostentation more frequently than the ostentatious must practice ignobility. This is [an important] principle with regard to curing [disorders within] character traits. Remember it.

For this reason, the pious would not [necessarily] direct their character traits to the median, but rather would bend slightly in the direction of excess or deficiency as a safeguard.[3] For example, a person would deviate slightly from restraint to a lack of desire, from assurance to rashness slightly, or from modesty to ostentatiousness slightly, or from humility to lowliness slightly. The same applies with regard to the other character traits. [Our Sages] alluded to this in their [emphasis on going] "beyond the measure of the law."[4]

At times, some of the pious have deviated toward an extreme at certain times by fasting, giving up sleep at night, refraining from

---

3. See *Hilchot De'ot* 1:5, where the Rambam develops similar concepts. Both the pious and a person of underdeveloped character deviate from the norm and tend to an extreme. The difference between them is that the deviation of the pious is carefully calculated, with the intent of refining his personality. An underdeveloped person, by contrast, deviates out of whim, without thought, as a natural response to his fancies.

4. *Berachot* 7a *et al.*

eating meat or drinking wine, shunning women, wearing [coarse] wool and sackcloth, living on mountains, or seeking solitude in the deserts. These [deeds] were performed to correct [their conduct, as explained above], or because of the degenerate nature of the people in their city - i.e., they saw that dealing with them and seeing their deeds impaired their [own conduct], and they feared that their character traits would also be corrupted through a relationship with them. Therefore, they departed from [these societies] to dwell in the deserts where there are no wicked people, as the prophet says,[5] "Would that I be granted a lodging place... in the desert."

[Nevertheless,] when the fools saw the pious perform the above activities, they did not comprehend their intent, and thought that the activities were good in their own right.[6] They began to emulate the behavior [of the pious], thinking that through this they would become like them, [attaining inner refinement]. [With this intent,] they began afflicting their bodies through many different types of penance, thinking that they had reached peaks [of divine service], and that this brings them close to God, as if God were the enemy of the body and desired to destroy and crush it.

They do not realize that these deeds are bad, and that they will lead a person to undesirable character traits. To use an analogy: They are like people who are untrained in medicine, who see an experienced physician administer potions of coloquintida, scammonial and aloe[7] to patients who are dangerously ill, and prevent them from eating ordinary food. [Through these herbs,] these patients were healed and saved from great danger.

These fools, however, jumped to the conclusion that if these foods could heal the ill, they could surely maintain and enhance the wellbeing of the healthy. Therefore, they began to use them at all times and to follow [the diet] of the ill.

---

5. Jeremiah 9:1. The conclusion of this verse: "And I will leave my people and go from them, for they are all adulterers, a faithless band," indicates that the Rambam is not merely borrowing Biblical phraseology. He is citing a verse that addresses itself specifically to the problem of living within a corrupt society.

See *Hilchot De'ot* 6:1, where the Rambam also cites this proof-text and states that we are obligated to leave cities and countries whose societies could corrupt our conduct. (See also *Iggeret HaSh'mad* where this subject is discussed.)

6. I.e., they did not appreciate that this extreme conduct was merely a means to an end. They considered it to be proper in its own right.

7. Our translation of these terms is taken from Rav Kapach's notes.

[Such a person] will surely become ill. Similarly, such people will become spiritually ill from using remedies while they are healthy. Our perfect Torah leads to our fulfillment, as one who knew it states,[8] "God's Torah is perfect, granting wisdom to the foolish, restoring the soul." [It] does not command us to follow any of these paths. Rather, it desires that man should live naturally, following the middle path, eating a moderate portion of food that he is permitted to eat, drinking a moderate portion of what he is permitted to drink, engaging in permitted sexual relations in a moderate way, and creating a society [based on] righteousness and justice.

He need not live in caves or on mountains, nor wear sackcloth and [coarse] wool. There is no need to weary the body, or to drain it or oppress it. Our Oral Tradition[9] has warned us against [such an approach in its interpretation of the Torah's indictment of] a Nazirite as one who "sinned against [his] soul."[10] Our Sages ask: How did the person "sin against his soul"? They explain: "He held himself back from [drinking] wine." Can we not extrapolate from this? If a person who refrains from drinking wine needs atonement, surely this would apply to one who holds himself back from involvement in other worldly things.

Similarly, the words of our prophets and the conduct of our Torah Sages [highlights] the importance of following the median and protecting one's life and body as the Torah obligates us. Indeed, when [the people] asked Zechariah whether they should continue to fast for one day each year: "Should I weep in the fifth month, abstaining as I have done for several years?"[11] God replied through His prophet:[12] "When you fasted in the fifth month and in the seventh month for these seventy years, have you fasted for Me? And when you eat and drink, is it for yourselves that you are eating and drinking?"

He commanded them to follow the median and [to seek to acquire] virtues, not to fast, saying [13] "Thus spoke the God of hosts: 'Execute true justice; and show kindness and mercy each man to his brother.'"

8. Psalms 19:8.
9. *Ta'anit* 11a; *Nedarim* 10a *et al.*
10. Numbers 6:11.
11. Zechariah 7:3. I.e., the people were asking whether should they continue to observe the fast of Tish'ah B'Av, which commemorates the Temple's destruction.
12. *Ibid.* 7:5-6.
13. *Ibid.* 7:9.

And subsequently, he said:[14] "Thus spoke the God of hosts: 'The
fast of the fourth month, the fast of the fifth month, the fast of
the seventh month, and the fast of the tenth month will be festivals
and [days of] rejoicing and happiness for the house of Judah. Love
truth and peace.'" Truth refers to the intellectual virtues, for they are
true and unchanging, as we mentioned in the second chapter. Peace
refers to the ethical virtues, for they will lead to peace in the world.
[These - peace and truth - and not fasts - are everlasting values.]

To return to our subject: If those of our faith whose conduct
resembles that of the gentiles[15] protest and say that my words do
not apply to them - that they are afflicting their bodies and refraining
from pleasure for the purpose of training their bodies' powers to
be inclined in a [desired] direction - as is proper for a person, and
as explained previously in this chapter, they are making a mistake,
as will be explained.

For the prohibitions of the Torah and its commandments stem from
this [principle]: to move further away from one extreme in order to
improve [one's nature].[16] [The purpose of] all the prohibitions against
forbidden foods, the prohibition against forbidden sexual relations
and relations with a harlot, and the obligation of a marriage contract,
the sanctification of the marriage bond, and the fact that [a person]
is not permitted [to have relations with his wife] at all times, [this]

---

14. *Ibid.* 8:19.
15. I.e., Jewish ascetics, whose conduct resembles the ascetic practices followed by
Christians and Moslems.
16. In the light of this statement and those that follow, it is worthwhile to refer to the
Rambam's statements at the conclusion of *Hilchot Temurah*:

Although all the statutes of the Torah are [Divine] decrees, it is proper to
contemplate them, as mentioned at the conclusion of *Hilchot Me'ilah*; whenever
it is possible to provide a reason, one should.... The majority of the laws
of the Torah are far-seeing counsel (cf. Isaiah 25:1) from He who is great in
counsel (cf. Jeremiah 32:19), to correct [our] character traits and rectify our
conduct.

This statement clarifies the Rambam's position with regard to a fundamental question
of Jewish thought. There is a difference of opinion between our Sages (*Berachot* 5:3)
whether the Torah's commandments are considered Divine decrees - i.e., edicts to
be fulfilled without questioning their rationale - or whether there are reasons for
the mitzvot. The statements quoted indicate that the Rambam favors merging both
opinions: On the one hand, the mitzvot are Divine decrees, for man can never fathom
the full measure of Divine will or wisdom. Nevertheless, He has communicated His
wisdom in the Torah, and this makes it possible for us - and obligates us - to
comprehend a certain dimension of His intent.

being forbidden [during and] after menstruation and childbirth - the
sole purpose God commanded us regarding all this was so that we
should turn far away from excessive desire, deviating from the median
in the direction of lack of desire to strengthen the quality of restraint
in our souls. [For this same reason,] our elders instituted further
restrictions to limit the frequency of intercourse - [e.g.,] not to have
intercourse during the day, as explained [in our commentary on the
tractate] *Sanhedrin*.[17]

Similarly, all the Torah's commandments regarding tithes,
leket,[18] *shich'chah*,[19] *pe'ah*,[20] *peret*,[21] *olelot*,[22] the laws of the Sabbatical
and Jubilee years, and [the obligation to give] charity until one satisfies
the needs of [the poor], draw us closer to the quality of profligacy, so
that we will turn far away from stinginess and strengthen the quality
of generosity.

Similarly, if one contemplates the majority of the mitzvot, one will
be able to appreciate that they all improve the powers of the soul. For
example, the prohibitions against vengeance and redeeming the blood
[of a slain person], as it is written[23] "Do not take vengeance or bear a
grudge," the mitzvot "You shall surely help,"[24] "you shall surely raise
up,"[25] weaken the qualities of wrath and anger. Similarly, the mitzvah
"you shall surely return"[26] was instituted to remove the quality of
selfishness. Similarly, the mitzvot, "Rise before a white-haired man
and show respect for an elder,[27] "Honor your father...,"[28] and "Do
not deviate from the instructions they give you,"[29] were instituted to

17. See Chapter 7, Mishnah 4. See also *Niddah* 17a; *Mishneh Torah, Hilchot Issurei
Bi'ah* 21:10.
18. Leaving fallen stalks of grain for the poor (Leviticus 19:9).
19. Leaving sheaves of grain that were forgotten, for collection by the poor
(Deuteronomy 24:19).
20. Leaving the ends of one's fields unharvested for the poor (Leviticus 19:9).
21. Leaving individual grapes that fall to be collected by the poor (*ibid.*:10).
22. Leaving incompletely formed grape clusters for the poor (*ibid.*).
23. Leviticus 19:18.
24. Exodus 23:5. This mitzvah involves helping a person unload a donkey that has
fallen under its burden. The verse specifically refers to "a donkey of your enemy."
25. Deuteronomy 22:4. This mitzvah requires helping a person reload a donkey that
has fallen under its burden.
26. *Ibid.*:1. This mitzvah requires the return of a lost article.
27. Leviticus 19:32.
28. Exodus 20:12.
29. Deuteronomy 17:11.

remove the quality of impudence. Similarly, we have been warned to keep a distance from the other extreme, reticence, as reflected in the commandment "You shall surely admonish your neighbor; do not bear sin because of him,"[30] and "Do not become inhibited in the face of any man."[31] These mitzvot steer us away from reticence and lead to the middle path.

If a foolish - and this adjective is correct without doubt - person decides to add [further stringencies] to these matters - e.g., he forbids partaking of food and beverages beyond those that are forbidden, or he forbids marrying women who are not prohibited [by the Torah], or he gives all his financial resources to the poor or consecrates them in [opposition to the guidelines of] charity and the consecration of articles [found in the Torah], he is doing an evil act. He has [deviated to] an extreme and departed entirely from the median.

Our Sages have made [many] brilliant statements about these matters, incomparable to any others I have seen. For example, the Jerusalem Talmud, the ninth chapter of *Nedarim*[32] condemns those who obligate themselves in oaths and vows to the extent that it is as if they are fettered. Among the statements there is the following: "Rav Iddi says in the name of Rabbi Yitzchak: 'Is it not enough for you what the Torah has forbidden?'" This is the concept that we have mentioned in concise terms, without adding or diminishing.

From our explanations in this chapter, a person should realize [the importance of] directing his conduct towards the middle path, and that it is improper to deviate to either extreme, except for the purpose of healing his conduct and acquiring the influence of the opposite trait. [To cite an example,] a person who is well-versed in medicine who sees his disposition change slightly should not ignore this and allow the infirmity to become stronger so that he will be forced to take very strong medications. Similarly, if a person knows that one of his limbs is weak, he should always take care of it, staying away from things that can harm him, and seeking things that will help heal that limb, or at least prevent it from becoming weaker.

Similarly, a person who has perfected his character should always analyze his personal qualities, weigh carefully his conduct and evaluate the inclination of his soul every day. If he sees that his soul tends toward

30. Leviticus 19:17.
31. Deuteronomy 1:17.
32. Chapter 9, Halachah 1.

either of the extremes, he should immediately seek to heal himself, without allowing the undesirable characteristics to entrench themselves through the repetition of undesirable acts, as we have explained.

Similarly, he should focus his attention on the most undesirable character traits that he possesses and try to heal them, as we have suggested. For every person surely possesses shortcomings. As the philosophers have said,[33] it is highly unlikely to find a person who by nature possesses all virtues - i.e., innately has both emotional and intellectual qualities that are developed.

The prophets have stressed [the fact that human beings, by nature, have shortcomings], as it is written,[34] "He does not trust His servants," and it is written,[35] "What merit will a man born of woman possess?" And King Solomon said definitively,[36] "There is no righteous man on the earth who does [only] good and does not sin."

And of the master of [all mankind, of both] the former and the latter generations, Moses, our teacher, it is written,[37] "Since you did not believe in Me, to sanctify Me before all the children of Israel...," "for you rebelled against My edict at the waters of Merivah," and "because you did not sanctify Me."[38]

He sinned, because his nature was inclined to one of the extremes of the emotional characteristics, showing anger [instead of the median, which is] patience, as it is written,[39] "Listen, you rebellious ones." God rebuked him, for a person like him should not have displayed anger toward the Jewish people in a situation where anger is not called for. For his level, this was considered a desecration of God's name.

[Why was every particular of Moses' conduct so important?] Because [the people] would learn from each of his deeds and words, and [by emulating his example,] they hoped to merit success in this world and in the world to come. How then could anger come from such a person? For anger is an improper act as explained, coming from an undesirable character trait.

With regard to this, it is written, "for you rebelled against My

---

33. See *Emunot V'De'ot*, essay 5, chapter 2ff; *Sefer HaMiddot*, essay 7, chapter 1.
34. Job 4:18.
35. *Ibid.* 25:4.
36. Ecclesiastes 7:20.
37. Numbers 20:12.
38. Deuteronomy 32:51.
39. Numbers 20:10.

edict," for the reasons I will explain: [Moses] was not speaking with a mass of common people, but rather with individuals on a high spiritual level. Our Sages say[40] that the lowest of their women was on the level of [the prophet] Ezekiel, the son of Buzi, and they would evaluate everything [Moses] said or did. When they saw that he became angry, [knowing] that he was not among those whose emotional qualities were impaired, they assumed that God had already become enraged against them for asking for water, and that they had already incurred God's rage. For [otherwise], Moses would not have become angry. [This was not the case, for] God did not show either anger or rage when speaking with him. He [merely] said,[41] "Take the staff... and give water to the congregation and their flocks." [Since Moses created a mistaken impression of God's will, it was considered a sin.]

(This is a departure from the contents of this chapter. It does, however, answer one of the questions many have asked with regard to the Torah. Many have discussed the issue and questioned: what sin did Moses commit? Compare our explanation of this passage with that of others.[42] The path of the truth will show its way.)

To return to the subject under discussion: If a person continually evaluates his conduct and directs it toward the mean, he will achieve the highest level of conduct possible for a mortal. In this way, he will draw close to God, and grasp His will. Our Sages have already spoken about this matter, saying:[43]

Whoever weighs his paths [of conduct] will merit the salvation of the Holy One, blessed be He, as it is written,[44] "To whoever positions his path will I show the salvation of God." Do not read *sam* ("positions"), but rather *sham* ("weigh").

Weighing means gauging and evaluating. This is the thrust of our statements in this chapter, and this is what we see necessary to explain concerning this matter.

40. *Mechilta, Parashat BeShalach; Devarim Rabbah* 7:9.
41. Numbers 20:8.
42. Perhaps the Rambam was referring to the interpretation of Rav Sa'adiah Gaon in his Commentary on the Torah, or to that of Rabbenu Chanan'el, quoted in the Commentary of the Ramban.
43. *Mo'ed Katan* 5b; *Sotah* 5b.
44. Psalms 50:23.

CHAPTER FIVE

DIRECTING OUR POWERS TO ONE GOAL

It is fitting for a person to control all the powers of his soul by his thought, as we mentioned in the previous chapter. He should place one goal before his eyes: the comprehension of God - glorified be He - to [the full extent of] mortal potential.[1] This means to know Him.

One should direct all of his activities, endeavors, and [even] his relaxation toward that goal, to the extent that none of his activities is purposeless - i.e., that they do not lead to this goal.

A person's intent when he eats, drinks, sleeps, engages in sexual relations, wakes, performs activity and relaxes should be for the sake of his physical health. And the intent of the pursuit of health should be that his soul will have healthy and whole vessels to use for study and for acquiring the intellectual and ethical virtues, so he will reach the above goal.[2]

In this way, his intent will not be solely for the sake of pleasure.[3] Instead of choosing the tastiest food and drink, he will choose those that are most beneficial [for his health]. If the result is that [the foods] he chooses are sweet, he will be satisfied; but if they are not sweet, he will not be upset.

There may be occasions when a person will seek to eat sweet foods as a therapeutic approach - e.g., he has lost desire for food, and

---

1. See *Hilchot Yesodei HaTorah* 1:10, where the Rambam explains that there are limits to a mortal's ability to comprehend Godliness. (See also *Hilchot Melachim* 12:5, where the Rambam mentions the comprehension of Godliness to the full extent of mortal potential as the consummation of the Messianic age.)
2. See *Hilchot De'ot*, Chapter 3, where the Rambam also emphasizes that a person's activities should be directed to physical health, and that health should serve as a medium leading to his spiritual development.
3. With the addition of the word "solely," the Rambam indicates that he is not critical of pleasure. On the contrary, he maintains that God has structured the makeup of man's nature in such a manner that beneficial activities bring about pleasure (Commentary on the Mishnah, *Sanhedrin* 7:3). What he criticizes are activities carried out for the sake of pleasure alone.

it is necessary to arouse such a craving by eating sweet and tastily seasoned foods. Similarly, if a person is overcome by melancholy, he should endeavor to purge himself of it by listening to songs and music, strolling through gardens and magnificent buildings, and frequenting attractive works of art.[4] [In these activities,] his intent should [not be for pleasure *per se*, but rather] be for his physical health. And the purpose of attaining physical health is to attain knowledge.

Similarly, when a person seeks to acquire wealth and property, his intent in these endeavors should be to use these resources for beneficial purposes, so that he will be able to maintain his personal existence. And the purpose of maintaining his existence should be to comprehend and know God to the fullest extent of his capacity.

In this context, medical knowledge is very important with regard to personal development, the knowledge of God, and the appreciation of true happiness. Its study and its practice should be considered of great importance, [rather than disparaged and relegated to a status] similar to weaving or carpentry. For [medical knowledge] enables us to direct our conduct in a manner that it will reflect our human potential and will be directed to personal development and truth.

For when a person approaches food and eats it because it is tasty, has a pleasant aroma, and is deemed desirable - even though it may damage him, and possibly cause severe sickness or even death - he and an animal are the same. This is not considered to be an act performed by man because he is human. On the contrary, it is an act performed by man because he is an animal, [to borrow a Biblical phrase,][5] "He is like the beasts and resembles them."

An expression of our human potential, [by contrast,] involves seeking only food that is beneficial, choosing that which is not sweet and rejecting the sweet [when doing so] is beneficial. This represents thoughtful conduct. Through such acts, a human being distinguishes himself from other [living beings]. Similarly, if a person engages in sexual relations whenever he desires without considering the benefit and the possible damage, he is conducting himself like an animal and not like a human being.

It is possible that a person will conduct himself only according to

---

4. Although the traditional interpretation of the Rambam's words is as above, based on *Hilchot Teshuvah* 8:6, it is possible to render the phrase "associating with attractive women."

5. Psalms 49:13, 21.

what is beneficial for [his health], as we explained, but [this will be a self-contained goal]. His only concern will be that he is healthy and not affected by disease. This is also not a sign of personal development. For just as one desires the pleasure of health and well-being, another desires the pleasure of food or of sex. None of these represents a true goal for our conduct.

Instead, it is proper that a person direct all his activities, his physical health, and the maintenance of his existence so that the limbs [of his body] serve as perfect media for his soul. Then his soul will be able to exercise the ethical and intellectual virtues without any impediment.

Needless to say, everything that a person learns in his studies and the sciences that leads to that purpose [is desirable]. Other [studies] that are not directly related to this purpose - e.g., algebra, mathematical equations, geometry, extensive inquiry into engineering, the study of weights and the like - should be directed toward the purpose of sharpening one's mind and training one's sense of logic to seek proofs, so that a person will grasp the power to distinguish one concept from another. This will provide him with a medium to reach the knowledge of the truth of His Being.

Similarly, with regard to speech: a person should speak only those words that are necessary to bring him a benefit or to ward away harm from his soul or body, to learn a positive virtue, to praise a virtue or a prominent man, or to criticize a fault or a wicked person. For the condemnation of people who possess faults and the decrying of their esteem is an obligation and a virtue when one's intent is to belittle them in people's eyes so that others will take heed and refrain from emulating their conduct. Indeed, we see this pattern within the Torah itself, as evidenced by the verse,[6] "[Do not copy] the deeds of the Land of Egypt or the deeds of the Land of Canaan..." and the story of the Sodomites' [conduct].[7] Everything that Scripture says in denunciation of wicked and inadequate people and in praise of the righteous is intended [to motivate] people to follow the paths of [the righteous] and avoid the paths of [the wicked].

When a person appreciates this concept, he will eliminate many actions and limit his speech greatly. For a person who has these goals will not seek to decorate his walls with gold, or to make a golden strand on a garment, unless his intent in such an act is to settle

6. Leviticus 18:3.
7. Genesis, Chapters 18 and 19.

his soul so that it will heal and remove its sickness, making it taintless and pure to receive knowledge, as [our Sages] said:[8] "An attractive dwelling, an attractive wife, attractive implements, and a made bed are appropriate for Torah scholars" and "expand a person's knowledge."[9]

For one's soul will weary and one's thought processes will become sluggish from constantly seeing unpleasant things, just as the body will become sick from draining labor until it regains its balance. In a similar way, the soul requires quiet and involvement in pleasant matters until languidness departs. As [our Sages] said,[10] "When the Sages became weary of studying, a humorous remark would be made." In a similar vein, I would say that certain activities - e.g., looking at paintings, sculpture, buildings, implements, and clothes - are not bad, nor are they wasteful.

This level [of conduct] is very elevated and hard [to reach]. It will be attained only by a select few, and only after much training. If a person who possesses these qualities exists, I would say that he is no less [developed] than the prophets. [I am referring to a person who] motivates all the powers of his soul and directs them to God alone, and who does not perform any act, whether important or insignificant, or say any word unless that act or word will bring him virtue. He contemplates and thinks regarding all his activities and movements, and evaluates whether they will lead him to that goal or not. Only afterwards does he act.

God charged us with [seeking] this intent with His [command]:[11] "And you shall love God, your Lord, with all your heart and with all your soul" - i.e., with all the elements of your soul, directing each one to a single intent: the love of God. Our prophets have also inspired our people to this end, saying:[12] "Know Him in all your ways." And our Sages said:[13] "This includes even a sin."[14] The intent of this statement is that a person should direct his activities to a purpose, the truth, even when there is a dimension of transgression involved in them.

8. *Shabbat* 25b.
9. *Berachot* 57b.
10. The exact source of the Rambam's statements is a matter of question. Some have referred to *Shabbat* 30b, where related statements are made.
11. Deuteronomy 6:5.
12. Proverbs 3:6.
13. *Berachot* 63a.
14. *Chesed L'Avraham* interprets this as a reference to Yael's seduction of Sisera

Our Sages have condensed this entire discussion into the most concise form possible, yet including the furthest extensions of the idea. When one contemplates how this concise statement includes this vast and prodigious concept, about which many texts were written without encompassing it totally, one realizes that without a doubt it was said with Divine inspiration. The intent is the statement mentioned in this tractate,[15] "All your deeds should be for the sake of Heaven." This is the concept explained in this chapter, and this is the content we have deemed appropriate to mention here based on the preface already provided.

(Judges, Chapter 4, as explained in *Nazir* 23b). Although her act was forbidden, it had a positive intent and was praised by God.
15. Chapter 2, Mishnah 11.

CHAPTER SIX

THE DIFFERENCE BETWEEN A PIOUS PERSON AND ONE WHO OVERCOMES HIS DESIRES

The philosophers have defined a person who overcomes his desires as one who does worthy acts and good deeds, even though he has a tendency towards base deeds and desires to perform them. He battles these tendencies and does the very opposite of what his soul-powers, natural desires, and disposition prompt him to do. Although he acts nobly, he suffers discomfort while doing so.

A pious person, by contrast, conducts himself according to the manner in which he is prompted by his desires and disposition. He performs worthy deeds because he wants to, and because this is his nature.

All philosophers agree that a pious person is on a higher rung than one who overcomes his desires. Nevertheless, one who overcomes his desires resembles a pious person in many ways. He is definitely on a lower level, for he desires to conduct himself basely. Although he does not actually do so, his desire to do so [reflects] a perverse trend in his soul. King Solomon spoke of this, saying:[1] "A wicked soul desires evil." And he said of the happiness a pious man [experiences] when doing good, and the discomfort [experienced] when a person who is not pious performs [good deeds]:[2] "Doing justice brings joy to the righteous, but it is the downfall of the workers of iniquity." This reflects a parallel between the words of the Prophets and the words of the philosophers.

[On the other hand,] when we researched our Sages' statements on this question, we found that a person who has an inclination to sin and desires to do so is on a higher and more complete level than one who has no desire for them and does not feel discomfort in spurning them. They said that however great a person is, his desire to sin and his discomfort in spurning sin will be greater. Indeed, they illustrated this

---

1. Proverbs 21:10.
2. *Ibid.* 21:15.

principle with stories,[3] and said,[4] "Whoever is greater than his colleague possesses an evil inclination that is greater than his." And they said that the reward given for overcoming one's desire is commensurate with the discomfort he felt in overcoming it. And they said,[5] "According to the discomfort is the reward." And they warned against saying, "By nature, I have no desire [to perform] such a sin, even had it not been forbidden by the Torah." Thus, they quote:[6]

Rabbi Shimeon ben Gamliel says: "A person should not say, 'It is impossible for me to eat milk and meat,' 'It is impossible for me to wear *sha'atnez*,' or 'It is impossible for me to engage in forbidden sexual relations.' Instead, he should say, 'It is possible for me, but what should I do? My Father in heaven decreed against it.'"

On the surface, these two approaches [that of the philosophers and that of our Sages] appear to contradict each other. This is, however, not true. They are both true, and there is no discrepancy between them at all. [The explanation is as follows:] The qualities that the philosophers deem evil and concerning which they say that a person who has no desire for them is more elevated than one who has a desire, but overcomes it, are those that all people will appreciate as evil - e.g., murder, theft, robbery, cheating, damaging a person who has performed no harm, repaying good with evil, demeaning one's parents, and the like.

These are commandments which, even if they had not been recorded [in the Torah], it would have been proper to inscribe them.[7] They are referred to by some of the wise men of the later generations who have fallen into the sickness of the sect of *medabrim*[8] as "rational commandments." There is no doubt that a soul that desires [to perform] any of these acts is a soul with depraved qualities. For a refined soul will not desire any of these base things at all, and will not suffer discomfort from holding back from them.

3. For example, see the story of Rav Amram, *Kiddushin* 81a, and that of Abbaye, *Sukkah* 52a.
4. *Sukkah, op. cit.*.
5. *Avot* 5:23. Note, however, that in his commentary on that *Mishnah*, the Rambam interprets the discomfort as referring to the rigor a person feels when laboring in Torah study.
6. *Sifra, Parashat Kedoshim.* There are, however, differences between the version of the text as it appears in the *Sifra* and the version quoted by the Rambam. For example, the present version of the *Sifra* attributes this teaching to Rabbi Eleazar ben Azariah.
7. Cf. *Yoma* 67b.
8. See the notes at the beginning of Chapter 1.

In contrast, the matters concerning which our Sages said that a
person who overcomes his natural inclination is greater and [thus
earns] a greater reward refer to mitzvot that require obedience. For in
truth, had the Torah not forbidden them, they would not be considered
evil at all. For this reason, our Sages said that a person should continue
to desire them, and should feel that the only thing preventing them is
the Torah's [decree].

Realize the greatness of their wisdom, by contemplating the examples
they gave. They did not say that a person should not say, "It is
impossible for me to kill..." or that "It is impossible for me to
steal..." or that "It is impossible for me to lie, but what can I do...
?" Instead, their quote mentions mitzvot that all require obedience:
[the avoidance of] milk and meat, wearing *sha'atnez*, and forbidden
sexual relations.

These mitzvot and the like are called *chukkim*, decrees, about which
it is said:[9] "These are decrees that I have established for you; you have
no permission to query about them. The nations of the world dispute
them, and the Satan accuses concerning them - e.g., the Red Heifer, and
the goat sent [to Azazel]." The commandments that the later thinkers
refer to as "rational" are called mitzvot by our Sages.

With the above, we have explained the nature of the sins concerning
which a person who has no desire for them will be more esteemed
than one who overcomes his desire, and the nature of the sins where
the opposite is true. This is a magnificent point, and an impressive
resolution of the two approaches. A careful look at the terminology
used also indicates the correctness of our explanations. This concludes
the contents of this chapter.

9. See *Yoma, loc. cit.*; *BaMidbar Rabbah* 19:3.

CHAPTER SEVEN

VEILS [OF OUR TRUE SELVES] AND HOW THEY OPERATE

In many places in the *Midrash* and the *Aggadah* - including some passages quoted in the Talmud - [it is stated] that there are prophets who see God [concealed] behind many veils and others [who see Him] behind fewer veils. [The difference depends] on the extent of their closeness to God and the elevated level of their prophecy. Thus, it is said that Moses saw God behind one clear and shining - i.e., transparent - veil.

This is what is meant by the expression[1] that "he [Moses] looked through the brilliant looking glass." The term "looking glass" refers to a lens made from a shining material like diamond or crystal, as mentioned at the conclusion of the tractate of *Keilim*.[2]

The intent of this statement is that, as explained in Chapter 2, there are intellectual virtues and ethical virtues. Conversely, there are intellectual shortcomings - e.g., foolishness, naivete, difficulty in understanding - and ethical shortcomings - e.g., gluttony, pride, anger, wrath, brashness, the love of money, and the like. Indeed, there are many of these, and we have mentioned the way to distinguish them in Chapter 4. All these shortcomings are veils that separate between man and God. This was alluded to in the prophet's statement,[3] "It is your sins that separate between you and your God." "Your sins" - i.e., the shortcomings mentioned are veils that separate between us and Him.

Know that a prophet will not prophesy until he has acquired all the intellectual virtues and most - including the more formidable - of the ethical virtues. This is implied by our Sages' statement,[4] "The spirit of

1. *Yevamot* 49b.
2. Chapter 30, Mishnah 2. Note the Rambam's Commentary on that Mishnah. (See also the Rambam's explanations of the difference between Moses and the other prophets in his introduction to the tenth chapter of *Sanhedrin* and in *Hilchot Yesodei HaTorah*, Chapter 7.)
3. Isaiah 59:2.
4. *Shabbat* 92a.

prophecy will rest solely on a wise man, who is valiant and wealthy."[5]

The term "wise man" surely includes all the intellectual virtues. The term "wealthy" includes all the ethical virtues; for it refers to the quality of satisfaction. [Our Sages] would call a person who is satisfied wealthy, as they stated:[6] "Who is rich? One who is happy with his portion" - i.e., one who is happy with what fortune presents him and does not grieve over what fortune does not present him.

Similarly, "valiant" refers to an ethical virtue - i.e., the ability to direct one's potentials in congruence with one's thought, as we explained in Chapter 5. This is implied by our Sages' statement,[7] "Who is valiant? One who conquers his natural inclination."

It is not necessary for a prophet to have mastered all the ethical virtues to the point that he does not possess any shortcomings at all. This is evidenced by the fact that [King] Solomon was a prophet, as the verse states,[8] "At Givon, God appeared [to Solomon]." And we find explicit reference to his having ethical shortcomings - i.e., overindulgence, [for he had] many wives; this comes as a result of the trait of overindulgence. Scripture explicitly [censures] him for this, as it is written:[9] "Did not Solomon, King of Israel, sin in this matter?"

Similarly, David was a prophet, as it is written,[10] "[The God of Israel] said to me, the Rock of Israel spoke." Nevertheless, we find that he was hardhearted. Although he directed this quality against the gentiles and killed those who deny God, and was merciful to the Jews, we nevertheless find in Chronicles that God did not find him fit to build the Temple because of the many people he slew, as it is written,[11] "You will not build a house for My name, because you shed much blood earthward before Me."

Similarly, we find that Elijah [the prophet] possessed the trait of anger. Although he directed it against the non-believers and would focus his wrath on them, our Sages explain[12] that God removed

---

5. Significantly, in his treatment of this subject in *Hilchot Yesodei HaTorah* 7:1, the Rambam makes reference to the same quote, but omits the term "wealthy."

6. *Avot* 4:1.

7. *Ibid.*.

8. I Kings 3:5.

9. Nechemiah 13:26.

10. II Samuel 23:3.

11. I Chronicles 22:8.

12. See *Sanhedrin* 113b and *Yalkut Shimoni*, Vol. II, Kings, sec. 217, which describe Elijah as prone to anger and rage. Indeed, this is evident from the Biblical narrative itself. See also *Tana D'bei Eliyahu Zuta*, sec. 8.

him [from the world], telling him that a person with his degree of zealousness is not fit to live among people, lest he cause them to be destroyed. Similarly, Samuel [had shortcomings, as evidenced by] his fear of Saul.[13] And Jacob feared Esau.[14]

[Despite their having these shortcomings, the prophets mentioned above were able to convey God's word.] The [undesirable] attributes [they possessed, nevertheless,] were like veils for them. Whoever had two or three qualities that deviated from the mean, as explained in Chapter 4, would see God behind two or three veils.

Do not wonder at the fact that a person's shortcomings with regard to his ethical development will reduce the level of his prophecy. For indeed we find that a lack of ethical development can prevent prophecy entirely. For example, anger, as our Sages said,[15] "Whoever displays anger, if he is a prophet, his prophecy will depart from him." They derived this concept from [the narrative] regarding Elisha, who did not receive a vision [from God] until he purged himself of anger, and therefore, he requested,[16] "Bring me a musician."

Similarly, worry and melancholy [prevent prophecy], as reflected by the fact that the spirit of prophecy did not rest upon Jacob throughout the years he mourned [for Joseph], until he received word that he was alive. Thus, the verse,[17] "And the spirit of Jacob, their father, was revived," is rendered by the *Targum* - which explains the interpretations received through tradition from Moses - as: "And the spirit of prophecy rested on Jacob, their father." And our Sages commented,[18] "Prophecy does not rest amidst laziness or sadness, only amidst joy."

Since Moses our teacher knew that there was no veil remaining that he had not rent, and that he had already acquired all the ethical and intellectual virtues, he sought to comprehend God and the Truth of His Being, for no hindrance remained. Thus, he asked Him,[19] "Show me Your glory."

God replied that this was impossible, for [Moses] still remained a mind contained in a material [body] - i.e., he was mortal. This is

13. I Samuel 16:2.
14. Genesis 32:8.
15. *Pesachim* 66b.
16. II Kings 3:15.
17. Genesis 45:27.
18. *Shabbat* 30b; *Pesachim* 117a.
19. Exodus 33:18. (See also a parallel explanation in *Hilchot Yesodei HaTorah* 1:10 and the Guide for the Perplexed, Vol. I, Chapters 21, 37-38.)

reflected in God's answer,[20] "No living man will see me." Nothing remained between him and the appreciation of God and the Truth of His Being except one pristine veil - mortal intellect. [This] can never be separated [from material consciousness].

After he made this request, God in His generosity granted him a greater measure of understanding than he had possessed previously. But He told him that the ultimate conception was impossible as long as he lived within a material body. [In His response, God] referred to the ultimate conception by using the allegory of seeing one's face. For when a person sees a colleague's face, his countenance becomes fixed in his memory, never to be confused with that of another person. When, by contrast, one sees a person's back, although it is possible to recognize him when seeing him, it is, nevertheless, possible for uncertainty to arise, and perhaps one will mistake him for another person.

Similarly, with regard to the true comprehension of God: For a soul to grasp the Truth of His Being in a manner that clearly distinguishes Him from all other types of existence, until His existence will be permanently affixed in his soul in a manner different from all other entities - this is impossible for a mortal. Moses, however, very nearly comprehended this. This is alluded to in the verse,[21] "And you will see My back." I will explain this concept in full in the Book of Prophecy.[22]

Since our Sages knew that these two shortcomings - i.e., our ethical and intellectual failings - separate man from God, and that this distinguished the prophets, they said[23] with regard to some of their colleagues, whose wisdom and ethical development they saw, "They are fit for the Divine Presence to rest upon them, as it rested on Moses our teacher." Do not err and think that by comparing them with him, they sought to equate them with him, heaven forbid. Similarly, they said with regard to others, [that they could be compared to] Joshua bin Nun. This is the concept that we desired to explain in this chapter.

20. Exodus 33:20.
21. *Ibid.*:23.
22. See the notes at the conclusion of Chapter 1.
23. *Sotah* 28a; *Bava Batra* 134a.

CHAPTER EIGHT

THE COMPOSITION OF HUMAN NATURE

It is impossible for a person to be born with personal virtues or shortcomings, just as it is impossible for a person to be born with professional skill in one of the crafts. It is, however, possible for a person to be born with a tendency to one of the virtues or one of the shortcomings - i.e., conduct [representative of this trait] will come easier to him than other types of conduct.

To illustrate: It is possible that a person's nature will tend more toward dryness. As such, his mind will be clearer, less inclined to moistness. This will grant this person greater facility with regard to memory and the comprehension of ideas than one whose nature is controlled by white gall-bladder secretions, and whose mind will be more phlegmatic. Nevertheless, if the person whose natural inclination puts him at an advantage acts sluggishly and fails to study or develop his potentials, he will surely remain foolish. Conversely, if the person who is by nature coarse and phlegmatic applies himself to study and conceptual activity, he will be able to learn and comprehend, albeit with greater difficulty and after expending more effort.

Similarly, there are those whose nature is more heated than the norm, who will be inclined to boldness. If [such a person] habituates himself to this form of conduct, it will come more readily to him. Conversely, a person whose nature is more cold-hearted than the norm will be inclined towards timidity and fear. If he habituates himself to these traits, he will acquire them faster, and it is only with great difficulty that he will be able to incline his conduct towards boldness. But if he trains himself in this direction, he will acquire this trait without a doubt.

I have explained these concepts for the purpose of negating the claims made by the astrologers, who maintain that the sign under which a person is born endows him with virtues and shortcomings and that a person must conduct himself according to these [natural] traits. It is well known, as taught by our [holy] Torah - and [proven by] Greek philosophy by empirical evidence - that every aspect of a person's conduct is dependent on his [free] will. He is under no compulsion whatsoever. There is no external force directing him to virtue or to inadequacy, except the natural inclination mentioned above. This makes a particular activity easier or more difficult. In no way, however, is he forced [to do anything] or prevented [from doing anything].

If a person were forced to conduct himself [in any way], all the commandments and prohibitions of the Torah would be purposeless and of absolutely no value. For a person would have no control over his behavior.[1] Similarly, this would negate the entire purpose of study and education, and even of training in the crafts. All this would be worthless, for a person - according to the belief of these people - would be compelled by an external force to conduct himself in a certain way, to know certain subjects, and possess certain traits.

Reward and punishment - either from mortals or from God - would be absolutely unjust. For if Shimon killed Reuven because he was compelled to do so, why should he be punished for this? How could we say that God, who is just and righteous, would punish a person for performing a deed that he was compelled to perform, one that he would be forced to perform even if he desired not to.

Moreover, [this approach] would negate the entire value of planning, building homes, preparing for one's livelihood, fleeing in a time of danger and the like. [Of what purpose would this be] if everything is fated?

Instead, this [entire approach] is empty, of absolutely no truth. It runs contrary to logic and to reality. It destroys the walls of the Torah and projects an unjust image of God, heaven forbid. Without any doubt, the truth is that every aspect of a person's conduct is subject to his [choice]. If he desires, he will act in one way. And if he desires not to, he will not. Nothing is forcing him or compelling him at all. Therefore, it is relevant to command [man], as it is written,[2] "Behold I have set before you today life and good, death and evil. Choose good." For God has given us choice in this regard.

Thus, it is necessary that there be reward for those who heed [God's command], and punishment for those who fail to heed, as it is written,[3] "If you will obey.... If you will not obey...." Similarly,

---

1. See *Hilchot Teshuvah* 5:1-4, where the Rambam makes similar statements.
2. Deuteronomy 30:15.
3. *Ibid.* 11:27-28.

it is fitting that [people] study and teach, as it is written,[4] "And you shall teach them to your children," and "You shall study them and be careful to observe them."[5] This is also obvious from all the other charges given with regard to the study [of the Torah] and the observance of the mitzvot.

Similarly, on this basis we are obligated [with regard to duties to others] and charged with taking necessary precautions, as the Book of Truth [the Torah] states,[6] "And you shall make a guardrail for your roof, lest a person fall," "[Let him go home] lest he die in war,"[7] "[Return it to him.... This alone is his covering...] in what will he sleep?"[8] "Do not take an upper millstone or a lower millstone [for that is taking a person's life as security]."[9] Similarly, we find many other verses in the Torah and the works of the prophets that emphasize the importance of taking precautions [within the context of the natural means available].

[There is no contradiction to this from the following] statement of our Sages:[10] "Everything is in the hands of heaven except the fear of heaven." This statement is true and conforms to the conceptual framework that we have explained. Nevertheless, many people err with regard to it and imagine that a person is fated with regard to many of the matters in which he is given free choice: e.g., whether he will marry a particular woman or acquire a sum of money through theft.[11]

This is absolutely not true. For if a person marries a woman, granting her a marriage contract and performing the rites of *kiddushin*, he is performing a mitzvah, and God does not decree that we will perform any mitzvot. Should the marriage be forbidden, [entering into it] is a sin, and God does not decree that we will perform any sins.

4. *Ibid.* 11:19.
5. *Ibid.* 5:1.
6. *Ibid.* 22:8.
7. *Ibid.* 20:5-7.
8. Exodus 22:26.
9. Deuteronomy 24:6. The Rambam's intent in citing these verses is to illustrate how the Torah takes the possibility of natural consequences into consideration instead of relying merely on fate. (See also the Guide for the Perplexed, Vol. III, Chapter 20.)
10. *Berachot* 33a *et al.*
11. The concluding words "through theft" are taken from Rav Kapach's translation of the Commentary on the Mishnah and are lacking in the standard published text. This intent is, however, clearly evident from the continuation of the text.

Similarly, if one robs money belonging to someone else, steals it, deceives him, denies possession of money [that was entrusted] and takes a [false] oath about it [this is a sin]. If one said that God decreed that this person should acquire this money, and that he should take it from the second person, [God would be] decreeing that [the person commit] a sin.

This is not true. Instead, the totality of a person's conduct is given over to him and is dependent on his choice; in this sphere, one finds compliance and defiance. As we explained in the second chapter, the commandments and prohibitions of the Torah apply only to those actions that a person has the choice whether to perform or not. That this element of the soul should be God-fearing is not in the "hands of heaven," but is rather given over to man's choice, as we have explained.

For when our Sages used the term "everything," their intent was merely the natural matters for which a person does not have the [potential to] choose - e.g., will the person be tall or short, will there be rain or a drought, will the air be murky or clear, and the like regarding matters that will take place in the world outside the realm of man's activity or lack of such.

This concept - that a person's compliance or defiance [with the Torah] is neither decreed or willed by God, but is dependent on the will of that particular person - is based on the words of Jeremiah:[12] "From the mouth of the Most High does not come forth evil or good." "Evil" refers to wicked deeds, and "good" to good deeds. [The prophet states that] God does not decree that a person perform evil deeds or good deeds. And as such, it is in truth correct for a person to grieve over his performance of sins and shameful acts, for he willfully performed these wicked deeds. And thus, the following verse continues, "For what should a living man grieve? A man for his sins."

[The prophet] continues in the following verses, stating that curing this impairment is also in our hands. Just as we have willfully rebelled against Him, so too, can we repent, [improving] our evil conduct, as it is written: "Let us examine our ways and explore them, and return to God. Let us lift our hearts with our hands to God in heaven."

[There is, however, a means of explaining the position that is] widely held among people and that appears to be supported by the words of our Sages and by certain verses: that how a person stands, sits,

12. *Eichah* 3:38. The Talmudic tradition attributes *Eichah* to Jeremiah.

and all of his actions are willed and desired by God. This is correct when understood in a certain way.

[To explain:] When a person throws a stone in the air and it descends it can be said that God desired that the stone descend. For God desired that the Earth be in the center [of the universe]. Therefore, wheneve a portion of it is thrown upward, it is propelled back to the center Similarly, all the elements of fire [by nature] rise upward as a resul of [God's original] desire that fire rise upward. It is not that at thi moment God desired that this part of the earth descend to the center

This is [one of] the differences between [our faith] and the sect o *medabrim*, who, it is reported, believe that God's desire is invested in every entity at all times. Our faith differs, maintaining that God's will [was determined at the time of] the six days of creation. [At tha time, He willed that] all entities continue to function according to their nature, as [implied by the verse][13] "What was, is what will be what has occurred will occur. There is nothing new under the sun."[14]

Therefore, with regard to all the miracles that took place - or tha will take place, as we have been promised - our Sages were forced to say[15] that the desire for them originated beforehand, during the six day of creation. [At that time,] all the extraordinary developments tha were to occur were implanted within [the scheme of] nature. It merely appeared that they were new developments at the time they occurred This, however, was not the case. This matter has been explained a length in the *Midrash* on Ecclesiastes and in other sources, and is also

---

13. Ecclesiastes 1:9.
14. The conceptual difficulty that the Rambam is attempting to resolve with this explanation is that one of the fundamental principles of faith - and logical imperatives - is that God does not change. (For change implies a cause and effect relationship, with the cause and the effect sharing a commonality, and that cannot be said about the Creator and any element of His creation.) Therefore, the Rambam explains that God's will is not changing, but is rather constant, established at the initial time of creation.
15. As a source, the commentaries point to *Bereishit Rabbah* 5:5, which states: "The Holy One, blessed be He, established a condition with the sea that it will split before the Jewish people.... Not only with the sea did the Holy One, blessed be He, establish a condition, but with all that was created in the six days of creation."

Afterwards, the *Midrash* mentions other miracles that took place in the course of Israel's national history. The point of the Rambam's statements here, as well, is to emphasize that these miracles do not represent a change in the Divine will. (See also the Rambam's commentary on *Avot* 5:6.)

pparent from our Sages' statement,[16] "The world proceeds according
‹ its pattern."

[Study of these sources] shows how our Sages were always reticent
‹ ascribe a particular Divine will to every particular entity at all times.
'hus, they would explain that if a person sits or stands, it was willed
y God that he do so. [The intent, however, is that] initially, when
ιan first came into being, he was granted the capacity to rise or sit
t will. It is not that at this time God desired that the person stand or
‹ot, just as there is no [new] Divine will that a stone fall or not.

Just as God desires that man stand upright, possess a broad chest,
ιnd that [his hands] have fingers, so too, He desires that he move and
est at will, and perform all his activities by choice, without anything
‹ompelling him or preventing him.

This is [implied by the] statement of the book of Truth (the
'orah):[17] "Thus, man has become unique, knowing good and evil."
'he *Targum* emphasizes that by "knowing good and evil," man
ιecomes "unique." For there is no other species in the world that
ιas this capacity - i.e., the ability to know oneself what is good and
ιhat is bad, and to choose either voluntarily, without any hindrance.
ιecause [man has this potential, there was apprehension] "lest he
xtend his hand, pick from this (the Tree of Life), partake of it, and
ιve forever."[18]

Since this is one of the fundamental aspects of human existence - that
ιne willfully performs good or evil as one desires - it is necessary to
each man the good path, to give him commands and prohibitions,
‹o reward him and to punish him and for this to be just. Similarly,
t becomes necessary for [man] to train himself to perform positive
ιctivities until he acquires [internal] virtue, and to shun undesirable
ιeeds until he removes the failings that he previously possessed.

He should not say that these shortcomings are already ingrained
ιn his character and cannot be removed. For in every situation a
ιerson has the choice of changing from good to bad, and from bad to

6. *Avodah Zarah* 54b. (See also the Rambam's comments on this matter in the Guide
‹or the Perplexed, Vol. II, Chapter 30.)
7. Genesis 3:22. Our translation of the verse follows the *Targum Onkelos*, as the
ιambam explains. The traditional rendition of the verse is "Thus, man has become
ıke one of us, knowing good and evil." The Rambam prefers the interpretation of
ιnkelos, because it highlights the quality of free choice.
8. Genesis, *loc. cit.*

good. The choice is in his hands. This is the basis of all our statements with regard to the fulfillment of God's will or the rebellion against it.

There is one more point that has to be explained in this context that certain verses appear to indicate that God decreed that [man] would rebel and thus He forces him to do so. This is absolutely false. [To clarify this point,] we will explain [these passages] for they have been the subject of much discussion by others.[19]

For example, it was promised to Abraham:[20] "And they shall enslave them [your descendants] and oppress them." Thus, it appears that it was decreed for the Egyptians to oppress Abraham's descendants. If so, why were they punished? They were compelled to oppress them as decreed. The answer to this question is that this [prophecy] can be compared to God's saying, "In the future, there will be those who heed [God's commandments] and those who do not, righteous men and wicked ones."

This is a true statement. It does not obligate that so and so, who is wicked, had to be wicked, or that so and so, who is righteous, had to be righteous. Instead, whoever acts wickedly does so on his own volition. Had he desired to be righteous, it would have been possible; there was nothing preventing him. Similarly, every righteous person could have been wicked; he was not hindered. The statement is not applied with regard to each particular individual so that he could rationalize and say that [his fate] was decreed. Instead, the statement is general in nature, allowing every individual to act voluntarily according to his own character.

Similarly, had any one of the Egyptians who wronged and oppressed the Jewish people desired not to wrong them, he would have been able to make this choice. For a decree was not made that any particular person would wrong [the Jews]. This same explanation can resolve the difficulty in the verse,[21] "[When] you sleep with your fathers, this nation will arise and stray after the foreign gods of the land." There is no difference between this [prophecy] and a statement that all who worship false gods will be destined to be treated in such and such a manner. For if there were never a person who transgressed, all these warnings would have no purpose. [Similarly,] all the curses

19. See *Hilchot Teshuvah*, Chapter 5, where the Rambam focuses on several of the passages he cites here and explains a similar concept.
20. Genesis 15:13.
21. Deuteronomy 31:16.

would have no purpose, as would all the punishments in the Torah. For the fact that there exists a law requiring stoning in the Torah does not justify the statement that a person who desecrates the Sabbath was compelled to desecrate it. Nor does the fact that the Torah includes curses [against those who worship false gods] justify the statement that a person who worships such gods was compelled to. Rather, whoever committed these transgressions committed them willingly and brought the punishment upon themselves. As it is written,[22] "They have chosen their own ways... and I will choose [torments for them]."

[A problem might be raised based on the verse,][23] "I will harden Pharaoh's heart." Afterwards, [as a result of Pharaoh's hardheartedness, God] punished him and destroyed him. This is the proper place to discuss this concept and explain a fundamental principle. Therefore, contemplate my words on this subject and pay attention to them. Afterwards, compare them to other interpretations that have been offered and select what you think is best.

[The concept can be explained] as follows: If the only sin committed by Pharaoh and his servants had been that they did not release the Jewish people, the matter would indeed have been difficult. For He prevented him from releasing them, as it is written,[24] "I have hardened his heart and the hearts of his servants." [How then] can He ask him to release them, when he is compelled not to release them, and then punish him for not releasing them, destroying him and his servants? [If this were the case,] it would be unfair and this would negate all that we have explained previously.

This, however, was not the case. Pharaoh and his servants rebelled against God willingly, without anyone's forcing them or compelling them. They oppressed the strangers in their land and treated them unjustly, as [the Torah] explicitly states,[25] "And he said to his people, 'Behold the Jewish people.... Let us act cleverly with them.'" This act they performed voluntarily, as a result of their own wicked thoughts; nothing compelled them to do so.

God punished them for this and prevented them from repenting, so that He would punish them as His justice dictates. The fact that they

22. Isaiah 66:3-4.
23. Exodus 14:4. (See also parallel explanations of this concept in *Hilchot Teshuvah*, Chapter 6; Guide for the Perplexed, Vol. III, Chapter 17.)
24. Exodus 10:1.
25. *Ibid.* 1:9-10.

were prevented from repenting was expressed in their failure to releas [the Jews].

God already explained this to [Pharaoh], informing him that had H merely desired to take the Jews out [of Egypt], He could have destroye him and his servants, and [the Jews] could have left. [God,] howevei desired that while taking the Jews out, He would punish [Pharaoh an his servants] for their previous wickedness, as He mentioned initiall [when telling Abraham of the enslavement and the exodus, as it i written],26 "And I will also judge the nation whom they will serve. Since it would be impossible to punish them if they repented, [God therefore prevented them from repenting, and thus they detained [th Jews] further. [This is reflected in the verses,27 "Would I now stretc forth My hand, [I could smite you and your people].... But for thi purpose, I have maintained you [to show My power through you]."

This concept - that God will punish a person by preventing him fron repenting and withholding the option of *teshuvah* - is not a foreign one For He knows [the severity of] the sins and His wisdom and justic determine the nature of the punishment received. There are thos whom He punishes merely in this world, others whom He punishes ir the World to Come, and others whom He punishes in both worlds Similarly, the type of punishment in this world varies. Some ar punished in their physical person, others through their finances, anc some through both these means. For example, as a punishment [God may nullify [the possibility for] a person to function in certain ways ir which he could have chosen to function previously. He might preven his hand from functioning, as He did with regard to Jeroboam,28 oi his eyes from seeing as He did to the inhabitants of Sodom whc congregated against Lot.29 Similarly, He may prevent the desire for repentance from arising, so that he will perish in his sins.

There is no necessity that we fathom His wisdom and comprehend why He chose to punish a particular person in this fashion and no in another. [This cannot be known,] just as we cannot know the reason that causes a particular species to be given this form, and not another one. The general principle is, however, that all His ways are just;30 He will punish a sinner according to the nature of his

26. Genesis 15:14.
27. Exodus 9:15-16.
28. I Kings 13:4.
29. Genesis 19:11.
30. Cf. Deuteronomy 32:4.

n, and reward those who act kindly according to the nature of
their kindness.

If you ask: why did [God] demand from [Pharaoh] to release the
Jews time after time although he was prevented from doing this?
Moreover, the plagues were brought against him while he was adamant
in his refusal, for, as we mentioned above, he was punished because
he remained adamant in refusal. Why would [God] needlessly demand
from him something that he could not perform?

This is also an expression of God's wisdom; to show [Pharaoh]
that God had the potential to negate his free choice. Therefore, He
told him, "I demand that you release them. If you release them,
you will be saved, but [I know that] you will not release them until
you perish."

[Pharaoh indeed] desired to consent so that it would appear that
he reversed the words of the prophet who said that he was prevented
from agreeing, and yet he could not. This was a great miracle and
brought [God] renown among all men, as it is written,[31] "[But for this
purpose, I have maintained you,...] so that My name will be proclaimed
throughout the earth." This made it known that God [may] punish
a person by withholding free choice from him. Thus, a person will
know [of this possibility] and will not be able to continue leading his
life [sinfully] and rely on the option of repentance.

A similar punishment was given to Sichon, king of Cheshbon.
Because he rebelled against God when he was not compelled to, God
punished him by preventing him from responding to the Jews and
forcing them to] wage war against him. As it is written,[32] "Sichon,
King of Cheshbon, did not desire to allow us to pass through [his
land], because God hardened his spirit." Many commentaries have
questioned this, asking why Sichon was punished for refusing to allow
the Jews to pass through his land, for seemingly he was compelled
[to refuse], just as [they asked why] Pharaoh and his servants were
punished for not sending forth the Jews.

The explanation is, however, as given previously: that Pharaoh and
his servants were punished by God for their previous wrongdoings
in that they were prevented from repenting so that they would be
punished by these plagues. And Sichon was punished for his previous
evil and unjust behavior in his kingdom in that he would be prevented
from responding to the Jews, so that they would kill him.

31. Exodus 9:16.
32. Deuteronomy 2:30.

God explained this concept in his words to the prophet Isaiah, telling
him that there are certain wicked people whom God will punish b
preventing them from repenting and withholding free choice from them
As it is written,[33] "Make the heart of the people fat and their ear
heavy... [lest] they repent and be healed." This is an explicit verse
which does not need any interpretation and which serves as a key to
open many locks.

This foundation serves as a basis for the explanation of the
statements of [the prophet] Elijah with regard to the sinners of his
generation:[34] "And You have turned their hearts backward." This
means that since they voluntarily rebelled, You punished them by
turning their hearts away from the paths of repentance so that they
would have no choice or will to forgo their sins. And they therefore
continued in their denial [of God].

Similarly, it is written,[35] "Ephraim is joined to idols, let him be"
- i.e., because he joined himself to idols voluntarily, in love for them,
his punishment should be that he continue in this love. A person who
has sensitivity to abstract thought will appreciate the wondrous nature
of this interpretation.

The statement of Isaiah,[36] "Why, God, have You made us stray
from Your ways, and hardened our hearts against fear of You?" is not
an extension of this concept. Indeed, it is totally unrelated. Instead,
it is connected with the concepts discussed previously and afterwards,
in which [Isaiah] pleads [because of the difficulties] for our exile,
wandering, and dispersion, and the fact that the gentile nations rule
over us. In his supplication, he says that when [our people] see this
situation - that those who deny [God's] rule over them - they will
be swayed from the path of truth and their hearts will drift from fear
of You. It will be as if You caused these fools to depart from the path
of truth. We find similar statements made by Moses:[37] "All the nations
who have heard of Your renown will say that it is impossible for
God...."

33. Isaiah 6:10.
34. I Kings 18:37.
35. Hoshea 4:17.
36. Isaiah 63:17.
37. Numbers 14:15-16. The Rambam is explaining that just as Moses issued a plea to God
based on the way God's deeds would be perceived in the world at large, so too,
Isaiah issued a plea based on the manner in which His deeds would be perceived by
the Jews.

[To emphasize the supplicatory aspect of his statements, Isaiah] continues:[38] "For Your servant's sake, return the tribes of Your inheritance" - i.e., so that there will not be a desecration of God's name. In a similar vein, we find in the works of the twelve [lesser prophets] statements concerning [the fate] of those who seek truth in the time of the exile, how they will be vanquished by the idolaters e.g.]:[39] "[You say; 'Everyone who does evil is good in the eyes of God and in them does He delight,' or 'Where is the God of judgment?'" And similarly, he tells of statements that will be made because of the difficulty of exile:[40] "You have said, 'It is futile to serve God; what profit is there in observing His charge, and in our having walked in darkness before the Lord of Hosts? Now we call the proud happy.'" And we are promised that God will ultimately clarify the truth, as it is written,[41] "And you shall return and see the difference between a righteous man and one who is wicked."

And so, we have explained all the difficult verses in the Torah and in Scripture that make it appear as though God compels one to sin. These explanations will certainly be found satisfactory by a person who contemplates them. Thus, the foundations we have established remain: That obedience and rebellion are in the hands of man, that he has free choice in his deeds. He will do what he desires to do, and will not do what he does not desire to do unless God will punish him for the performance of a sin by negating his will, as we have explained. Therefore, it is proper that he eagerly seek to acquire virtues, for there is no external force that will arouse him to them. And this is the lesson communicated by the teaching in this tractate:[42] "If I am not for myself, who will be for me?"

In this context, there remains only one concept that is worthwhile to discuss to complete the subject matter of this chapter, In truth, I would not like to discuss this matter at all, but I feel the necessity to do so. [The subject is] God's knowledge of the future. For the people who maintain that man is compelled to obey or disobey God's will and that man has no free choice with regard to his conduct, because his will is dependent on God's will, come to this conclusion [for the following reasons].

38. *Loc. cit.*:17.
39. Malachi 2:17.
40. *Ibid.* 3:14-15.
41. *Ibid.*:18.
42. 1:13.

They ask: Does God know that a certain person will be righteous or wicked, or does He not know? If we say that He knows, [they maintain,] this would mean that the person is obligated to come to that state that God knew beforehand. If not, His knowledge would be imperfect. And if we say that He does not know [what the person would do] beforehand, this would obligate an awesome and strange set of notions and destroy the walls [of faith]. Therefore, listen to the principles that I will explain and contemplate them at length, for they are undoubtedly true.

As explained by the science of Godly knowledge - i.e., metaphysics - that God does not know with [ordinary] knowledge, or live with [ordinary] life in a manner that He and His life are two separate entities, as are a man and His knowledge.[43] For a person exists independently of his knowledge and knows independently of his existence; they [man and his knowledge] are two separate entities. If God knew with knowledge [of this type], there would of necessity be a multitude of eternal entities: God, His knowledge, His life, His potential, and all His other qualities.

I have shown a simple proof of this concept, one that will be understood by the general public. Nevertheless, the proofs and rebuttals that negate this concept [that God knows through ordinary knowledge] are very strong and openly evident.

Thus, it is apparent that He is one with His attributes and His attributes are one with Him, to the extent that we can say that He is the Knower, He is the Knowledge, and He is what is known. He is life; He is the one living, and He is the one who draws down life to Himself. The same applies with regard to His other attributes. These concepts are difficult to comprehend. A person cannot expect to gain a complete understanding of the matter from two or three of my lines. He will gain merely a general conception.[44]

43. See also *Hilchot Yesodei HaTorah* 2:10 and the Guide for the Perplexed, Vol. I, Chapters 68 and 72, where the Rambam also discusses this matter.
44. The Rambam's intent is that, not only is this a very difficult concept, which can be understood only after much intellectual contemplation; moreover, it is something which man, by definition, cannot understand. Our very mortal condition prevents us from ever grasping this concept in its entirety.

Nevertheless, although we cannot fully appreciate the principle, we can understand the premises on which it is based. We exist in the context of an environment separate from ourselves. Therefore, though man can use his knowledge to conceive of other entities, that connection, as any bond with an external entity, cannot be complete, and there is no possibility for complete oneness. With regard to God, *Bereishit Rabbah* 68:9 states, "He is the the place of the world," i.e., the existence of all other entities is not

On this basis, we can [appreciate a grammatical concept] in Hebrew. We do not say חֵי יְהֹוָה (*chei HaShem*,[45] "By the life of God"), as one would say *chei nafsh'cha* ("By the life of your soul")[46] or *chei Pharaoh* ("By the life of Pharaoh");[47] i.e., that [life is] an additional quality [to the person himself], the person and this additional dimension being two separate entities.

[This is not true with regard to God,] for there is nothing that can be appended to His essence. For God's life is His essence, and His essence is His life; it is not a separate entity. Therefore, it is written:[48] חַי יְהֹוָה (*chai HaShem*, "As God lives"),[49] the intent being that He and His life are one.

It has already been explained in Metaphysics[50] that our minds do not have the capacity to attain complete knowledge of His existence, because of the perfection of His being and the limits of our minds. For His Being is not caused by external factors through which He could be known.

---

apart from Him. Therefore, when knowing them, He does not know a separate entity, He knows Himself, and thus there is nothing to prevent true unity. Nevertheless, the concept in its totality cannot be comprehended by man, because there is no way that we can conceive of an existence above the frame of creation.

An analogy for the manner in which God knows existence can be taken from our dreams. When we dream, we create within our minds a world that did not exist previously. The existence of that dream world is totally dependent upon our imagination and vanishes when our attention focuses on something else. All the entities within the dream exist by virtue of our powers of thought alone.

(There are, however, many differences between the existence of the world within God's thought and our dreams. Among them:
(a) God's thought creates actual, material existence and not dreamlike entities; and
(b) None of the entities in our dreams are totally new creations. The dream world is new for the dreamer. However, the entities within are taken from or combined from different elements of his experience.)

See also the Guide for the Perplexed, Vol. III, Chapter 21, where the Rambam explains this concept with the simile of an engineer who perceives the entire structure of a mechanism in his mind before drawing up the blueprints for it.

45. Using a *tzeireh* (..) as the punctuation sign under the *chet* in the word *chei*.
46. I Samuel 1:26.
47. Genesis 42:15.
48. E.g., I Kings 18:15; Jeremiah 38:16. These proof-texts are quoted in the standard printed texts of the Rambam's Commentary on the Mishnah. They do not, however, appear in the authoritative manuscripts of that text. There are many other such verses throughout Scripture.
49. Using a *patach* (-) as the punctuation sign under the *chet* in the word *chai*.
50. The intent appears to be Aristotle's Metaphysics, Vol. XII, Chapter 9.

The limits of our knowledge of Him can be compared with the limit of our eyes to perceive sunlight. This is not a result of the weaknes of the sun's light. [Instead, the opposite is true.] It is a stronger ligh than one desires to perceive. This subject is explained at length [ir Metaphysics], and all his words are clear and direct.

The summary of this discussion is that we do not comprehenc His knowledge, nor do we fathom its extent at all, for He is His knowledge and His knowledge is Him. This is a wondrous concept which is not grasped [by many]. Although [these same individuals admit that His Being is the ultimate of all perfection, which canno be grasped. Nevertheless, they tried to grasp His knowledge, thinking that they would be able to comprehend it. But this is impossible, since if they were able to know His knowledge, they would know His Being for they are all one. For the perfection of His knowledge involve: grasping His Being, together with His knowledge, His potential, Hi will, His life, and His other wondrous qualities.

As we have explained, the thought of comprehending His knowledge is absolute foolishness. We know that He knows just as we know that He exists. If one asked: what is the nature of His knowledge? We should reply that just as we do not grasp His Being perfectly, so too, we cannot grasp His knowledge perfectly. Those who thought they could comprehend Him have already been rebuked, as it is written,[51] "Can your research find God?"

Thus, it has been explained that [every] person's actions are given over to him, and it is within his potential to be righteous or wicked There is no compulsion from God with regard to either of these two paths. Therefore, it is necessary that there be commandments, study, preparation, reward, and punishment. The manner in which He knows and comprehends is beyond our [mortal] comprehension, as explained.

These are the concepts I had intended to explain with regard to this chapter. The time has come to cease this explanation and begin interpreting the tractate for which these prefaces were necessary.

51. Job 11:7.

PIRKEI AVOT / פרקי אבות

with the commentary of the Rambam

CHAPTER ONE

1. Moses received the Torah from Sinai and passed it on to Joshua; Joshua [passed it on] to the elders; the elders to the Prophets; the Prophets passed it on to the Men of the Great Assembly.

They [the men of the Great Assembly] made three statements: Be deliberate in judgment; raise up many students; and make a fence around the Torah.

2. Shimon the Righteous was one of the last of the Men of the Great Assembly. He used to say: The world stands on three things - on the Torah, service, and deeds of kindness.

3. Antigonus of Socho received [the oral tradition] from Shimon the Righteous. He used to say: Do not be like servants who serve their master for the sake of receiving a grant, but rather be like servants who serve their master without the intent of receiving a grant; and let the fear of Heaven be upon you.

Moses received - In the introduction to this text,[1] we already explained the order of the [Oral] Tradition, and how it was transmitted. Therefore, my intent [in these notes] will be merely to explain these ethical statements, to encourage the acquisition of these qualities, for they are of great value. We will also elaborate in admonishment against certain negative traits, for they cause great loss. On other occasions, I will explain the meaning of the words and some of the concepts.

Be deliberate in judgment - [Judges] should be patient in coming to a decision, and should not hastily issue a ruling without contemplating it in depth. For it is possible that later they will realize concepts that were not apparent to them in their original conception of the matter.

And make a fence around the Torah - I.e., institute decrees and ordinances that will separate a person from sin. As God said,[2] "And you shall observe My ordinances," which was interpreted by our Sages[3] to mean, "Make a safeguard for My ordinances."

On [the study of] Torah, the [Temple] service, and deeds of kindness - Torah refers to knowledge [intellectual virtue]. Deeds of kindness [reflect] ethical virtue. [Service

1. I.e., the introduction to the Rambam's Commentary on the Mishnah.
2. Leviticus 18:30.
3. *Mo'ed Katan* 5a.
4. I.e., the introduction to that chapter, where the Rambam speaks of the Thirteen Principles of Faith. (See also the tenth chapter of *Hilchot Teshuvah*.)
5. Deuteronomy 6:13.
6. Jerusalem Talmud, *Berachot* 9:7.

פֶּרֶק רִאשׁוֹן

א מֹשֶׁה קִבֵּל תּוֹרָה מִסִּינַי, וּמְסָרָהּ לִיהוֹשֻׁעַ, וִיהוֹשֻׁעַ לִזְקֵנִים, וּזְקֵנִים לִנְבִיאִים, וּנְבִיאִים מְסָרוּהָ לְאַנְשֵׁי כְנֶסֶת הַגְּדוֹלָה. הֵם אָמְרוּ שְׁלֹשָׁה דְבָרִים: הֱווּ מְתוּנִים בַּדִּין, וְהַעֲמִידוּ תַלְמִידִים הַרְבֵּה, וַעֲשׂוּ סְיָג לַתּוֹרָה.

ב שִׁמְעוֹן הַצַּדִּיק הָיָה מִשְׁיָרֵי כְנֶסֶת הַגְּדוֹלָה. הוּא הָיָה אוֹמֵר: עַל שְׁלֹשָׁה דְבָרִים הָעוֹלָם עוֹמֵד: עַל הַתּוֹרָה, וְעַל הָעֲבוֹדָה, וְעַל גְּמִילוּת חֲסָדִים.

ג אַנְטִיגְנוֹס אִישׁ סוֹכוֹ קִבֵּל מִשִּׁמְעוֹן הַצַּדִּיק. הוּא הָיָה אוֹמֵר: אַל תִּהְיוּ כַעֲבָדִים הַמְשַׁמְּשִׁין אֶת הָרַב עַל מְנָת לְקַבֵּל פְּרָס, אֶלָּא הֱווּ כַעֲבָדִים הַמְשַׁמְּשִׁין אֶת הָרַב שֶׁלֹּא עַל מְנָת לְקַבֵּל פְּרָס, וִיהִי מוֹרָא שָׁמַיִם עֲלֵיכֶם.

refers to] the observance of the mitzvot, [more particularly] the sacrificial worship [in the Temple]. The continued improvement of the world and its stable existence in the most perfect manner possible [depend on these three modes of devotion].

Grant - This refers to the award with which a person is endowed when he performs a deed that he is not obligated to perform. For example, a person who tells his servant, his younger son, or his wife, "Do this or this and I will give you a *dinar* or two *dinarim*." This is the difference between the words פרס ("grant") and שכר ("remuneration"). For a reward is given for fulfilling an obligation.

This pious man [Antigonus, teaches]: Do not serve God for the sake of the beneficence and kindness He will grant you. For then, you are pursuing compensation and carrying out your service for its sake. Instead, serve Him as do servants who are not concerned with the kindness and good that they receive. His intention is that one should serve [God] out of love, as explained in the tenth chapter of *Sanhedrin*.[4]

Despite this [stress on love], he did not free [his disciples] from [the obligation of] fear. [He emphasized that] although you serve God with love, you should not neglect fear entirely. [Rather,] ...

Let the fear of Heaven be upon you. - For the Torah also includes a commandment to fear, as it is written,[5] "And you shall fear God, your Lord." And our Sages said,[6] "Serve Him with love and serve Him with fear." And it is said,[7] "One who loves [God] will not neglect the commandment, and one who fears [God] will not

7. The *Torah Temimah* cites the Rambam's source for this quote as the passage in the Jerusalem Talmud cited previously. Nevertheless, an examination of that source reveals textual differences. Rav Kapach maintains that the Rambam is referring to a well-known Arab ethical dictum.

4. Yosse ben Yo'ezer of Tzreidah and Yosse ben Yochanan of Jerusalem received [the Oral Tradition] from them. Yosse ben Yo'ezer of Tzreidah said: Let your house be a meeting place for sages; sit in the dust at their feet: and drink in their words thirstily.

5. Yosse ben Yochanan of Jerusalem said: Let your house be wide open [for guests]. Treat the poor as members of your household, and do not indulge excessively in conversation with the woman.

This was said concerning one's own wife; how much more so does it apply to the wife of another. Hence, the Sages have declared: Anyone who indulges excessively in conversation with a woman causes evil to himself, neglects the study of Torah, and ultimately will inherit Hell.

6. Yehoshua ben Perachiah and Nittai of Arbel received [the Oral Tradition] from them. Yehoshua ben Perachiah said: Provide yourself

transgress [His] warning." Thus, fear plays a great role [as a spur to the observance of] the negative commandments, particularly those mitzvot that emphasize obedience.[8]

Antigonus had two students, Tzadok and Boethus. When they heard this teaching, they departed his presence and without understanding his intent said to each other, "The master has stated that there is no reward, nor punishment, nor hope."

They continued speaking to each other until they denied the Torah. To each was attracted a following, whom the Sages referred to as Sadducees and Boethusians. When they saw that they could not draw the masses to the faith that they conceived - for this wicked creed creates division among those united, instead of joining together those dispersed - they changed tactics, and declared the truth of the Written Torah, for they could not deny it before the masses. [Indeed,] had they denied its truth, they would have been executed.

Each of them tried to create the impression among his followers that he believed in the Written Torah, but challenged the Oral Tradition, saying that it was not genuine, the intent being to free themselves [of the restrictions] of the mitzvot transmitted through that tradition, and the Rabbinic decrees and enactments. For they saw that it was impossible for them to renounce the totality [of our heritage], the Written Law and the Oral Tradition.

Moreover, this approach left room for interpretation. For if there is no [accepted] interpretation transmitted by tradition, the matter is left to will. One can be lenient when one desires and stringent when one desires, according to one's own intents, since one does not believe in the fundamental matter at all. In this manner, they sought an approach that would be attractive to certain people.

After these cursed sects arose, they were followed by other groups of non-believers, including those who are called Karaites in this land - Egypt. The Sages would refer to all these [types of deviants with the general terms,] Sadducees and Boethusians.

8. I.e., the *chukkim*, the mitzvot whose observance depends on the acceptance of God's will, rather than on morals whose value can be appreciated by human logic. See the sixth introductory chapter.

ד יוֹסֵי בֶן יוֹעֶזֶר אִישׁ צְרֵדָה וְיוֹסֵי בֶן יוֹחָנָן אִישׁ יְרוּשָׁלַיִם קִבְּלוּ מֵהֶם. יוֹסֵי בֶן יוֹעֶזֶר אִישׁ צְרֵדָה אוֹמֵר: יְהִי בֵיתְךָ בֵּית וַעַד לַחֲכָמִים, וֶהֱוֵי מִתְאַבֵּק בַּעֲפַר רַגְלֵיהֶם, וֶהֱוֵי שׁוֹתֶה בַצָּמָא אֶת דִּבְרֵיהֶם.

ה יוֹסֵי בֶן יוֹחָנָן אִישׁ יְרוּשָׁלַיִם אוֹמֵר: יְהִי בֵיתְךָ פָתוּחַ לִרְוָחָה, וְיִהְיוּ עֲנִיִּים בְּנֵי בֵיתֶךָ, וְאַל תַּרְבֶּה שִׂיחָה עִם הָאִשָּׁה. בְּאִשְׁתּוֹ אָמְרוּ, קַל וָחֹמֶר בְּאֵשֶׁת חֲבֵרוֹ. מִכָּאן אָמְרוּ חֲכָמִים: כָּל זְמַן שֶׁאָדָם מַרְבֶּה שִׂיחָה עִם הָאִשָּׁה, גּוֹרֵם רָעָה לְעַצְמוֹ, וּבוֹטֵל מִדִּבְרֵי תוֹרָה, וְסוֹפוֹ יוֹרֵשׁ גֵּיהִנֹּם.

ו יְהוֹשֻׁעַ בֶן פְּרַחְיָה וְנִתַּאי הָאַרְבֵּלִי קִבְּלוּ מֵהֶם. יְהוֹשֻׁעַ בֶן פְּרַחְיָה אוֹמֵר: עֲשֵׂה לְךָ רַב, וּקְנֵה לְךָ חָבֵר, וֶהֱוֵי דָן אֶת כָּל הָאָדָם לְכַף זְכוּת.

These are the individuals who sought to question the Oral Tradition and interpret the verses as they saw fit without listening to the wise men at all, disregarding God's directive:[9] "Act according to the laws, about which you will be instructed, and the judgments that will be told you. Do not deviate from the word that you will be told right or left."

A meeting place - A gathering place; i.e., you should structure your home [environment] so that it will be a place where sages frequently gather, like a synagogue or house of study. [The distinction of one's home for this purpose should be so powerful] that when one sage says to another, "Where will we meet?", the other will reply, "At so and so's house."

Be wide open - So that you should have a gate open to wayfarers, so that any traveler that needs anything, or who is hungry or thirsty, will enter your home without hesitation.

Treat the poor as members of your household - I.e., [employ] the poor and the indigent as your servants instead of purchasing slaves. The Sages would thus criticize those who purchase servants and praise those employ the poor, for they are of one's people and are one's family.

Do not indulge excessively in conversation with the woman - By and large, a man's conversation with women will revolve around sex. Therefore, [the teaching] states that excessive talk with [one's wife] is forbidden, because one...

causes evil to himself - i.e., he habituates himself to undesirable character traits - e.g., desire.

neglects the study of Torah - This is obvious, for he will spend his time involved with other matters.

and ultimately will inherit Hell - The rebellion against God that comes as a result of this idle talk will require that the person be punished.

Provide yourself with a master - I.e.,[10] even if the person is not worthy of being

9. Deuteronomy 17:11.
10. The Hebrew term עשה also has the connotation of "force." Even if you would not naturally accept this person as a teacher, force yourself to do so.

with a master; acquire for yourself a friend; and judge every person favorably.

7. Nittai of Arbel said: Keep away from a bad neighbor; do not fraternize with a wicked man; and do not abandon belief in [Divine] retribution.

8. Yehudah ben Tabbai and Shimon ben Shetach received [the Oral Tradition] from them. Yehudah ben Tabbai said: Do not act as a

your teacher, accept him as your teacher, so that you will confer and debate with him. In this manner, you will retain your studies. For one cannot compare the effect of individual study to that of study with another person. [Subject matter studied with] another person will be retained better and will be clarified more. This applies even if the other person is on one's own level of wisdom and even when he is on a lower level. This is the intent of this charge.

acquire for yourself a friend - [The *mishnah*] uses the expression "acquire," not "provide yourself with a friend," or "make friends with others." [This emphasizes the importance of friendship.] For a person should always have a friend who will [help him] better all aspects of his conduct, as our Sages commented,[11] "Either comradeship or death." If one does not find one easily, one must make efforts in this direction. If necessary, one should procure his friendship until [true] friendship is established. One should not cease accomodating oneself to the other person's nature until such friendship has been established. Thus, the ethical masters have taught, "Do not establish friendship according to your nature; establish friendship according to your friend's nature."

When each of the friends conducts himself according to this directive, the desire of each one will be to fulfill the will of his colleague. Thus, they will both share a single goal. How appropriate is the statement of Aristotle,[12] "Your other friend is really yourself."[13]

In general, there are three types of friends:[14] a friend befriended for the sake of benefit, a friend befriended for the sake of satisfaction, and a friend befriended for the sake of a higher purpose. Examples of friends befriended for the sake of benefit are two partners, or the relationship between a king and his army.

There are two types of friends befriended for the sake of satisfaction: a friend whom one trusts and a friend who grants one pleasure. An example of a friend who grants one pleasure is the relationship between men and women during marriage.

A friend whom one trusts refers to a person on whom one can rely without withholding anything from him, neither deed nor word. He reveals to him all his matters - both good and bad - without worrying that he will shame him - either

11. *Ta'anit* 23a.
12. Nicomethean Ethics, Discourse 9, Chapter 4.
13. Aristotle states that a person's first friend is himself, for a person must take responsibility for his conduct. His second friend, although another person, also identifies fully with him, for the development of friendship leads to a fusion of identity among people.

ז נִתַּאי הָאַרְבֵּלִי אוֹמֵר: הַרְחֵק מִשָּׁכֵן רָע, וְאַל תִּתְחַבֵּר לָרָשָׁע, וְאַל תִּתְיָאֵשׁ מִן הַפֻּרְעָנוּת.

ח יְהוּדָה בֶן טַבַּאי וְשִׁמְעוֹן בֶּן שָׁטַח קִבְּלוּ מֵהֶם. יְהוּדָה בֶן טַבַּאי אוֹמֵר: אַל תַּעַשׂ

in private or in public. When a person is able to trust a colleague so thoroughly, he will derive tremendous satisfaction from talking to him and sharing his company.

A friend befriended for the sake of a higher purpose refers to a situation where both desire and focus on a single objective: doing good. Each will desire to draw strength from his colleague, and to attain this good for them both. This is the type of friend [the *mishnah*] commanded us to acquire - for example, the comradeship between a teacher and his disciple, and between a disciple and his teacher.

and judge every person favorably - I.e., [the intent is as follows:] a person's character is unknown to you and you are not aware whether he is righteous or wicked. You saw that he performed a deed or made a statement that could, according to a given set of circumstances, be defined as good, but could also be interpreted as being bad. [The *mishnah* is teaching,] judge the person favorably, and do not think evil about him.

When, however, a person is known to be righteous, and is renowned for his good deeds, but one nevertheless saw him perform a deed that looks wicked from all vantage points, and could be interpreted as a good deed only with great difficulty and in a farfetched manner, one is obligated to interpret it positively, since there is the possibility of doing so. It is forbidden to suspect him, and in this regard our Sages said,[15] "A person who suspects the worthy will be punished."

Similarly, if a person is wicked, and his [evil] deeds are well known, but he performed a deed that looks positive from all vantage points, and it is only with great difficulty and in a farfetched manner that it could be interpreted as evil, one should take precautions and not believe that it is good, since it has the possibility of being evil. Concerning this, it is written:[16] "Even when he lifts his voice in supplication, do not believe him, for there are seven abominations in his heart." If, however, the person's identity is unknown, and his conduct could be interpreted in either manner, it is an obligation [for those who follow] the path of piety to judge him in a favorable manner.

Do not fraternize with a wicked man - [I.e., avoid] any type of association so that you do not learn from his conduct. As explained in the previous chapters,[17] undesirable traits are acquired through association with the wicked.

do not abandon belief in [Divine] retribution - [The *mishnah* also teaches] that if you have sinned or have seen others sin, do not become lax and say that God's punishment will be only in the World to Come. Instead, do not abandon belief that one will suffer Divine retribution in this world for that sin.

14. Here also the Rambam is borrowing concepts from Aristotle, Nicomethean Ethics, Discourse 8, Chapters 2-4.
15. *Shabbat* 97a.
16. Proverbs 26:25.
17. See the fourth introductory chapter.

counselor [when sitting as a judge]; when the litigants stand before you, regard them both as guilty; but when they leave, having accepted the judgment, regard them both as guiltless.

9. Shimon ben Shetach said: Examine the witnesses thoroughly; and be cautious with your words, lest through them they learn to speak falsehood.

10. Shemayah and Avtalion received [the Oral Tradition] from them. Shemayah said: Love work; abhor taking high office; and do not seek intimacy with the ruling power.

11. Avtalion said: Sages, be careful with your words. For you may incur the penalty of exile and be banished to a place of evil waters, and the disciples who follow you there will drink and die, and consequently God's name will be desecrated.

12. Hillel and Shammai received [the Oral Tradition] from them. Hillel said: Be of the disciples of Aaron, loving peace and pursuing peace, loving the created beings, and bringing them near to the Torah.

As a counselor - [i.e., an advocate] who knows how to assert claims, who receives power of attorney to act on a person's behalf in a dispute. They devise questions so that if the judge replies one way, the answer will be such, and if the litigant makes a certain claim, such a reply will be given. It is as if they are arraying the position of the judges and litigants before them. This is the meaning of the term עורך דין, one who positions the judges, as it were.

[The *mishnah*] advises against conducting oneself in such a manner - i.e., one should not advise a litigant to assert a claim that will benefit him [more than the truth] or to defend himself, by saying such and such or denying the claim. This applies even when one knows that he is being exploited and that the other litigant is making a false claim. It is, nevertheless, forbidden to teach him a [false] claim that will advance his interests.

The ruling power - This is the meaning of the word רשות.

These three directives will bring one benefit with regard to both one's divine service and one's worldly activity. For when a person does not work, he will become destitute, and will steal and act with deceit.

And when a person seeks position he will face many challenges and difficult situations. For he will become jealous of others. [Similarly,] he will be forced to take a stand

---

18. This statement is also quoted by the *Baal HaTurim* (gloss on Numbers 1:50). Its source is a matter of question among the commentaries, for no explicit statement to this effect has

עַצְמְךָ כְּעוֹרְכֵי הַדַּיָּנִין, וּכְשֶׁיִּהְיוּ בַּעֲלֵי דִינִים עוֹמְדִים לְפָנֶיךָ יִהְיוּ בְעֵינֶיךָ כִּרְשָׁעִים, וּכְשֶׁנִּפְטָרִים מִלְּפָנֶיךָ יִהְיוּ בְעֵינֶיךָ כְּזַכָּאִין, לִכְשֶׁקִּבְּלוּ עֲלֵיהֶם אֶת הַדִּין.

ט שִׁמְעוֹן בֶּן שָׁטַח אוֹמֵר: הֱוֵי מַרְבֶּה לַחְקֹר אֶת הָעֵדִים, וֶהֱוֵי זָהִיר בִּדְבָרֶיךָ, שֶׁמָּא מִתּוֹכָם יִלְמְדוּ לְשַׁקֵּר.

י שְׁמַעְיָה וְאַבְטַלְיוֹן קִבְּלוּ מֵהֶם. שְׁמַעְיָה אוֹמֵר: אֱהֹב אֶת הַמְּלָאכָה, וּשְׂנָא אֶת הָרַבָּנוּת, וְאַל תִּתְוַדַּע לָרָשׁוּת.

יא אַבְטַלְיוֹן אוֹמֵר: חֲכָמִים הִזָּהֲרוּ בְדִבְרֵיכֶם, שֶׁמָּא תָחוּבוּ חוֹבַת גָּלוּת, וְתִגְלוּ לִמְקוֹם מַיִם הָרָעִים, וְיִשְׁתּוּ הַתַּלְמִידִים הַבָּאִים אַחֲרֵיכֶם וְיָמוּתוּ, וְנִמְצָא שֵׁם שָׁמַיִם מִתְחַלֵּל.

יב הִלֵּל וְשַׁמַּאי קִבְּלוּ מֵהֶם. הִלֵּל אוֹמֵר: הֱוֵי מִתַּלְמִידָיו שֶׁל אַהֲרֹן: אוֹהֵב שָׁלוֹם

against his enemies and in doing so, will lose his faith. [In this vein,] our Sages said,[18] "When a person becomes a leader on this earthly plane, he is deemed wicked on the spiritual plane."

Similarly, familiarity with a king [creates dangers] that are difficult to evade and harms one's faith, for the person seeks only those things that will endear him to the ruler. The case of Do'eg [the Edomite][19] serves as an example of this. And in that instance, the king to whom he drew close was referred to as "God's anointed"[20] and "God's chosen";[21] and he served as a prophet.[22]

Evil waters - This is an analogy for heresy. [The *mishnah*] counsels [the Sages] to be careful with their public statements, lest they leave room for misinterpretation. Non-believers may be present and they will interpret it according to their dogma. Since the students will have heard this teaching from you, they may turn to heresy thinking that this was your intent. This will cause a desecration of God's name, as happened with regard to Antigonus of Socho and [his students,] Tzadok and Boethus.

Be of the disciples of Aaron - The following narrative is told about Aaron. When he would feel or hear that a person had wickedness within him, or that he would commit

been found in the Talmud or *Midrashim*. Rav Tzvi Hirsch Chayyut points to *Sanhedrin* 103b, which in the standard text reads "When a person becomes poor (רש) on the material plane, he has been deemed wicked on the spiritual plane," and suggests that the Rambam's version of the text read ראש, "a leader," rather than רש, "poor."
19. See I Samuel, Chapter 22, which relates how Do'eg told Saul how the priests of Nov provided David with refuge and thus caused those priests to be killed.
20. I Samuel 10:1.
21. II Samuel 21:6.
22. I Samuel 10:11.

He used to say: He who seeks renown loses his reputation; he who does not increase [his knowledge of the Torah] decreases it; he who does not study [the Torah] deserves death; and he who exploits the crown [of the Torah for his own ends] shall perish.

13. He used to say: If I am not for myself, who is for me? And if I am only for myself, what am I? And if not now, when?

14. Shammai said: Make your study of Torah a fixed priority; say little and do much; and receive every person with a cheerful countenance.

15. Rabban Gamliel said: Provide yourself with a master and free yourself of doubt. And do not tithe by estimation, even giving in excess of the required amount.

---

sins, he would [always] greet him first, become friendly with him, and speak with him frequently.

This would cause the other person to become embarrassed and say, "Woe is me. If Aaron knew my inner thoughts or were aware of my deeds, he would not let himself see me; how much more so would he not speak to me. Surely he considers me to be pious. I will make his conception true, and repent and become one of his students again."

With regard to this lofty quality, God said:[23] "He walked with Me in peace and uprightness, and he turned many away from sin." It was to this notable quality that Hillel referred.

Hillel continued, saying that the fact that a person has achieved renown and greatness is a sign that his existence will cease. And further, he continued saying that a person who does not increase his studies will die by God's hand. If, however, someone has not studied at all, he deserves to be killed.

He who exploits the crown [of the Torah for his own ends] shall perish - The intent is a person who uses the Torah as a means to derive a livelihood. This is the meaning of this teaching, as will be explained later in this tractate.[24]

[The word תגא] can also be interpreted as an acronym for the words תלמיד גברא אחרינא - "The student of another man." [The *mishnah* is teaching that] it is forbidden to make use of a Torah scholar unless he is one's own student.

If I am not for myself - [In this *mishnah*, Hillel] teaches that [a person should say]: if I will not be the one who rouses me to virtue, who else will arouse me? For, as explained in the eighth introductory chapter, there are no external motivators to

---

23. Malachi 2:6.
24. Chapter 4, *Mishnah* 7.
25. Proverbs 22:6.
26. Genesis, Chapter 18.

וְרוֹדֵף שָׁלוֹם, אוֹהֵב אֶת הַבְּרִיּוֹת וּמְקָרְבָן לַתּוֹרָה. הוּא הָיָה אוֹמֵר: נְגֵד שְׁמָא, אֲבַד
שְׁמֵהּ; וּדְלָא מוֹסִיף, יָסֵף; וּדְלָא יָלֵף, קְטָלָא חַיָּב; וּדְאִשְׁתַּמֵּשׁ בְּתָגָא, חָלָף.

יג הוּא הָיָה אוֹמֵר: אִם אֵין אֲנִי לִי, מִי לִי? וּכְשֶׁאֲנִי לְעַצְמִי, מָה אֲנִי? וְאִם לֹא
עַכְשָׁו, אֵימָתָי?

יד שַׁמַּאי אוֹמֵר: עֲשֵׂה תוֹרָתְךָ קֶבַע, אֱמֹר מְעַט וַעֲשֵׂה הַרְבֵּה, וֶהֱוֵי מְקַבֵּל אֶת כָּל
הָאָדָם בְּסֵבֶר פָּנִים יָפוֹת.

טו רַבָּן גַּמְלִיאֵל אוֹמֵר: עֲשֵׂה לְךָ רַב, וְהִסְתַּלֵּק מִן הַסָּפֵק, וְאַל תַּרְבֶּה לְעַשֵּׂר אֲמָדוֹת.

divine service. Rather, it is the person himself who must turn himself to either side,
as he desires.

And if I am only for myself - [I.e., knowing this,] what have I accomplished? Which
good deeds have I performed? Belittling himself, [Hillel] asks:

What am I - What is my contribution? I have not reached personal fulfillment,
although as above, I knew [that it is within my reach]. And he continues: If I will
not acquire virtues now - when I am young - when will I attain them? When I
grow old and white?

No. [That is unlikely,] for then it is harder to change one's tendencies, for one's
habits have already become set, and one has slackened to seek either virtue or vice. In
this vein, the wise man said,[25] "Educate a youth according to his way ... ."

Set a fixed time - I.e., make Torah study the primary element [of your life], and
all your other activities secondary. [Regard them nonchalantly.] If they come, it is
good; and if they do not come, nothing is lost because of their absence.

[The *mishnah*] teaches that the righteous make a small commitment and do much.
For example, Abraham our Patriarch promised [the angels] a loaf of bread and brought
them butter, milk, a calf and three cakes of fine flour.[26] The wicked, by contrast, make
impressive promises and do nothing. For example, Efron promised to give everything
[without charge]; in practice, he did not forego even one *dinar* of [the property's]
worth.[27]

a cheerful countenance - i.e., amenably, and graciously.

Provide yourself with a master - The intent is not a teacher, but one who issues
halachic decisions. [The *mishnah*] teaches: select a person as an authority so that you
will rely on him as to what is permitted and what is forbidden, and you will thus not
be beset by doubt. In this vein, the Jerusalem Talmud states,[28] "Bring a sage from

---

27. *Loc. cit.*, Chapter 23. The comparison between the two is found in *Bava Metzia* 87a.
28. *Mo'ed Katan* 1:6. It is significant to compare this *mishnah* to *Mishnah* 6, where the same
advice is given in a slightly different context.
With regard to tithing by approximation, see *Hilchot Ma'aser* 1:14.

16. Shimon his son said: All my days I grew up among the Sages and did not find anything better for one's person than silence. Study is not the essential thing - deed is; and whoever engages in excessive talk brings on sin.

the marketplace upon whose opinion I will rely, and I will permit this for you." Similarly, [the admonition against] separating tithes by approximation is to avoid doubt.

Excessive talk - The man of wisdom has already said,[29] "In the multitude of words, sin will not be lacking." The rationale [behind these statements] is that most of the things [we] say are superfluous and sinful, as will be explained.

When a person speaks excessively, he will surely sin, because within his words, there will surely be at least one concept that was unnecessary to mention. One of the ways of detecting a wise man is to see whether he speaks with measured words, as it is said,[30] "Silence is a fence for wisdom." And excessive talk is an indication of foolishness, as it is written,[31] "A fool's voice is known by a multitude of words." Similarly, our Sages have said[32] that a sign of revered lineage is restraint from speaking, and with regard to a person of revered lineage they said, "His lineage is reflected in his silence."

The Book of Ethics[33] tells of a wise man who cherished silence and would speak only on rare occasions. He was asked why he preferred silence, and he explained that he probed the nature of speech and found that there are four categories of talking:

a) The first category is only damaging and does not possess any positive virtue - e.g., curses and vile speech. Such speech is utter foolishness.

b) The second category is damaging, but also contains virtue - e.g., to praise a person so that one may derive benefit from him, and yet this praise will anger the person's enemy. This causes damage to the person who was praised. Therefore, one should refrain from making statements of this nature, and one should not speak matters that fall into this category.

c) The third category is one that neither has virtue nor is damaging - i.e., most of the talk of the masses describing how the wall of a city was built, how a particular palace was built, a description of the beauty of a particular house or the abundance of produce in a particular land. These and other similar matters are all superfluous. And this entire category is thus immaterial and lacking virtue.

d) The fourth category of speech includes matters that are of genuine value - e.g., talk about wisdom or ethical development, and a person's statements with regard to matters necessary to maintain his existence.

29. Proverbs 10:19.
30. Chapter 3, *Mishnah* 13.
31. Ecclesiastes 5:2.
32. *Kiddushin* 71b.
33. The identity of the text cited by the Rambam is a matter of question. It does not refer to Aristotle's *Nicomethean Ethics*. Significantly, Rabbi Shlomo Ibn Gabirol also quotes the same concepts in his book, "Chosen Pearls."

טז שִׁמְעוֹן בְּנוֹ אוֹמֵר: כָּל יָמַי גָּדַלְתִּי בֵּין הַחֲכָמִים, וְלֹא מָצָאתִי לַגּוּף טוֹב מִשְּׁתִיקָה;
וְלֹא הַמִּדְרָשׁ הוּא הָעִקָּר, אֶלָּא הַמַּעֲשֶׂה; וְכָל הַמַּרְבֶּה דְבָרִים, מֵבִיא חֵטְא.

"These are the matters," [the wise man said,] "about which it is worthy to speak.
Whenever I hear something, I evaluate it. If I find that it is included in the fourth
category, I speak about it. If it is part of the others, I remain silent."

The people concerned with ethical development said, "Contemplate this person's
[behavior]. In his wisdom, he has eliminated three-fourths of the subject of our talk.
This is wisdom that should be emulated."

I say that from the standpoint of our Torah, speech is divided into five categories:
a) what we are commanded to speak, b) what we are forbidden to speak, c) speech
that should be eschewed, d) speech that is desirable, and e) speech that is left to
our discretion.

a) The first category, what we are commanded to speak: This refers to the reading of
the Torah, its study, and the research into its meaning. This is a positive commandment
that we have been commanded to fulfill, as it is written:[34] "And you shall speak of
them." It is equivalent to all the other mitzvot.[35] There have been enough powerful
words of encouragement stated regarding the study [of the Torah] that this text could
not include even a [significant] portion of them.

b) The second category, speech that is forbidden - e.g., false testimony, lies, gossip,
curses. The Torah specifies what is included in this category. This also includes vile
speech and slander.

c) The third category, speech that should be eschewed, refers to speech that brings no
benefit to the person whatsoever, and involves neither the observance nor the negation
[of God's commandments]. For example, the stories of the masses describing events
that took place, how a particular king would conduct himself in his palace, why did
so-and-so die, or how so-and-so became wealthy. The Sages referred to this as idle
talk, and the pious would strive to avoid such matters. Rav, the student of Rabbi
Chiyya, was praised as "never having engaged in idle talk in his life."[36] Also included
in this category is disparaging a positive virtue or acclaiming an undesirable trait.

d) The fourth category, desirable speech, refers to speech in praise of positive virtues,
whether intellectual or ethical, and the deprecation of undesirable qualities of either
type. This includes inspiring the soul with addresses and songs, and the use of
these same media to encourage the shunning of undesirable traits.

Similarly, [this category] includes the praise of the wise and the description of
the importance of their virtues, to endear their conduct to people at large and [to
encourage] them to emulate it. By the same token, it encompasses the denigration
of the wicked and their undesirable traits in the public's eye, so that they will shun

34. Deuteronomy 6:7. See *Sefer HaMitzvot* (Positive Commandment 11); *Hilchot Talmud
Torah*, Chapter 1.
35. *Pe'ah* 1:1. In this instance, we have based our translation on the translation of Ibn Tibbon.
Rav Kapach renders this phrase as "It is like the other mitzvot." In his notes, however, he states
that Ibn Tibbon's rendition might be correct.
36. See also *Hilchot De'ot* 2:4. The commentaries have not been able to locate a source that praises
Rav in this manner. *Sukkah* 28a ascribes such praise to Rabbi Eliezer and Rabbi Yochanan ben
Zakkai.

them and not emulate their behavior. Some have referred to this category - i.e., training in positive attributes and the avoidance of vulgar attributes - as *derech eretz*, lit. "the way of the world."

e) The fifth category is speech that is left to our discretion - i.e., matters concerning a person's commercial affairs, his earning of a livelihood, his food and drink, his clothing, and his other needs. These matters are neither desired nor eschewed. If a person desires, he may speak of these matters as much as he wants, and if he desires, he may be silent. [Nevertheless,] it is praiseworthy for a person to minimize the amount he speaks, [even] with regard to this category. Similarly, our ethical texts warn against indulging heavily in such talk. With regard to the categories that are forbidden or deemed undesirable, there is no need to speak of the matter. There is no necessity to command [a person or to advise him] that it is proper to remain mute with regard to these matters entirely.

With regard to the [categories of speech that are] commanded and deemed desirable, by contrast, if a person spoke about them throughout his entire life - this would be the ultimate purpose [of his existence]. There are, however, two conditions. First, his conduct must match his words, as it is said,[37] "It is beautiful when words are spoken by one who practices them." With regard to this concept, it is said here:

Study is not the essential thing, deed is - Our Sages said[38] to a pious man who taught positive virtues: "Speak. For you it is befitting to speak." And the prophet said,[39] "May the righteous rejoice in God; it is fitting for the upright to offer praise."

The second quality is brevity. A person should always endeavor to speak few words with much content, and not the converse. This is implied by our Sages' statement:[40] "A person should always teach his students in a concise form."

[In this context, it is worthy to note that] songs, regardless of the language in which they are composed, are judged according to their content. We should follow the same guidelines with regard to them as mentioned above with regard to the five categories of speech.

Although this point of clarification is obvious, it is necessary to mention it [specifically], because I have seen men of stature and pious individuals from our nation [ignoring it]. When they attend a party, a wedding, or [a celebration of] that like, and a person desires to sing a song in Arabic, they object and refuse to allow the song to be sung. This is true even when the song praises courage or forthrightness - i.e., it is in the category of desired speech - or it praises wine. If, by contrast, a singer sings a Hebrew song, no one will object, nor will they remonstrate even though the content of the song concerns subjects that are forbidden or that should be eschewed.

This is utter foolishness. For the decision whether a particular subject is forbidden or permitted, desirable or objectionable, is not dependent on the language in which it is spoken, but rather on its content. If the content of a song is inspiring, it is necessary to sing it, regardless of the language in which it is written. And if its subject matter is corrupt, we are obligated to shun it, regardless of the language in which it is written.

---

37. *Tosefta, Yevamot*, Chapter 8.
38. *Bava Batra* 75a. The phrase is borrowed somewhat out of context.
39. Psalms 33:1.
40. *Pesachim* 3b.

I feel, however, that there is a further point to be added in this regard. When there are two songs that both arouse sensual desire, extol it, and draw the soul in this direction, this is [surely] a shortcoming. And this is the category of speech that should be eschewed, for it arouses and and stimulates a crude quality, as we explained in the fourth [introductory] chapter. When one of the songs was composed in Hebrew and the other in Arabic or Persian, hearing the Hebrew song and speaking of these matters in that language is less desirable according to the Torah. Because of the holiness of the language,[41] it is not fitting to use it except for refined purposes. Surely, the above applies if the person [incorporates] a verse from the Torah or the Song of Songs. This causes [the song] to move from the undesirable category to the forbidden. For the Torah has forbidden the use of the words of prophecy for songs about crude and lowly matters.[42]

Since we have mentioned *lashon hara* (which includes harmful gossip) in the category of forbidden speech, I will elaborate on the matter,[43] mentioning some of our Sages' statements, for it is as if people are utterly blind with regard to this matter. This is the most serious transgression that a person will frequently commit. And thus, our Sages said,[44] "The shade of *lashon hara* - a person is not delivered from it each day." Would that this were true [regarding only] the shade of *lashon hara*, but not *lashon hara* itself.

Lashon hara refers to divulging a person's shortcomings and faults, and denigrating a Jew in any manner whatsoever. This applies even when [the person] is in fact as base as was described. For *lashon hara* does not mean telling lies about a person and ascribing to him deeds that he did not perform. This is called *motzi shem ra*. *Lashon hara* is the degradation of a person even for acts that we know he has performed.

The person who speaks [*lashon hara*] sins, as does the one who listens. Our Sages said,[45] "*Lashon hara* kills three people: the one who speaks it, the one who listens to it, and the person about whom it is spoken." And our Sages said,[46] "The person who accepts it is more severely [affected] than the one who speaks it."

The shade of *lashon hara* indicates the allusion to a person's faults without explicitly mentioning them. With regard to a person who makes such allusions, but feigns not to know that his colleague understands his words, as if this were not his intent at all, King Solomon said,[47] "As a madman who throws firebrands, arrows, and death and then says: 'I am only joking.'"

Similarly, one of the Sages once praised the penmanship of a particular scribe that he showed at a large celebration. [The Sages'] master rebuked him for this, saying "Stop speaking *lashon hara*." His intent was that by praising the scribe in public, you will cause him dishonor. For both his friends and his enemies were attending [that celebration], and when his enemies hear him being praised, they will begin telling of his shortcomings. This is a great safeguard against *lashon hara*.

41. See the Guide for the Perplexed, Vol. III, Chapter 8, where the Rambam discusses the holiness of the Hebrew language.
42. See *Sanhedrin* 101a.
43. See also Chapter 7 of *Hilchot De'ot* for the Rambam's rulings regarding this subject.
44. *Bava Batra* 164b.
45. *Arachin* 15b; Jerusalem Talmud (*Pe'ah* 1:1).
46. See *Shabbat* 56b and *Pesachim* 118a.
47. Proverbs 26:18-19.

17. Rabban Shimon ben Gamliel said: The world endures by virtue of three things - justice, truth, and peace - as it is written:[59] "Administer truth, justice, and peace in your gates."

CHAPTER TWO

1. Rabbi said: Which path is the right one, that a man should choose for himself? That which is honorable to himself and brings him honor from man.

Be as careful [in the performance of a seemingly] minor mitzvah as of a major one, for you do not know the reward given for the mitzvot.

The Mishnah states:[48] "The judgment against our ancestors in the desert was sealed only because of *lashon hara*" - i.e., the sin of the spies, about whom it is said,[49] "They issued a false report of the land." Our Sages said:[50] These individuals made slanderous statements merely about trees and stones and yet were given such punishment. How much more so for someone who speaks disparagingly of a colleague.

The *Tosefta* states:[51] "For three sins, retribution is taken from a person in this world, and yet he is denied a portion in the World to Come: the worship of false gods, forbidden sexual relations and murder. *Lashon hara* is equivalent to all of them."

The Talmud[52] states that the word *gadol* ("great") is used in connection with the worship of false gods, as it is written,[53] "Please, for this nation has committed a great sin." Similarly, the word *gadol* is used with regard to the sin of forbidden sexual relations, as it is written,[54] "How could I commit such a great evil?" And this same word is used with regard to the sin of murder, as it is written,[55] "Is my sin too great to bear?" But with regard to *lashon hara*, the word *gedolot* [the plural term] is used, indicating that it is equivalent to all three, as it is written,[56] "[May God cut off all guileful lips,] the tongues that speak great things."

Our Sages have spoken very much about this cursed sin. The ultimate of all their statements is the following:[57] "Whoever speaks *lashon hara* denies God, as it is

---

48. *Arachin* 3:5.
49. Numbers 13:32.
50. *Arachin* 15a.
51. A source for this quote in the *Tosefta* has not been found. This wording is found in the Jerusalem Talmud, *Pe'ah* 1:1.
52. *Arachin* 15b.
53. Exodus 32:31.
54. Genesis 39:9.
55. *Ibid.* 4:13.
56. Psalms 12:4.
57. *Arachin* 15b.

יז רַבָּן שִׁמְעוֹן בֶּן גַּמְלִיאֵל אוֹמֵר: עַל שְׁלֹשָׁה דְבָרִים הָעוֹלָם עוֹמֵד: עַל הַדִּין וְעַל הָאֱמֶת וְעַל הַשָּׁלוֹם, שֶׁנֶּאֱמַר: אֱמֶת וּמִשְׁפַּט שָׁלוֹם שִׁפְטוּ בְּשַׁעֲרֵיכֶם.

פֶּרֶק שֵׁנִי

א רַבִּי אוֹמֵר: אֵיזוֹהִי דֶרֶךְ יְשָׁרָה שֶׁיָּבֹר לוֹ הָאָדָם? כֹּל שֶׁהִיא תִפְאֶרֶת לְעוֹשֶׂיהָ, וְתִפְאֶרֶת לוֹ מִן הָאָדָם.

וֶהֱוֵי זָהִיר בְּמִצְוָה קַלָּה כְּבַחֲמוּרָה, שֶׁאֵין אַתָּה יוֹדֵעַ מַתַּן שְׂכָרָן שֶׁל מִצְוֹת.

written,[58] 'Those who said: With our tongues we will prevail; our lips are our own. Who is lord over us?' "

I have cited some of the sources that speak about this sin. Although I have elaborated, my intent was that a person eschew it to the full extent of his potential, and set as a goal to refrain from this type of utterance entirely.

justice - This refers to governing a country with fairness.
As explained in the fourth [introductory] chapter,
truth - is one of the intellectual virtues, while
peace - is one of the ethical virtues. When these three virtues are attained, [our] existence will, without any doubt, reach the ultimate level of fulfillment possible.

Chapter 2
Which path is the right one - The "right path" refers to the positive activities we mentioned in the fourth [introductory] chapter. They represent balanced conduct,[1] and it is through them that a person acquires a developed personality and improves his relations with his fellow man. This is reflected in the [continuation of the] *mishnah's* statement:
That which is honorable to himself and brings him honor from man.
Afterwards, the *mishnah* emphasizes that one should be as careful in the performance of those mitzvot that appear to be of minor importance - e.g., rejoicing in the festivals or studying the Holy Tongue[2] - as in the performance of those mitzvot whose severity has been made known - e.g., circumcision, *tzitzit* or the Paschal sacrifice. The *mishnah* then explains the rationale:
for you do not know the reward given for the mitzvot. - The explanation of this concept is as follows: The Torah contains both positive commandments and negative

---

58. Psalms 12:5.
59. Zechariah 8:16.

1. See also the first chapter of *Hilchot De'ot.*
2. See the *Sifre's* comment on Deuteronomy 11:19, which states that when a child begins to be able to talk, his father should speak to him in the Holy Tongue.

Calculate the loss incurred [by the violation of] a mitzvah [in order to know] the reward [for its fulfillment], and the gain [derived] from [refraining from committing] a sin [by comparing it to] the loss [incurred by committing] it.

Reflect upon three things and you will not come to sin: Know what is above you - an Eye that sees, an Ear that hears - and [know] that all your deeds are recorded in a book.

commandments. With regard to the negative commandments, in almost all instances the Torah has explicitly stated the punishment a person will receive for their violation. For some, a person is liable for capital punishment; for some, *karet*;[3] for others, death by God's hand; and for others, lashes.

From the punishments given for violation of the negative commandments, we can determine which transgression is more severe and which is less severe. [In particular,] there are eight levels:

the first level, the most severe transgressions, are those for which one is liable to be executed by being stoned to death;

the level below that [includes those transgressions] for which one is liable to be executed by being burned to death;[4]

the third level [includes those transgressions] for which one is liable to be executed by decapitation;

the fourth level [includes those transgressions] for which one is liable to be executed by strangulation;

the fifth level [includes those transgressions] for which one is liable for *karet*;

the sixth level [includes those transgressions] for which one is liable for death by God's hand;

the seventh level [includes those transgressions] for which one is liable for lashes; and the eighth level [includes those transgressions] for which one is not liable even for lashes.

From the scale of the punishments received for transgressions, one can appreciate the severity of certain sins, and the less severe nature of others. With regard to the positive commandments, by contrast, [the Torah] did not explicitly make known to us the nature of the reward we will be granted before God, so that we could realize which are most severe and which are not as significant. Instead, He commanded us to obey all the various commandments without revealing which will bring a greater reward. Therefore, it is fitting to apply ourselves to the performance of all of them.

This is the basis for [our Sages'] ruling[5] that a person who is occupied in the performance of one mitzvah is not obligated to perform another, without distinguishing between the mitzvah in which the person is involved and the mitzvah whose observance

3. *Mo'ed Katan* 28a relates that this involves death before the age of fifty at the hand of God. In *Hilchot Teshuvah* 8:1, the Rambam explains that *karet* involves more than premature death. In addition, the soul is "cut off" and does not receive a portion in the World to Come.
4. This does not mean that the person was burned at the stake. Instead, molten lead was poured down his throat, killing him instantly (*Hilchot Sanhedrin* 15:3).
5. *Sukkah* 25a.

וֶהֱוֵי מְחַשֵּׁב הֶפְסֵד מִצְוָה כְּנֶגֶד שְׂכָרָהּ, וּשְׂכַר עֲבֵרָה כְּנֶגֶד הֶפְסֵדָהּ.

וְהִסְתַּכֵּל בִּשְׁלֹשָׁה דְבָרִים, וְאֵין אַתָּה בָא לִידֵי עֲבֵרָה; דַּע מַה לְמַעְלָה מִמְּךָ: עַיִן

רוֹאָה, וְאֹזֶן שׁוֹמַעַת, וְכָל מַעֲשֶׂיךָ בַּסֵּפֶר נִכְתָּבִים.

he foregoes. [Similarly,] for this reason, [our Sages] said:[6] "One should not bypass a mitzvah"; i.e., if by circumstance you are presented with the fulfillment of a mitzvah, do not bypass it so that you can fulfill another mitzvah.

[The *mishnah* continues,] stating that although the order of priority of the mitzvot has not been explained, it is possible to make a projection. For [there are many positive commandments that are coupled with a negative commandment;] whenever the negative commandment associated with a mitzvah involves a severe obligation, one can assume that the reward for observing the positive commandment is also great.

For example, circumcision, the Paschal sacrifice, resting on the seventh day, and constructing a guardrail are all positive commandments. A person who performs [a forbidden] labor on the Sabbath is liable to be stoned to death. A person who negates the mitzvah of circumcision or the mitzvah of offering the [Paschal] sacrifice at its proper time is liable for *karet*. And a person who creates a dangerous situation in his home violates a negative commandment [but does not incur punishment]. From this, one can assume that the reward for resting on the Sabbath is greater than the reward for circumcision. Similarly, the reward for circumcision is greater before God than the reward for making a guardrail.

This [explanation] is implied [by the continuation of the *mishnah*]:
Calculate the loss incurred [by the violation of] a mitzvah [in order to know] the reward [for its fulfillment].

[The *mishnah* continues] explaining that you can appreciate the nature of the reward given for not violating a transgression - although this also has not been explicitly stated - from the punishment given for its violation. For the transgressions that are associated with severe punishments, one receives a greater reward - the extent of the reward being in proportion to the severity of the punishment. This is implied by the statement in [the tractate of] *Kiddushin*:[7] "Whoever remains passive and does not violate a transgression will be given a reward as if he performed a mitzvah." We have already explained this.[8]

[**An Eye that sees... -**] It is explicitly stated in the Torah that our deeds are known by Him in the unique manner in which He knows[9] them, as [alluded to in the verse,][10] "[Wipe me out] from the book that You have written."

6. *Pesachim* 64b.
7. *Kiddushin* 39b.
8. This teaching is also included in the Mishnah (*Makkot* 3:15), and the Rambam explains that teaching in his Commentary on the Mishnah.
9. I.e., God's perfect knowledge differs from mortal knowledge, as explained in the eighth introductory chapter.
10. Exodus 32:32. Note the Rambam's mention of this prooftext in the eleventh of his principles of faith, which cites this as the basis for the belief in God's awarding just reward and punishment.

2. Rabban Gamliel, the son of Rabbi Yehudah HaNasi, said: It is good [to combine] the study of Torah with an occupation, for the effort required by both of them keeps sin out of mind; while all Torah-study that is not combined with work will ultimately cease and will lead to sin.

All who occupy themselves with the affairs of the community should engage in them for the sake of Heaven, for the merit of their fathers assists them and their righteousness endures forever. And upon you [says God], I will bestow a great reward, as though you had accomplished [many mitzvot].

3. Be wary of those in power, for they befriend a person only for their own benefit; they seem to be friends when it is to their advantage, but they do not stand by a man in his hour of need.

4. He used to say: Make His will your own will, so that He may fulfill your will as though it were His will. Set aside your will because of His will, so that He may set aside the will of others before your will.

5. Hillel said: Do not separate yourself from the community; do not be sure of yourself until the day you die. Do not condemn your fellow man until you have stood in his place; do not make an [ambiguous] statement that is not readily understood, [with the hope] that it will ultimately be understood. And do not say, "When I have free time I will study," for perhaps you will never have free time.

An occupation - This is the meaning of the term ארץ דרך in this context.

And will lead to sin - as we explained in another place.[11] Our Sages said[12] that ultimately such a person will rob others.

And upon you [says God] I will bestow a great reward - God makes this statement to those people who are working for the communal welfare because [it is possible] that at times they will be prevented from carrying out a mitzvah because of their involvement. [God assures them] that, although they were prevented from performing a mitzvah, He grants them a reward as if they had performed it, because they are involved in communal welfare projects for the sake of heaven.

---

11. Some commentaries have cited the Rambam's comments on Chapter 1, *Mishnah* 10, which speaks of the depravity that results from failure to work. Others point to Chapter 4, *Mishnah* 7, where the Rambam elaborates on the impropriety of benefiting from one's Torah study.
12. *Kiddushin* 29a.

ב רַבָּן גַּמְלִיאֵל בְּנוֹ שֶׁל רַבִּי יְהוּדָה הַנָּשִׂיא אוֹמֵר: יָפֶה תַלְמוּד תּוֹרָה עִם דֶּרֶךְ אֶרֶץ, שֶׁיְּגִיעַת שְׁנֵיהֶם מְשַׁכַּחַת עָוֹן. וְכָל תּוֹרָה שֶׁאֵין עִמָּהּ מְלָאכָה, סוֹפָהּ בְּטֵלָה וְגוֹרֶרֶת עָוֹן.

וְכָל הָעֲמֵלִים עִם הַצִּבּוּר, יִהְיוּ עֲמֵלִים עִמָּהֶם לְשֵׁם שָׁמַיִם, שֶׁזְּכוּת אֲבוֹתָם מְסַיַּעְתָּן, וְצִדְקָתָן עוֹמֶדֶת לָעַד. וְאַתֶּם, מַעֲלֶה אֲנִי עֲלֵיכֶם שָׂכָר הַרְבֵּה כְּאִלּוּ עֲשִׂיתֶם.

ג הֱווּ זְהִירִים בָּרָשׁוּת, שֶׁאֵין מְקָרְבִין לוֹ לָאָדָם אֶלָּא לְצֹרֶךְ עַצְמָן; נִרְאִין כְּאוֹהֲבִים בִּשְׁעַת הֲנָאָתָן, וְאֵין עוֹמְדִין לוֹ לָאָדָם בִּשְׁעַת דָּחְקוֹ.

ד הוּא הָיָה אוֹמֵר: עֲשֵׂה רְצוֹנוֹ כִּרְצוֹנְךָ, כְּדֵי שֶׁיַּעֲשֶׂה רְצוֹנְךָ כִּרְצוֹנוֹ; וּבַטֵּל רְצוֹנְךָ מִפְּנֵי רְצוֹנוֹ, כְּדֵי שֶׁיְּבַטֵּל רְצוֹן אֲחֵרִים מִפְּנֵי רְצוֹנֶךָ.

ה הִלֵּל אוֹמֵר: אַל תִּפְרֹשׁ עַצְמְךָ מִן הַצִּבּוּר, וְאַל תַּאֲמֵן בְּעַצְמְךָ עַד יוֹם מוֹתְךָ, וְאַל תָּדִין אֶת חֲבֵרְךָ עַד שֶׁתַּגִּיעַ לִמְקוֹמוֹ, וְאַל תֹּאמַר דָּבָר שֶׁאִי אֶפְשָׁר לִשְׁמֹעַ, שֶׁסּוֹפוֹ לְהִשָּׁמֵעַ. וְאַל תֹּאמַר לִכְשֶׁאֶפָּנֶה אֶשְׁנֶה, שֶׁמָּא לֹא תִפָּנֶה.

Those in power - This is the meaning of the word רשות, as explained above.[13] [The *mishnah*] describes the tendencies of these people and warns [of contact with them].

[Do not separate yourself from the community -] As mentioned in the fourth [introductory] chapter, it is not proper to separate from the community, except for the following reason: because of their [undesirable habits of] conversation, as explained there.

[Do not be sure of yourself... -] Although a person has acquired refined qualities and has reinforced them, he should not cease seeking to perform good deeds, so that he will continue to strengthen [his positive traits]. He should not become overconfident and think that he has already acquired refined qualities, and it is impossible that he will forfeit them. [One should always remain wary], as [the *mishnah*] says...

until the day you die.

Do not make an [ambiguous] statement - i.e., a statement whose simple meaning appears farfetched and of no value, but whose correctness can be perceived by a person who offers it deeper contemplation. The *mishnah* warns against making such statements, as if to say "Do not speak in a manner that will require an abstract explanation and much contemplation before it is understood."

When I have free time - i.e., when I can free myself from my business concerns

I will study - This resembles the admonition of his colleague Shammai:[14] "Make your study of Torah a fixed priority."

---

13. Chapter 1, *Mishnah* 10.
14. Chapter 1, *Mishnah* 14.

6. He used to say: A crude person cannot be sin-fearing, nor can a common person be pious. A bashful person will not learn, nor can the short-tempered teach; neither can anyone who is over-occupied in trade become a scholar.

In a place where there are no men, strive to be a man.

7. He also saw a skull floating on the water; he said to it: Because you drowned others, they drowned you; and ultimately those who drowned you will themselves be drowned.

8. He used to say: Increasing flesh increases worms; increasing possessions increases worry; increasing [the number of] wives increases sorcery; increasing maidservants increases lewdness; increasing man servants increases thievery.

[But] increasing Torah increases life; increasing assiduous study increases wisdom; increasing counsel increases understanding; increasing charity increases peace.

One who has acquired a good name has acquired it for himself; one who has acquired for himself Torah knowledge, has acquired for himself life in the World to Come.

9. Rabban Yochanan ben Zakkai received [the oral tradition] from Hillel and Shammai. He used to say: If you have studied much Torah, do not claim special credit for yourself; for this very purpose were you created.

A **crude person** - A person who possess neither wisdom nor developed ethical qualities.

A **common person** - One who does not possess intellectual virtues, but does possess certain ethical qualities.[15]

A **bashful person** - one who is reticent.[16]

The **short-tempered** - One who is angered easily.

Strive - Striving refers to struggling with oneself, stretching oneself to acquire virtues. Where there are no teachers, a person must serve as his own teacher. [This interpretation is borne out by the manner in which] Onkelos translates [the verse:][17] "And a man wrestled with him." [He renders] ויאבק as ואשתדל.

[**Neither can anyone who is over-occupied in trade become a scholar** -] The *mishnah*

15. See the Rambam's commentary on Chapter 5, *Mishnayot* 6 and 13, for a more detailed definition of these terms.
16. The Rambam uses the same Arabic term as he uses in the fourth introductory chapter for a person who sways from the mean of reservation and fears involvement with others.
17. Genesis 32:25.

ו הוּא הָיָה אוֹמֵר: אֵין בּוּר יְרֵא חֵטְא, וְלֹא עַם הָאָרֶץ חָסִיד, וְלֹא הַבַּיְשָׁן לָמֵד, וְלֹא הַקַּפְּדָן מְלַמֵּד, וְלֹא כָל הַמַּרְבֶּה בִסְחוֹרָה מַחְכִּים, וּבְמָקוֹם שֶׁאֵין אֲנָשִׁים הִשְׁתַּדֵּל לִהְיוֹת אִישׁ.

ז אַף הוּא רָאָה גֻּלְגֹּלֶת אַחַת שֶׁצָּפָה עַל פְּנֵי הַמָּיִם. אָמַר לָהּ: עַל דַּאֲטֵפְתְּ אַטְפוּךְ וְסוֹף מְטִיפַיִךְ יְטוּפוּן.

ח הוּא הָיָה אוֹמֵר: מַרְבֶּה בָשָׂר, מַרְבֶּה רִמָּה. מַרְבֶּה נְכָסִים, מַרְבֶּה דְאָגָה. מַרְבֶּה נָשִׁים, מַרְבֶּה כְשָׁפִים. מַרְבֶּה שְׁפָחוֹת, מַרְבֶּה זִמָּה. מַרְבֶּה עֲבָדִים, מַרְבֶּה גָזֵל מַרְבֶּה תוֹרָה, מַרְבֶּה חַיִּים. מַרְבֶּה יְשִׁיבָה, מַרְבֶּה חָכְמָה. מַרְבֶּה עֵצָה, מַרְבֶּה תְבוּנָה מַרְבֶּה צְדָקָה, מַרְבֶּה שָׁלוֹם. קָנָה שֵׁם טוֹב, קָנָה לְעַצְמוֹ. קָנָה לוֹ דִבְרֵי תוֹרָה, קָנָה לוֹ חַיֵּי הָעוֹלָם הַבָּא.

ט רַבָּן יוֹחָנָן בֶּן זַכַּאי קִבֵּל מֵהִלֵּל וּמִשַּׁמַּאי. הוּא הָיָה אוֹמֵר: אִם לָמַדְתָּ תּוֹרָה הַרְבֵּה, אַל תַּחֲזִיק טוֹבָה לְעַצְמְךָ, כִּי לְכָךְ נוֹצָרְתָּ.

teaches that Torah knowledge will not be found among the proud and the haughty, nor among those who journey to distant places. Our Sages[18] homiletically appended this teaching to the verse:[19] "It [the Torah] is not in the heavens, nor is it across the sea." [They said: Torah scholarship] is not found among the haughty, [whose heads are in the sky,] nor among those who journey across the sea.

Because you drowned others, they drowned you... - I.e., you were killed because you killed others, and those who killed you will themselves be killed. The intent is that evil activities return to plague those who performed them, as it is written:[20] "His own iniquities will trap the wicked man." And it is written:[21] "He has made a pit, digging it out, and he shall fall into the ditch he has made." And our Sages said:[22] "According to the measure by which the person measures [others], he himself is measured."

This is evident and common in all places and times: that whoever performs a wicked act and brings about crookedness and flaws will ultimately suffer harm from those wicked activities that he himself has spread. For he promotes the activities that will bring harm to himself and others.

Conversely, a person who promotes virtuous qualities and one who brings about good deeds will ultimately derive benefit from this activity, for he has promoted doing things that will benefit himself and others. This was wisely stated in the verse:[23] "A person's labors will be his recompense."

18. *Eruvin* 55a.
19. Deuteronomy 30:12.
20. Proverbs 5:22.
21. Psalms 7:16.
22. *Sanhedrin* 90a; *Sotah* 1:7.
23. Job 34:11.

10. Rabban Yochanan ben Zakkai had five [outstanding] disciples, and they were: Rabbi Eliezer ben Horkanos, Rabbi Yehoshua ben Chanania, Rabbi Yosse the priest, Rabbi Shimon ben Netan'el, and Rabbi Eleazar ben Arach.

He used to enumerate their praiseworthy qualities: Rabbi Eliezer ben Horkanos - a cemented cistern that does not lose a drop; Rabbi Yehoshua ben Chanania - happy is she who bore him; Rabbi Yosse the priest - he is pious; Rabbi Shimon ben Netan'el - sin-fearing; and Rabbi Eleazar ben Arach - like a spring that flows with ever- increasing strength.

11. He used to say: If all the Sages of Israel were on one side of the scale, and Eliezer ben Horkanos were on the other, he would outweigh them all. Abba Shaul said in his name: If all the Sages of Israel, including even Eliezer ben Horkanos, were on one side of the scale, and Eleazar ben Arach were on the other, he would outweigh them all.

12. He said to them: Go and see which is the good way to which a man should adhere. Rabbi Eliezer said: a good eye; Rabbi Yehoshua said: a good friend; Rabbi Yosse said: a good neighbor; Rabbi Shimon said: one who sees the consequences [of his actions]; Rabbi Eleazar said: a good heart. [Rabban Yochanan ben Zakkai] said to them: I prefer the words of Eleazar ben Arach to all of yours, for in his words, yours are included.

He said to them: Go and see which is the evil path from which a man should keep far away. Rabbi Eliezer said: an evil eye; Rabbi Yehoshua said: a wicked friend; Rabbi Yosse said: a wicked neighbor; Rabbi Shimon said: He who borrows and does not repay - one who borrows from man is as one who borrows from God - as it is stated:[24] "The

---

[He used to enumerate their praiseworthy qualities -] [He] praised Rabbi Eliezer for his memory, Rabbi Yehoshua ben Chanania for his ethical virtues, Rabbi Yosse the priest for his intellectual and ethical virtues, Rabbi Shimon ben Netan'el for his austerity, and Rabbi Eleazar ben Arach for his clarity of conception and broad understanding. Every difficult concept would appear to him to be easy, for his abilities of comprehension would prevail in all matters.

A good eye - For a person to be satisfied with what he possesses. This is an ethical virtue.

24. Psalms 37:21.

י חֲמִשָּׁה תַלְמִידִים הָיוּ לְרַבָּן יוֹחָנָן בֶּן זַכַּאי, וְאֵלּוּ הֵן: רַבִּי אֱלִיעֶזֶר בֶּן הוּרְקָנוֹס
וְרַבִּי יְהוֹשֻׁעַ בֶּן חֲנַנְיָא, וְרַבִּי יוֹסֵי הַכֹּהֵן, וְרַבִּי שִׁמְעוֹן בֶּן נְתַנְאֵל, וְרַבִּי אֶלְעָזָר בֶּן
עֲרָךְ.

הוּא הָיָה מוֹנֶה שִׁבְחָן: רַבִּי אֱלִיעֶזֶר בֶּן הוּרְקָנוֹס, בּוֹר סוּד שֶׁאֵינוֹ מְאַבֵּד טִפָּה; רַבִּי
יְהוֹשֻׁעַ בֶּן חֲנַנְיָה, אַשְׁרֵי יוֹלַדְתּוֹ; רַבִּי יוֹסֵי הַכֹּהֵן, חָסִיד; רַבִּי שִׁמְעוֹן בֶּן נְתַנְאֵל
יְרֵא חֵטְא; וְרַבִּי אֶלְעָזָר בֶּן עֲרָךְ, כְּמַעְיָן הַמִּתְגַּבֵּר.

יא הוּא הָיָה אוֹמֵר: אִם יִהְיוּ כָל חַכְמֵי יִשְׂרָאֵל בְּכַף מֹאזְנַיִם, וְרַבִּי אֱלִיעֶזֶר בֶּן
הוּרְקָנוֹס בְּכַף שְׁנִיָּה — מַכְרִיעַ אֶת כֻּלָּם.

אַבָּא שָׁאוּל אוֹמֵר מִשְּׁמוֹ: אִם יִהְיוּ כָל חַכְמֵי יִשְׂרָאֵל בְּכַף מֹאזְנַיִם, וְרַבִּי אֱלִיעֶזֶר בֶּן
הוּרְקָנוֹס אַף עִמָּהֶם, וְרַבִּי אֶלְעָזָר בְּכַף שְׁנִיָּה — מַכְרִיעַ אֶת כֻּלָּם.

יב אָמַר לָהֶם: צְאוּ וּרְאוּ אֵיזוֹהִי דֶרֶךְ יְשָׁרָה שֶׁיִּדְבַּק בָּהּ הָאָדָם. רַבִּי אֱלִיעֶזֶר
אוֹמֵר: עַיִן טוֹבָה. רַבִּי יְהוֹשֻׁעַ אוֹמֵר: חָבֵר טוֹב. רַבִּי יוֹסֵי אוֹמֵר: שָׁכֵן טוֹב. רַבִּי
שִׁמְעוֹן אוֹמֵר: הָרוֹאֶה אֶת הַנּוֹלָד. רַבִּי אֶלְעָזָר אוֹמֵר: לֵב טוֹב. אָמַר לָהֶם: רוֹאֶה
אֲנִי אֶת דִּבְרֵי רַבִּי אֶלְעָזָר בֶּן עֲרָךְ, שֶׁבִּכְלָל דְּבָרָיו דִּבְרֵיכֶם.

אָמַר לָהֶם: צְאוּ וּרְאוּ אֵיזוֹהִי דֶרֶךְ רָעָה שֶׁיִּתְרַחֵק מִמֶּנָּה הָאָדָם. רַבִּי אֱלִיעֶזֶר אוֹמֵר:
עַיִן רָעָה. רַבִּי יְהוֹשֻׁעַ אוֹמֵר: חָבֵר רָע. רַבִּי יוֹסֵי אוֹמֵר: שָׁכֵן רָע. רַבִּי שִׁמְעוֹן אוֹמֵר:
הַלֹּוֶה וְאֵינוֹ מְשַׁלֵּם; אֶחָד הַלֹּוֶה מִן הָאָדָם, כְּלֹוֶה מִן הַמָּקוֹם, שֶׁנֶּאֱמַר: לֹוֶה רָשָׁע

A bad eye - The opposite of the above, that a person looks at the abundance he possesses as being meager, and fervently seeks to increase [his property].

One who sees the consequences [of his actions -] i.e., one who learns from the past about the future. The intent is not abstract thinking, for the term does not refer to an intellectual virtue that enables a person to learn about the hidden from what has been revealed. Instead, the intent is that a person [has the ability to take] an overview of his own conduct in the [day-to-day] activities necessary to maintain his existence; that he sees the consequences of his behavior.[25] As the antithesis to this trait, [Rabbi Shimon] mentions...

He who borrows and does not repay - For he will not receive a loan in the future. This [trait] is an ethical shortcoming.

As we mentioned in the second introductory chapter to this tractate, the ethical virtues are relevant only with regard to the element of the soul [that governs] stimulation. Similarly, it is with regard to [this element of the soul] that the ethical shortcomings apply. In the fourth [introductory] chapter, we explained that positive

25. The Rambam's intent is to show that this is an ethical virtue, and thus that it is included in the expression, "a good heart."

wicked one borrows and does not repay, but the righteous one acts graciously and gives." Rabbi Eleazar said: a wicked heart. [Rabban Yochanan ben Zakkai] said to them: I prefer the words of Eleazar ben Arach to all of yours, for in his words, yours are included.

13. They [each] said three things. Rabbi Eliezer said: Cherish the honor of your colleague as your own, and do not become angered easily. Repent one day before your death. Warm yourself by the fire of the sages, but beware of their glowing embers lest you be burned - for their bite is the bite of a fox, their sting is the sting of a scorpion, their hiss is the hiss of a serpent, and all their words are like fiery coals.

deeds refer to those deeds that follow the mean, and that they stem from the ethical virtues.

Similarly, it is known to the philosophers and the physicians that the soul is aroused through the heart, and that the heart is its abode. Therefore, [the soul] is referred to [by the term "heart"]. Although a correct conception appreciates that all the various powers emanate from the heart, and that the heart is their source [there is a difference between these other powers, and the element of the soul that governs stimulation]. The element [of the soul governing] stimulation does not issue forth from the heart to other limbs. [For example,] as explained in the first [introductory] chapter, the element of the soul [that governs] digestion extends from the heart to the liver.

To summarize what we have explained: The expression...

A good heart - refers to the ethical virtues that [give rise to] good deeds - i.e., deeds that reflect the middle path. They include being satisfied with one's lot, fellowship with good people, and the other ethical qualities. This is the intent of [the continuation of the *mishnah*]:[26]

For in his words, yours are included. - Conversely,

A bad heart - i.e., ethical shortcomings. These include all the other [particular qualities] the Sages warned about.

Do not become angered easily. - Do not put yourself in a state that arouses wrath and anger. [Our Sages] have expounded with regard to the vice of anger, stating:[27] "Whoever becomes angry is considered as if he worshiped false gods." They derived this teaching from the [conjunction of the clauses in] the verse:[28] "Do not

26. I.e., all the ethical virtues mentioned by the other Sages are particular qualities and they are included in the general statement, "a good heart."
27. *Shabbat* 105b.
28. Psalms 81:10.
29. *Shabbat, loc. cit.,* interprets the term "foreign power" as referring to the evil inclination, the source of anger.

וְלֹא יְשַׁלֵּם, וְצַדִּיק חוֹנֵן וְנוֹתֵן. רַבִּי אֶלְעָזָר אוֹמֵר: לֵב רָע. אָמַר לָהֶם: רוֹאֶה אֲנִ
אֶת דִּבְרֵי רַבִּי אֶלְעָזָר בֶּן עֲרָךְ, שֶׁבִּכְלַל דְּבָרָיו דִּבְרֵיכֶם.

יג הֵם אָמְרוּ שְׁלֹשָׁה דְבָרִים. רַבִּי אֱלִיעֶזֶר אוֹמֵר: יְהִי כְבוֹד חֲבֵרְךָ חָבִיב עָלֶיךָ
כְּשֶׁלָּךְ, וְאַל תְּהִי נוֹחַ לִכְעֹס, וְשׁוּב יוֹם אֶחָד לִפְנֵי מִיתָתָךְ, וֶהֱוֵי מִתְחַמֵּם כְּנֶגֶד אוּרָ
שֶׁל חֲכָמִים, וֶהֱוֵי זָהִיר בְּגַחַלְתָּן שֶׁלֹּא תִכָּוֶה, שֶׁנְּשִׁיכָתָן נְשִׁיכַת שׁוּעָל, וַעֲקִיצָתָ
עֲקִיצַת עַקְרָב, וּלְחִישָׁתָן לְחִישַׁת שָׂרָף, וְכָל דִּבְרֵיהֶם כְּגַחֲלֵי אֵשׁ.

allow a foreign power within you;[29] do not bow down to an alien god." This indicates that the two [anger and alien worship] are equivalent.

Repent one day before your death. - Since a person does not know when he will die, he will thus spend his entire life in repentance.[30]

Warm yourself by the fire of the sages - This statement is not one of the ethical teachings authored by Rabbi Eliezer himself, but rather a teaching that he heard from a colleague and would repeat. Therefore, it is not included in [the sum of] his teachings.[31]

The intent of this charge is to teach you that if you associate with sages and men of virtue, do not act frivolously in their presence, nor feel that one may act without reservation with regard to them. One should not become over-familiar with them. Rather come close to them and approach them to the degree that they draw you close, and respect the limitations they set for you. Do not seek to draw any closer, lest they no longer think positively of you, and turn their love [for you] to hate, [denying] you the benefit that you had hoped for.

To offer an analogy: A person warms himself by a fire. If he sits a certain distance from it, he will benefit from its warmth and make use of its light. If, however, he is careless and comes closer [to the fire], he will be burned. This the analogy implied by the wording:

Warm yourself by the fire of the sages, but beware of their glowing embers... - The [*mishnah* continues,] arousing fear by stating...

[Their hiss is the hiss of a serpent -] Do not think that if they smart you with their tongue, you can fool them by talking with guile. They will not be deceived, as [implied by] the verse:[32] "They will not harken unto the voice of charmers." See what transpired with regard to Geichazi and his master [Elisha],[33] and Jesus the Nazarite and Yehoshua ben Perachiah.[34]

---

30. *Shabbat* 153a.

31. The Rambam's intent is that this is the fourth teaching mentioned in the name of Rabbi Eliezer. Since the *mishnah* states: "They [each] said three things," the Rambam feels it necessary to explain the nature of this fourth teaching.

32. Psalms 58:6.

33. See II Kings 5:20-27 and *Sanhedrin* 107b, which explain that after Geichazi took gifts from Na'aman the Aramean, Elisha cursed him, stating that he would be afflicted with Na'aman's leprosy.

34. The uncensored version of Sanhedrin 107b relates that Jesus was one of Rabbi Yehoshua's

14. Rabbi Yehoshua said: The evil eye, the evil inclination and hatred of one's fellow drive a man from the world.

15. Rabbi Yosse said: Let the money of your fellow man be as dear to you as your own. Prepare yourself for the study of Torah, for it does not come to you through inheritance; and let all your deeds be for the sake of Heaven.

16. Rabbi Shimon said: Be meticulous in reading the *Shema* and in prayer. When you pray, do not make your prayer a routine act, but rather an entreaty for mercy and a supplication before God, as it is stated:[36] "For He is gracious and compassionate, slow to anger and abounding in lovingkindness, and relenting of the evil decree."
And do not see yourself as wicked in your own eyes.

17. Rabbi Eleazar said: Be diligent in the study of Torah; know what to answer an unbeliever; and know before whom you toil, and who your Employer is who will pay you the reward of your labor.

18. Rabbi Tarfon said: The day is short, the work is much, the workmen are lazy, the reward is great and the Master is pressing.

[The evil eye... -] [The *mishnah*] states that the burning desire for money, craving for material pleasure and an unfriendly approach are sicknesses caused by depression.[35] This causes a person to despise seeing other men and to hate them, preferring solitude and dwelling in forests, deserts and desolate places. These will surely bring ruin to a person.

[Prepare yourself... -] In the eighth [introductory] chapter, we explained what is meant by self-preparation, and that a person should direct himself towards achieving virtue.
Let all your deeds be for the sake of Heaven. - We explained this concept in the fifth [introductory] chapter.

[A routine act -] We have already explained the concept of קבע[37] - i.e., that he will regard prayer as a heavy burden, a task that someone else compels him to do, [from which he desires] to rest.

students. Once he incurred Rabbi Yehoshua's anger, and Rabbi Yehoshua drove him away forcefully.
35. We have chosen a popular translation of the Hebrew *marah shechorah*, which literally means "a black gall bladder secretion." Such a physical condition was interpreted as the cause of depression and the other emotional shortcomings mentioned by the Rambam.
36. Joel 2:13.
37. In the Commentary on the Mishnah, *Berachot* 4:4.

יד רַבִּי יְהוֹשֻׁעַ אוֹמֵר: עַיִן הָרָע, וְיֵצֶר הָרָע, וְשִׂנְאַת הַבְּרִיּוֹת, מוֹצִיאִין אֶת הָאָדָם מִ
הָעוֹלָם.

טו רַבִּי יוֹסֵי אוֹמֵר: יְהִי מָמוֹן חֲבֵרְךָ חָבִיב עָלֶיךָ כְּשֶׁלָּךְ; וְהַתְקֵן עַצְמְךָ לִלְמֹד תּוֹרָה
שֶׁאֵינָהּ יְרֻשָּׁה לָךְ; וְכָל מַעֲשֶׂיךָ יִהְיוּ לְשֵׁם שָׁמָיִם.

טז רַבִּי שִׁמְעוֹן אוֹמֵר: הֱוֵי זָהִיר בִּקְרִיאַת שְׁמַע וּבִתְפִלָּה. וּכְשֶׁאַתָּה מִתְפַּלֵּל, אַל תַּעַשׂ
תְּפִלָּתְךָ קֶבַע, אֶלָּא רַחֲמִים וְתַחֲנוּנִים לִפְנֵי הַמָּקוֹם, שֶׁנֶּאֱמַר: כִּי (אֵל) חַנּוּן וְרַחוּם
הוּא אֶרֶךְ אַפַּיִם וְרַב חֶסֶד וְנִחָם עַל הָרָעָה, וְאַל תְּהִי רָשָׁע בִּפְנֵי עַצְמֶךָ.

יז רַבִּי אֶלְעָזָר אוֹמֵר: הֱוֵי שָׁקוּד לִלְמֹד תּוֹרָה, וְדַע מַה שֶּׁתָּשִׁיב לְאֶפִּיקוֹרוֹס, וְדַע
לִפְנֵי מִי אַתָּה עָמֵל, וְנֶאֱמָן הוּא בַעַל מְלַאכְתְּךָ שֶׁיְּשַׁלֶּם לְךָ שְׂכַר פְּעֻלָּתֶךָ.

יח רַבִּי טַרְפוֹן אוֹמֵר: הַיּוֹם קָצָר, וְהַמְּלָאכָה מְרֻבָּה, וְהַפּוֹעֲלִים עֲצֵלִים, וְהַשָּׂכָר
הַרְבֵּה, וּבַעַל הַבַּיִת דּוֹחֵק.

[Do not see yourself as wicked in your own eyes. -] When a person considers himself wicked, [he will not hesitate to transgress]. There will be no sin that he will consider too severe to transgress.

[Know what to answer an unbeliever -] Study the matters that will enable you to reply to the gentile non-believers, so that you will be capable of refuting them and answering them if they question you.

Our Sages stated[38] that this refers to a gentile non-believer, but not to a Jewish non-believer, for [such discussion] will cause the latter to increase his mockery and scorn [for Jewish values]. It is proper not to argue with such a person at all, for he will never be restored. There is no cure for him, as it is written:[39] "None that go to her will return; they will never regain the paths of life."[40]

[The mishnah] teaches that although a person may study the wisdom of the gentiles in order to reply to them, he must be careful that none of the matters [he studies] enters his heart. [This is accomplished when one] knows that he is serving One who knows his secret thoughts. This is alluded to by the continuation [of the mishnah]:

Know before Whom you toil.

[The day is short... -] This [mishnah] is an analogy to the brevity of the human life span, the immensity of the knowledge to be gained and the laziness of people in seeking it out despite the great reward promised for it. It also alludes to the encouragement and commandments of the Torah to seek out wisdom and knowledge.

---

38. Sanhedrin 38b.
39. Proverbs 2:19.
40. See similar statements in Hilchot Avodat Kochavim 2:5. Note, however, the Rambam's expression of tolerance for the children of such people in Hilchot Mamrim 3:3. There he states

19. He used to say: It is not incumbent upon you to complete the work, yet you are not free to desist from it; if you have studied much Torah, much reward will be given to you; and your Employer is trustworthy to pay you the reward for your labor, but know that the rewarding of the righteous will be in the Future.

CHAPTER THREE

1. Akavya ben Mahalal'el would say: Reflect upon three things and you will never come to sin: Know from where you came, to where you are going and before whom you are destined to give an accounting.

"From where you came" - from a putrid drop; "to where you are going" - to a place of dust, maggots and worms; "and before whom you are destined to give an accounting" - before the King of kings, the Holy One, blessed be He.

2. Rabbi Chanina, the deputy High Priest, would say: Pray for the welfare of the [ruling] kingdom, for were it not for the fear of it, men would swallow one another alive.[1]

3. Rabbi Chanina ben Teradion would say: If two sit together and no words of Torah are exchanged between them, it is a company of mockers, as it is stated:[2] "He does not sit among the company of mockers." But if two sit together and exchange words of Torah, the Divine Presence rests in their midst, as it is written:[3] "Then the God-fearing conversed with one another, and God listened and heard, and a book of remembrance was written before Him for those who fear God and meditate upon His name."

[The Future -] I.e., the World to Come. We have already explained the concept of the World to Come in the the tenth chapter of the tractate of *Sanhedrin* to the proper extent within the limits of this present commentary.

that the fact that they have been raised in an environment where Jewish knowledge was not taught absolves them of guilt for their conduct. "They should be drawn close with words of peace until they return to the Torah's rock-bed strength."

See also the conclusion of *Iggeret HaSh'mad*, where the Rambam urges patience and openheartedness to those who have strayed from Jewish practice.

יט הוּא הָיָה אוֹמֵר: לֹא עָלֶיךָ הַמְּלָאכָה לִגְמֹר, וְלֹא אַתָּה בֶן חוֹרִין לְהִבָּטֵל מִמֶּנָּה. אִם לָמַדְתָּ תּוֹרָה הַרְבֵּה, נוֹתְנִים לְךָ שָׂכָר הַרְבֵּה; וְנֶאֱמָן הוּא בַעַל מְלַאכְתְּךָ, שֶׁיְּשַׁלֶּם לְךָ שְׂכַר פְּעֻלָּתֶךָ. וְדַע, שֶׁמַּתַּן שְׂכָרָן שֶׁל צַדִּיקִים לֶעָתִיד לָבוֹא.

פֶּרֶק שְׁלִישִׁי

א עֲקַבְיָא בֶן מַהֲלַלְאֵל אוֹמֵר: הִסְתַּכֵּל בִּשְׁלשָׁה דְבָרִים, וְאֵין אַתָּה בָא לִידֵי עֲבֵרָה: דַּע מֵאַיִן בָּאתָ, וּלְאָן אַתָּה הוֹלֵךְ, וְלִפְנֵי מִי אַתָּה עָתִיד לִתֵּן דִּין וְחֶשְׁבּוֹן.

מֵאַיִן בָּאתָ? מִטִּפָּה סְרוּחָה; וּלְאָן אַתָּה הוֹלֵךְ? לִמְקוֹם עָפָר רִמָּה וְתוֹלֵעָה; וְלִפְנֵי מִי אַתָּה עָתִיד לִתֵּן דִּין וְחֶשְׁבּוֹן? לִפְנֵי מֶלֶךְ מַלְכֵי הַמְּלָכִים הַקָּדוֹשׁ בָּרוּךְ הוּא.

ב רַבִּי חֲנִינָא סְגַן הַכֹּהֲנִים אוֹמֵר: הֱוֵי מִתְפַּלֵּל בִּשְׁלוֹמָהּ שֶׁל מַלְכוּת, שֶׁאִלְמָלֵא מוֹרָאָהּ, אִישׁ אֶת רֵעֵהוּ חַיִּים בְּלָעוֹ.

ג רַבִּי חֲנַנְיָא בֶן תְּרַדְיוֹן אוֹמֵר: שְׁנַיִם שֶׁיּוֹשְׁבִים וְאֵין בֵּינֵיהֶן דִּבְרֵי תוֹרָה, הֲרֵי זֶה מוֹשַׁב לֵצִים, שֶׁנֶּאֱמַר: וּבְמוֹשַׁב לֵצִים לֹא יָשָׁב. אֲבָל שְׁנַיִם שֶׁיּוֹשְׁבִין וְיֵשׁ בֵּינֵיהֶם דִּבְרֵי תוֹרָה, שְׁכִינָה בֵינֵיהֶם, שֶׁנֶּאֱמַר: אָז נִדְבְּרוּ יִרְאֵי ה' אִישׁ אֶל רֵעֵהוּ וַיַּקְשֵׁב ה' וַיִּשְׁמָע, וַיִּכָּתֵב סֵפֶר זִכָּרוֹן לְפָנָיו לְיִרְאֵי ה' וּלְחשְׁבֵי שְׁמוֹ.

[**Reflect upon three things... -**] When a person contemplates from where he came, he will be moved to humility. When he contemplates his destiny, he will lose all concern for matters of this world. And contemplation of the greatness of the One who gave the commandments will make him eager to fulfill those commandments. And when a person attains these three qualities, he will not sin at all.

[**A company of mockers -**] The proof that any company that does not speak of the virtues of the Torah is considered to be a company of mockers is from the conclusion of the verse, "rather his desire was for the Torah of God." It is as if it said that a person

1. In the Yemenite manuscripts of the Rambam's Commentary on the Mishnah, there is a restatement of this *mishnah* in Arabic, since it conforms to a common Arabic proverb. In the Hebrew translations, this was deleted to avoid redundancy.
2. Psalms 1:1.
3. Malachi 3:16.

[From this verse, we learn] only that this is so with regard to two people. From which source do we know that even when one person sits and expounds upon the Torah, he is considered as if he fulfilled the entire Torah?[4] From the verse,[5] "He sits alone and [studies] in stillness; he takes it unto himself."

4. Rabbi Shimon would say: When three eat at one table without speaking words of Torah there, it is as if they ate of offerings to the dead, for it is written,[9] "For all tables are full of filthy vomit when there is no [mention of] the Omnipresent." When, by contrast, three sit at one table and speak words of Torah, it is as if they had eaten from the table of the Omnipresent, for it is written,[10] "And he said to me: 'This is the table before God.'"

5. Rabbi Chanina ben Chachinai said: A person who awakes during the night or who travels alone on a journey and turns his heart to empty matters, is liable to lose his life.

---

whose desire is for the Torah of God will shun a company that is not concerned with God's Torah.[6]

[Studies] in stillness - The meaning of וידום is to whisper in a still small voice.[7] This

4. Our translation is based on Rav Kapach's Yemenite manuscripts of the Rambam's Commentary on the Mishnah. The standard printed text reads: "One who sits and occupies himself with the Torah, the Holy One, blessed be He, allots a reward for him..." We have chosen to follow Rav Kapach's version, because it fits the Rambam's interpretation of the proof-text more closely.
5. *Eichah* 3:28.
6. The standard published text of the Commentary on the Mishnah includes the following quote from *Berachot* 6a:
> Which is the source that teaches that even one person who sits and occupies himself with the Torah, the Divine Presence consorts with him? It is written (Exodus 20:24): "In every place where I have My Name mentioned I will come to you and bless you."
> Since I know this about one individual, is it necessary to mention that this applies with regard to two? With regard to two - they are recorded in the book of remembrance. One is not recorded in the book of remembrance.
> Since I know this about two individuals, is it necessary to mention that this applies with regard to three? You might think that a judgment is intended merely to bring about peace in the world, and the Divine Presence does not manifest itself. The verse teaches that a judgment is also Torah.
> Since I know this about three individuals, is it necessary to mention that this applies with regard to ten? When there are ten, the Divine Presence precedes the gathering. When there are three, [it does not manifest itself] until they sit.
We have not chosen to include this passage in our text, because it is lacking in the authoritative manuscripts and does not fit the style of the Rambam's commentary.
7. Cf. I Kings 19:12.

אֵין לִי אֶלָּא שְׁנַיִם, מִנַּיִן שֶׁאֲפִלּוּ אֶחָד שֶׁיּוֹשֵׁב וְעוֹסֵק בַּתּוֹרָה, שֶׁהַקָּדוֹשׁ בָּרוּךְ הוּא קוֹבֵעַ לוֹ שָׂכָר? שֶׁנֶּאֱמַר: יֵשֵׁב בָּדָד וְיִדֹּם כִּי נָטַל עָלָיו.

ד רַבִּי שִׁמְעוֹן אוֹמֵר: שְׁלֹשָׁה שֶׁאָכְלוּ עַל שֻׁלְחָן אֶחָד וְלֹא אָמְרוּ עָלָיו דִּבְרֵי תוֹרָה, כְּאִלּוּ אָכְלוּ מִזִּבְחֵי מֵתִים, שֶׁנֶּאֱמַר: כִּי כָּל שֻׁלְחָנוֹת מָלְאוּ קִיא צֹאָה בְּלִי מָקוֹם.

אֲבָל שְׁלֹשָׁה שֶׁאָכְלוּ עַל שֻׁלְחָן אֶחָד וְאָמְרוּ עָלָיו דִּבְרֵי תוֹרָה, כְּאִלּוּ אָכְלוּ מִשֻּׁלְחָנוֹ שֶׁל מָקוֹם, שֶׁנֶּאֱמַר: וַיְדַבֵּר אֵלַי זֶה הַשֻּׁלְחָן אֲשֶׁר לִפְנֵי ה'.

ה רַבִּי חֲנִינָא בֶּן חֲכִינַאי אוֹמֵר: הַנֵּעוֹר בַּלַּיְלָה, וְהַמְהַלֵּךְ בַּדֶּרֶךְ יְחִידִי, וְהַמְפַנֶּה לִבּוֹ לְבַטָּלָה — הֲרֵי זֶה מִתְחַיֵּב בְּנַפְשׁוֹ.

is reflected in Onkelos' Aramaic translation of the phrase וידום אהרון as "And Aharon praised."[8]

The proof that such a person is considered as if he accepted the entire Torah is from the phrase: "he takes it unto himself" - i.e., it is as if he took the entire Torah for himself alone.

Offerings to the dead - This refers to offerings to false divinities, as the term is used in the verse,[11] as we mentioned in the third chapter of the tractate, *Avodah Zarah*.[12] [The verse] refers to such a table as "filthy vomit," just as false divinities are called "feces and abominations."[13] The verse that precedes the proof-text [from Isaiah] describes people who are involved in eating and drinking, while forsaking the Torah and its study. Therefore, all their tables are considered as if disgusting matter and filth were eaten upon them - i.e., foods associated with the worship of false divinities.

As the preceding verse states: "Also these are confused because of wine, become lost because of strong drink. Priest and prophet become confused because of strong drink, become derelict because of wine. Their vision is confused, their judgment confounded."

[Rabbi Chanina ben Chachinai -] teaches that when a person wakes from sleep at night, or travels alone and [instead of trusting in God,] conceives of thoughts involving the denial of religious beliefs, he is liable for punishment by the hand of God.[14]

---

8. The *Targum Onkelos* included in most *chumashim* states *ushteik*, but some ancient manuscripts state *ushvach* as in our translation. See also the Meiri's commentary on *Pirkei Avot*, which offers a similar interpretation to that of the Rambam and cites the *Targum Yerushalmi* as a source. The standard printed texts of the Rambam's Commentary on the Mishnah state *ushteik*.
9. Isaiah 28:8.
10. Ezekiel 41:22.
11. Psalms 106:28: "And they joined themselves to Baal Pe'or and they ate of offerings to the dead."
12. *Mishnah* 8.
13. See II Kings 23:24.
14. This commentary is lacking in the standard editions of the Rambam's Commentary on the Mishnah and is added based on the authoritative Yemenite manuscripts of the text.

6. Rabbi Nechunia ben Hakaneh said: All who take upon themselves the yoke of Torah, will have the yoke of government and the yoke of worldly affairs removed from them. All who, by contrast, cast off the yoke of Torah, will have the yoke of government and the yoke of worldly affairs imposed upon them.

7. Rabbi Chalafta ben Dosa of Kefar Chanania said: If ten people sit together and occupy themselves with Torah, the Divine Presence rests among them, as it is said:[19] "God stands in the assembly of the Lord."

Which verse teaches that the same is true even of five? It is said:[20] "He has founded His band upon the earth." Which verse teaches that the same is true even of three? It is said:[21] "Among the judges He renders judgment."

Which verse teaches that the same is true even of two? It is stated:[22] "Then the God-fearing conversed with one another, and God hearkened and heard." Which verse teaches that the same is true even of one? It is said:[23] "In every place where I have My name mentioned I will come to you and bless you."

8. Rabbi Eleazar [ben Yehudah] of Bartota said: Give Him of that which is His, for you and whatever is yours are His. And so it was said by David:[26] "For all things are from You, and from Your own we have given You."

9. Rabbi Ya'akov said: When a person walks on a journey reviewing [a passage of the Torah], interrupts his study and remarks, "How beautiful is this tree! How beautiful is this plowed field!" [the Torah] considers him as if he were guilty of a mortal sin.

---

the yoke of Torah - the obligation to study.[15]

the yoke of government - the rigors imposed by a king and subservience to him.

and the yoke of worldly affairs - the rigors of circumstance.

[The *mishnah*] teaches that as a reward for the acceptance of the yoke of the Torah, God will save a person from the rigors imposed by kings and make the rigors of circumstance lighter.

Cast off the yoke of Torah - This refers to a person who states: "The Torah was given from heaven,[16] and I want no part of it."

---

15. Our translation is based on Rav Kapach's. Ibn Tibbon renders the phrase "diligent study."

16. Our translation is based on authoritative texts of the Rambam's Commentary on the Mishnah and is based on the Jerusalem Talmud (*Pe'ah* 1:1). The standard text reads "One who says the Torah was not given from heaven."

ו רַבִּי נְחוּנְיָא בֶן הַקָּנָה אוֹמֵר: כָּל הַמְקַבֵּל עָלָיו עֹל תּוֹרָה, מַעֲבִירִין מִמֶּנּוּ עֹל מַלְכוּת וְעֹל דֶּרֶךְ אֶרֶץ; וְכָל הַפּוֹרֵק מִמֶּנּוּ עֹל תּוֹרָה, נוֹתְנִין עָלָיו עֹל מַלְכוּת וְעֹל דֶּרֶךְ אֶרֶץ.

ז רַבִּי חֲלַפְתָּא אִישׁ כְּפַר חֲנַנְיָא אוֹמֵר: עֲשָׂרָה שֶׁיּוֹשְׁבִין וְעוֹסְקִין בַּתּוֹרָה, שְׁכִינָה שְׁרוּיָה בֵּינֵיהֶם, שֶׁנֶּאֱמַר: אֱלֹהִים נִצָּב בַּעֲדַת אֵל.

וּמִנַּיִן אֲפִלּוּ חֲמִשָּׁה? שֶׁנֶּאֱמַר: וַאֲגֻדָּתוֹ עַל אֶרֶץ יְסָדָהּ.

וּמִנַּיִן אֲפִלּוּ שְׁלֹשָׁה? שֶׁנֶּאֱמַר: בְּקֶרֶב אֱלֹהִים יִשְׁפֹּט.

וּמִנַּיִן אֲפִלּוּ שְׁנַיִם? שֶׁנֶּאֱמַר: אָז נִדְבְּרוּ יִרְאֵי ה' אִישׁ אֶל רֵעֵהוּ וַיַּקְשֵׁב ה' וַיִּשְׁמָע וְגוֹמֵר.

וּמִנַּיִן אֲפִלּוּ אֶחָד? שֶׁנֶּאֱמַר: בְּכָל הַמָּקוֹם אֲשֶׁר אַזְכִּיר אֶת שְׁמִי אָבוֹא אֵלֶיךָ וּבֵרַכְתִּיךָ.

ח רַבִּי אֶלְעָזָר אִישׁ בַּרְתּוֹתָא אוֹמֵר: תֶּן לוֹ מִשֶּׁלּוֹ, שֶׁאַתָּה וְשֶׁלְּךָ שֶׁלּוֹ. וְכֵן בְּדָוִד הוּא אוֹמֵר: כִּי מִמְּךָ הַכֹּל וּמִיָּדְךָ נָתַנּוּ לָךְ.

ט רַבִּי יַעֲקֹב אוֹמֵר: הַמְהַלֵּךְ בַּדֶּרֶךְ וְשׁוֹנֶה, וּמַפְסִיק מִמִּשְׁנָתוֹ וְאוֹמֵר: מַה נָּאֶה אִילָן זֶה! מַה נָּאֶה נִיר זֶה! מַעֲלֶה עָלָיו הַכָּתוּב כְּאִלּוּ מִתְחַיֵּב בְּנַפְשׁוֹ.

On the verse,[17] "engraved on the tablets," our Sages comment,[18] "[Do not read 'engraved (חרות) on the tablets;' read] 'freedom (חירות) on the tablets;'" i.e., freedom from the rigors of circumstance and the rigors of kings is granted to one who accepts what is written on the tablets upon himself.

The assembly - In the beginning of the tractate of *Sanhedrin*,[24] we explained that the term "assembly" is used to refer to no fewer than ten people. There we also explained that a court consists of no fewer than three [judges], and they are referred to with the term *elohim* with regard to a judgment.

The term *agudah* refers to objects that a person binds together with his hands. He performs this binding process with the five fingers of his hand. Moreover, making a fist with one's five fingers is also referred to as an *agudah*.[25]

17. Exodus 32:16.
18. *Eruvin* 54a.
19. Psalms 82:1.
20. Amos 9:6.
21. Psalms, *loc. cit.*
22. Malachi 3:16.
23. Exodus 20:21.
24. Chapter 1, *Mishnah* 6.
25. See *Hilchot Chovel UMazik* 3:9.
26. I Chronicles 29:14.

10. Rabbi Dostai bar Rabbi Yannai said in the name of Rabbi Meir: Whenever anyone forgets any of his Torah knowledge, the Torah considers it as if he were guilty of a mortal sin, for it is said:[27] "But beware and guard your soul scrupulously, lest you forget the things that your eyes have seen."

One might think that this applies even if the subject matter proved too difficult for him [and therefore he forgot]; hence, the Torah adds:[28] "And lest they be removed from your heart all the days of your life." One is not guilty of a mortal sin until he intentionally removes them from his heart.

11. Rabbi Chanina ben Dosa said: Whenever a person's fear of sin comes before his wisdom, his wisdom will endure; but when a person's wisdom comes before his fear of sin, his wisdom will not endure.

12. He used to say: Whenever a person's [good] deeds exceed his wisdom, his wisdom will endure; but when a person's wisdom exceeds his [good] deeds, his wisdom will not endure.

He used to say: Whenever a person's fellow men are pleased with him, God is also pleased with him; but when a person's fellow men are not pleased with him, God is also not pleased with him.

13. Rabbi Dosa ben Horkinas said: Sleeping during the [late] morning, wine at midday, children's prattle and sitting in the gathering places of the ignorant drive a man from the world.

14. Rabbi Eleazar of Modi'in said: A person who profanes consecrated articles, degrades the festivals, publicly humiliates his colleague, abrogates the covenant of our Patriarch Avraham, or publicly violates

---

[Whenever a person's... -] This concept is also accepted by the philosophers. For when the regular exercise of refined qualities precedes wisdom and a firm habit is established, the wisdom that the person learns afterwards will encourage him to maintain these positive attributes. This, in turn, will motivate him to intensify his connection with wisdom, inspiring him with a love and enthusiasm for it, for this encourages an ingrained habit.

When, by contrast, bad tendencies are ingrained before one learns wisdom, the wisdom that one learns [creates a conflict, for it] prevents a person from [indulging] the desires to which he is accustomed. This will cause him [to see wisdom] as a burden and to abandon it.

27. Deuteronomy 4:9.
28. *Ibid.*

י רַבִּי דוֹסְתַּאי בַּר יַנַּאי מִשּׁוּם רַבִּי מֵאִיר אוֹמֵר: כָּל הַשּׁוֹכֵחַ דָּבָר אֶחָד מִמִּשְׁנָתוֹ, מַעֲלֶה עָלָיו הַכָּתוּב כְּאִלּוּ מִתְחַיֵּב בְּנַפְשׁוֹ, שֶׁנֶּאֱמַר: רַק הִשָּׁמֶר לְךָ וּשְׁמֹר נַפְשְׁךָ מְאֹד פֶּן תִּשְׁכַּח אֶת הַדְּבָרִים אֲשֶׁר רָאוּ עֵינֶיךָ.

יָכוֹל אֲפִלּוּ תָּקְפָה עָלָיו מִשְׁנָתוֹ? תַּלְמוּד לוֹמַר: וּפֶן יָסוּרוּ מִלְּבָבְךָ כָּל יְמֵי חַיֶּיךָ; הָא אֵינוֹ מִתְחַיֵּב בְּנַפְשׁוֹ עַד שֶׁיֵּשֵׁב וִיסִירֵם מִלִּבּוֹ.

יא רַבִּי חֲנִינָא בֶן דּוֹסָא אוֹמֵר: כָּל שֶׁיִּרְאַת חֶטְאוֹ קוֹדֶמֶת לְחָכְמָתוֹ, חָכְמָתוֹ מִתְקַיֶּמֶת; וְכָל שֶׁחָכְמָתוֹ קוֹדֶמֶת לְיִרְאַת חֶטְאוֹ, אֵין חָכְמָתוֹ מִתְקַיֶּמֶת.

יב הוּא הָיָה אוֹמֵר: כָּל שֶׁמַּעֲשָׂיו מְרֻבִּין מֵחָכְמָתוֹ, חָכְמָתוֹ מִתְקַיֶּמֶת; וְכָל שֶׁחָכְמָתוֹ מְרֻבָּה מִמַּעֲשָׂיו, אֵין חָכְמָתוֹ מִתְקַיֶּמֶת.

הוּא הָיָה אוֹמֵר: כָּל שֶׁרוּחַ הַבְּרִיּוֹת נוֹחָה הֵימֶנּוּ, רוּחַ הַמָּקוֹם נוֹחָה הֵימֶנּוּ; וְכָל שֶׁאֵין רוּחַ הַבְּרִיּוֹת נוֹחָה הֵימֶנּוּ, אֵין רוּחַ הַמָּקוֹם נוֹחָה הֵימֶנּוּ.

יג רַבִּי דוֹסָא בֶן הַרְכִּינַס אוֹמֵר: שֵׁנָה שֶׁל שַׁחֲרִית, וְיַיִן שֶׁל צָהֳרַיִם, וְשִׂיחַת יְלָדִים, וִישִׁיבַת בָּתֵּי כְנֵסִיּוֹת שֶׁל עַמֵּי הָאָרֶץ, מוֹצִיאִין אֶת הָאָדָם מִן הָעוֹלָם.

יד רַבִּי אֶלְעָזָר הַמּוֹדָעִי אוֹמֵר: הַמְחַלֵּל אֶת הַקֳּדָשִׁים, וְהַמְבַזֶּה אֶת הַמּוֹעֲדוֹת, וְהַמַּלְבִּין פְּנֵי חֲבֵרוֹ בָּרַבִּים, וְהַמֵּפֵר בְּרִיתוֹ שֶׁל אַבְרָהָם אָבִינוּ, וְהַמְגַלֶּה פָנִים בַּתּוֹרָה

[**Sleeping in the late morning... -**] I.e., these [forms of conduct] negate a person's virtues until he departs from this world. And then he perishes.[29]

Publicly humiliates his colleague - embarrasses and shames him

Publicly violates Torah law - A person who violates the commandments of the Torah in public, in a manner that becomes well known. This is the ultimate expression of the denial [of the Torah], as it is written:[31] "When a soul [transgresses] in a highhanded manner...."

The phrase מגלה פנים, literally "reveals the face," means "acts cheekily." This interpretation is based on the wording of the [Jerusalem] Talmud, *Pe'ah* [1:1], which states: "המגלה פנים בתורה - This is one who transgresses the words of the Torah publicly, as did Yehoyakim, the son of Yoshiyahu."

[**Abrogates the covenant of our Patriarch Avraham -**] This is one who continues

---

29. Our translation is based on that of Ibn Tibbon, which is interpreted to mean that the person does not receive a share in the World to Come.
30. In Rav Kapach's Yemenite manuscripts of the Rambam's Commentary on the Mishnah, the word "Torah" is omitted. That version also changes the order of the sins mentioned in the Mishnah.
31. Numbers 15:30.

Torah law - even though he may possess Torah[30] and good deeds, he has no share in the World to Come.

15. Rabbi Yishmael said: Be readily submissive to a superior and be calm with a younger person; receive every person cheerfully.

16. Rabbi Akiva said: Laughter and frivolity accustom a man to lewdness. The Oral Tradition is a fence around the Torah; tithes are a fence for riches;[34] vows are a fence for restraint; a fence for wisdom is silence.

17. He used to say: Beloved is man, for he was created in the image [of God]; an even greater expression of love is that it was made known to him that he was created in the image [of God], as it is stated: "For in the image of God He made man."[36]

Beloved are the people Israel, for they are called children of God; an even greater expression of love is that it was made known to them that they are called children of God, as it is said: "You are the children of God Your Lord."[37]

Beloved are the people Israel, for a precious article was given to them; an even greater expression of love is that it was made known to them that they were given a precious article, as it is said: "I have given you good teaching; do not forsake My Torah."[38]

[living with] a foreskin, a person who was not circumcised as a child and who does not circumcise himself after attaining majority.

And the source mentioned above states that with regard to all the sins for which our Sages said that the violator has no portion in the World to Come - should the person repent, there is nothing that can stand in the way of a *baal-teshuvah*. It is only when they do not repent and die in suffering [that they do not receive a portion in the World to Come]. Thus, the severity of the sins for which it is said that the violator has no portion in the World to Come in comparison with other sins, is that suffering and death do not atone for them.

Be calm - i.e., composed and patient.
This directive teaches that if you meet a highly developed person, you should

32. Chapter 1, *Mishnah* 14.
33. To this *mishnah*, Ibn Tibbon adds the following translator's note: "From the master's wording, it would appear that he interprets the word מקבל [rendered as 'receive'] as meaning 'confront.' A source can be seen in Onkelos' translation of the phrase מקבילות הלולאות (Exodus 26:5) as 'the loops being opposite each other.' Similarly, in Arabic, the expression is used: 'I met so and so with happiness,' or 'I met so and so in anger.'"
34. This phrase is lacking in several texts of the Rambam's Commentary on the Mishnah.

שֶׁלֹּא כַהֲלָכָה — אַף עַל פִּי שֶׁיֵּשׁ בְּיָדוֹ תּוֹרָה וּמַעֲשִׂים טוֹבִים, אֵין לוֹ חֵלֶק לָעוֹלָם
הַבָּא.

טו רַבִּי יִשְׁמָעֵאל אוֹמֵר: הֱוֵי קַל לָרֹאשׁ, וְנוֹחַ לַתִּשְׁחֹרֶת, וֶהֱוֵי מְקַבֵּל אֶת כָּל הָאָדָם
בְּשִׂמְחָה.

טז רַבִּי עֲקִיבָא אוֹמֵר: שְׂחוֹק וְקַלּוּת רֹאשׁ מַרְגִּילִין לְעֶרְוָה. מַסֹּרֶת סְיָג לַתּוֹרָה.
מַעַשְׂרוֹת סְיָג לָעשֶׁר. נְדָרִים סְיָג לַפְּרִישׁוּת. סְיָג לַחָכְמָה שְׁתִיקָה.

יז הוּא הָיָה אוֹמֵר: חָבִיב אָדָם שֶׁנִּבְרָא בְצֶלֶם. חִבָּה יְתֵרָה נוֹדַעַת לוֹ שֶׁנִּבְרָא בְצֶלֶם,
שֶׁנֶּאֱמַר: כִּי בְּצֶלֶם אֱלֹהִים עָשָׂה אֶת הָאָדָם.

חֲבִיבִין יִשְׂרָאֵל שֶׁנִּקְרְאוּ בָנִים לַמָּקוֹם. חִבָּה יְתֵרָה נוֹדַעַת לָהֶם שֶׁנִּקְרְאוּ בָנִים לַמָּקוֹם,
שֶׁנֶּאֱמַר: בָּנִים אַתֶּם לַה' אֱלֹהֵיכֶם.

חֲבִיבִין יִשְׂרָאֵל שֶׁנִּתַּן לָהֶם כְּלִי חֶמְדָּה. חִבָּה יְתֵרָה נוֹדַעַת לָהֶם שֶׁנִּתַּן לָהֶם כְּלִי
חֶמְדָּה שֶׁבּוֹ נִבְרָא הָעוֹלָם, שֶׁנֶּאֱמַר: כִּי לֶקַח טוֹב נָתַתִּי לָכֶם תּוֹרָתִי אַל תַּעֲזֹבוּ.

make yourself flexible, serving him as he desires and devoting yourself to his service. If, conversely, you meet a person of dark hair - i.e., a younger man - you should not do this. You should be earnest with him and need not be as flexible or as unpretentious.

[The *mishnah*] continues, explaining that you should not think that the warning against being unpretentious with a younger man requires you to receive him with animosity or anger. This is not so. Instead, you should receive every person - whether older or younger, free man or slave, every human being with happiness and joy. This is a more [demanding charge] than Shammai's instruction,[32] "Receive every person with a cheerful countenance."[33]

[Vows are a fence for restraint -] [The *mishnah*] teaches that taking and maintaining vows to abstain from certain elements ingrains in a person the tendency to bridle the [desires] he seeks to curb. This tendency will continue and it will be easy to acquire the quality of restraint - i.e., the tendency to protect oneself from impurity. [The interpretation of פרישות as self-control lest one come in contact with undesirable elements is supported by the teaching] in the tractate *Chaggigah*:[35] "The clothes of the common people are considered as a *midras* [a source of impurity] for the *perushim*."

[An even greater expression of love is that it was made known -] [The *mishnah*] teaches that making known the value of the favor[s] that [mankind and Israel] were

35. Chapter 2, *Mishnah* 7.
36. Genesis 9:6.
37. Deuteronomy 14:1.
38. Proverbs 4:2.

18. Everything is foreseen, yet freedom of choice is granted; the world is judged with goodness, and everything is according to the preponderance of [good] deeds.

19. He used to say: Everything is given on collateral and a net is spread over all the living; the shop is open, the Shopkeeper extends credit, the ledger is open, the hand writes, and whoever wishes to borrow may come and borrow. The collectors make their rounds regularly, each day, and exact payment from man with or without his knowledge [of his debt], and they have on what to rely. The judgment is a judgment of truth, and everything is prepared for the feast.

20. Rabbi Eleazar ben Azaryah said: If there is no Torah, there is no proper social conduct; if there is no proper social conduct, there is no

granted is itself an additional favor. For there are times when out of mercy for him, a person is granted a favor, and yet he is not appraised of the value of what was done for him, because [his benefactor] looks down at him with disdain.

[This teaching] includes very profound concepts and indeed was fit to be authored by none other than Rabbi Akiva. To follow is the explanation - albeit in brief - of the teaching. [Its comprehension is] dependent on the concepts mentioned in the introductory chapters.

It states that everything [that occurs] in the world is known before Him, and He foresaw its [occurrence]. This is the intent of the phrase...

Everything is foreseen - Nevertheless, one should not think the fact that God knows of all [our] deeds implies predetermination, that a person is compelled to perform any particular deed. This is not true. Instead, all people are given the initiative with regard to their conduct. This is implied by the phrase...

Freedom of choice is granted - i.e., to every individual, as explained in the eighth [introductory] chapter.

[the world is judged with goodness -] [The *mishnah*] continues, stating that God judges men with kindness, and not as befits their conduct according to the strict measure, as indicated by [our Sages' interpretation][39] of His attributes, "slow to anger and abounding in lovingkindness,"[40] as meaning: "slow to anger for both the righteous and the wicked." And the prophet describes him, saying:[41] "God is good to all."

[and everything is according to the preponderance of [good] deeds. -] With this, [the *mishnah*] explains that positive character traits are acquired not through the performance of great deeds, but rather through the performance of a deed many times.

39. *Eruvin* 22a.
40. Exodus 34:6.

יח הַכּל צָפוּי, וְהָרְשׁוּת נְתוּנָה, וּבְטוֹב הָעוֹלָם נִדּוֹן, וְהַכּל לְפִי רֹב הַמַּעֲשֶׂה.

יט הוּא הָיָה אוֹמֵר: הַכּל נָתוּן בְּעֵרָבוֹן, וּמְצוּדָה פְרוּסָה עַל כָּל הַחַיִּים. הַחֲנוּת פְּתוּחָה, וְהַחֶנְוָנִי מֵקִיף, וְהַפִּנְקָס פָּתוּחַ, וְהַיָּד כּוֹתֶבֶת, וְכָל הָרוֹצֶה לִלְווֹת יָבוֹא וְיִלְוֶה, וְהַגַּבָּאִים מַחֲזִירִין תָּדִיר בְּכָל יוֹם, וְנִפְרָעִין מִן הָאָדָם מִדַּעְתּוֹ וְשֶׁלֹּא מִדַּעְתּוֹ, וְיֵשׁ לָהֶם עַל מַה שֶּׁיִּסְמֹכוּ, וְהַדִּין דִּין אֱמֶת, וְהַכּל מְתֻקָּן לַסְּעֻדָּה.

כ רַבִּי אֶלְעָזָר בֶּן עֲזַרְיָה אוֹמֵר: אִם אֵין תּוֹרָה, אֵין דֶּרֶךְ אֶרֶץ; אִם אֵין דֶּרֶךְ אֶרֶץ, אֵין

For positive character traits are acquired solely through the repetition of good deeds many times. This is the way a person acquires a tendency toward [such conduct], and not through performing one good deed of great dimensions. For this deed will not habituate a person to this tendency.

For example, if a person gave 1000 *dinarim* to one person to whom it was fitting to give them, this one great deed will not accustom him to the quality of generosity to the same degree as if he gave 1000 *dinarim* to 1000 different people, [giving each one *dinar*, provided] he gave every *dinar* with a generous spirit. For by repeating the deed of generosity 1000 times, he establishes a firm tendency [within his character]. By contrast, the one great deed represents a single time in which his soul was aroused to positive activity, and afterwards this desire is no longer felt.

Similarly, with regard to the Torah's [scales of judgment]: The reward a person receives for redeeming one captive for 100 *dinarim* or giving a poor person 100 *dinarim* and thus satisfying his needs is not equivalent to the reward he would receive for redeeming ten captives or satisfying the needs of ten poor people, even if he gave each one only ten *dinarim*. This is implied by the expression "the preponderance of [good] deeds," and not "according to the greatness of the [good] deeds."

Extends credit - This is the meaning of the Hebrew term מקיף, to give on loan for an extended period without demanding payment immediately. The analogy intended is obvious. By saying...

Whoever wishes to borrow may come and borrow - [the *mishnah*] reinforces the concept stated previously, that there is no predetermination, nor is a person forced [to act in any way]. Instead, a person acts voluntarily, conducting himself on his own initiative.

The collectors make their rounds... - This is an analogy for death and other punishments that may be visited on a person.

Everything is prepared for the feast - i.e., the culmination of all this is the life of the World to Come.

[If there is no..., there is no... -] The intent is that each element of the pair facilitates the existence of the other and brings it to perfection.

41. Psalms 145:9.

Torah. If there is no wisdom, there is no fear [of God]; if there is no fear [of God], there is no wisdom. If there is no knowledge, there is no understanding; if there is no understanding, there is no knowledge. If there is no flour, there is no Torah; if there is no Torah, there is no flour.

21. He used to say: Anyone whose wisdom exceeds his [good] deeds - to what can he be compared? To a tree whose branches are numerous, but whose roots are few. The wind will come and uproot it and turn it upside down; as it is stated: "And he shall be like a lonely tree in arid land and shall not see when good comes; he shall dwell on parched soil in the wilderness, on salt-land, which is not inhabitable."[43]

In contrast, anyone whose [good] deeds exceed his wisdom - to what can he be compared? To a tree whose branches are few, but whose roots are numerous, so that even if all the winds in the world came and blew against it, they could not move it from its place; as it is stated: "And he shall be like a tree planted by waters, toward the stream spreading its roots, and it shall not feel when the heat comes, and its foliage shall be verdant; in the year of drought it shall not worry, nor shall it cease from yielding fruit."[44]

Rabbi Eliezer (ben) Chisma said:[45] The laws pertaining to the bird-sacrifices and the calculation of the onset of the *niddah* state - these are essentials of Torah law; the calculation of the heavenly cycles and geometry are condiments to wisdom.

The statement with regard to knowledge (דעת) and understanding (בינה) reflects a very abstract philosophical concept. I will mention it [in brief], relying on the understanding of those who have already studied such concepts.

The knowledge[42] that we reach and that we acquire is not really the [true] conception that would be grasped through seeing the abstract form of the concept and grasping it or through comprehending forms [e.g., spiritual entities,] whose very existence is ideal.

42. Our translation of the following passage is based on Ibn Tibbon's text. We have remained true to the literal meaning of his words, because, with justified humility, we do not profess to understand the precise intent of the abstractions explained by the Rambam.
43. Jeremiah 17:6. Although included in the standard published text, this proof-text is lacking in several texts of the Rambam's Commentary on the Mishnah.

תּוֹרָה. אִם אֵין חָכְמָה, אֵין יִרְאָה; אִם אֵין יִרְאָה, אֵין חָכְמָה. אִם אֵין בִּינָה, אֵין
דַּעַת; אִם אֵין דַּעַת, אֵין בִּינָה. אִם אֵין קֶמַח, אֵין תּוֹרָה; אִם אֵין תּוֹרָה, אֵין
קֶמַח.

כא הוּא הָיָה אוֹמֵר: כֹּל שֶׁחָכְמָתוֹ מְרֻבָּה מִמַּעֲשָׂיו, לְמָה הוּא דוֹמֶה? לְאִילָן
שֶׁעֲנָפָיו מְרֻבִּין וְשָׁרָשָׁיו מֻעָטִין, וְהָרוּחַ בָּאָה וְעוֹקַרְתּוֹ וְהוֹפַכְתּוֹ עַל פָּנָיו, שֶׁנֶּאֱמַר:
וְהָיָה כְּעַרְעָר בָּעֲרָבָה וְלֹא יִרְאֶה כִּי יָבוֹא טוֹב, וְשָׁכַן חֲרֵרִים בַּמִּדְבָּר אֶרֶץ מְלֵחָה
וְלֹא תֵשֵׁב.

אֲבָל כֹּל שֶׁמַּעֲשָׂיו מְרֻבִּין מֵחָכְמָתוֹ, לְמָה הוּא דוֹמֶה? לְאִילָן שֶׁעֲנָפָיו מֻעָטִין
וְשָׁרָשָׁיו מְרֻבִּין, שֶׁאֲפִלּוּ כָל הָרוּחוֹת שֶׁבָּעוֹלָם בָּאוֹת וְנוֹשְׁבוֹת בּוֹ, אֵין מְזִיזִין אוֹתוֹ
מִמְּקוֹמוֹ, שֶׁנֶּאֱמַר: וְהָיָה כְּעֵץ שָׁתוּל עַל מַיִם וְעַל יוּבַל יְשַׁלַּח שָׁרָשָׁיו וְלֹא יִרְאֶה כִּי
יָבוֹא חֹם, וְהָיָה עָלֵהוּ רַעֲנָן וּבִשְׁנַת בַּצֹּרֶת לֹא יִדְאָג וְלֹא יָמִישׁ מֵעֲשׂוֹת פֶּרִי.

רַבִּי אֱלִיעֶזֶר בֶּן חִסְמָא אוֹמֵר: קִנִּין וּפִתְחֵי נִדָּה, הֵן הֵן גּוּפֵי הֲלָכוֹת; תְּקוּפוֹת
וְגִימַטְרִיָּאוֹת פַּרְפְּרָאוֹת לַחָכְמָה.

[With regard to the latter,] their very existence is knowledge, regardless of whether we comprehend them as knowledge. [Our process of] comprehension is referred to as understanding and it [leads to] knowledge. Conversely, knowledge [leads] us to understand, making it possible for us to grasp what we comprehend.

Thus, it is as if [the *mishnah*] were saying: If we do not comprehend a concept, there is no way we will come to [true] knowledge of it. And conversely, if there is no [true] knowledge, there is no way we can comprehend, for our understanding stems from knowledge.

The comprehension of the above concept is very difficult, even from texts written to communicate this idea; surely this applies with regard to this text. Nevertheless, [the explanations] we [have given] prepare a straight path toward it.

[Anyone whose wisdom exceeds his good deeds -] These concepts were already explained in this chapter with regard to the words of Rabbi Chanina ben Dosa.[46]

---

44. *Ibid.* 17:8. Although included in the standard published text, this proof-text is lacking in several texts of the Rambam's Commentary on the Mishnah.
45. Although included in the standard published text, this entire teaching is lacking in the authoritative texts of the Rambam's Commentary on the Mishnah.
46. *Mishnah* 12.

CHAPTER FOUR

1. Ben Zoma said: Who is wise? He who learns from every person, as it is stated:[1] "From all those who have taught me, I have gained wisdom."

Who is valiant? He who subdues his [natural] inclination, as it is stated:[2] "A patient person is better than a mighty man, and he who masters his spirit is better than one who conquers a city."

Who is rich? He who is happy with his portion, as it is stated:[3] "When you eat of the labor of your hands, you will be happy, and it will be good for you." "You will be happy" - in this world; "it will be good for you" - in the World to Come.

Who is honored? He who honors others, as it is stated:[4] "I will honor those who honor Me, and those who despise Me will be degraded."

2. Ben Azzai said: Run to [perform even] an easy mitzvah, and flee from transgression; for one mitzvah brings about another mitzvah, and one transgression brings about another; for the reward for a mitzvah is the mitzvah, and the recompense for a transgression is a transgression.

3. He would say: Do not regard anyone with contempt, and do not reject anything, for there is no man who does not have his hour and no thing that does not have its place.

4. Rabbi Levitas of Yavneh said: Be of an exceedingly humble spirit, for the expectation of mortal man is but worms.[10]

[Who is wise... -] We have explained these concepts in the introductory chapters.[5]

[Run to [perform even] an easy mitzvah -] We have already explained this statement in [the commentary on] the tenth chapter of *Sanhedrin*.

Our Sages have already called attention to the shining example given in the Torah that inspires the performance of mitzvot, the verse:[6] "At that time, Moses set aside three cities...." It was known that this action was of no immediate consequence, because the laws of a city of refuge would not apply to them until they had separated

1. Psalms 119:99.
2. Proverbs 16:32.
3. Psalms 128:2.
4. I Samuel 2:30.
5. The Rambam is referring to his explanations in Chapters 2 and 7 of the introductory chapters. In the standard printed texts of the Rambam's Commentary on the Mishnah, this statement is

פֶּרֶק רְבִיעִי

א בֶּן זוֹמָא אוֹמֵר: אֵיזֶהוּ חָכָם? הַלּוֹמֵד מִכָּל אָדָם, שֶׁנֶּאֱמַר: מִכָּל מְלַמְּדַי הִשְׂכַּלְתִּי.

אֵיזֶהוּ גִבּוֹר? הַכּוֹבֵשׁ אֶת יִצְרוֹ, שֶׁנֶּאֱמַר: טוֹב אֶרֶךְ אַפַּיִם מִגִּבּוֹר, וּמוֹשֵׁל בְּרוּחוֹ מִלֹּכֵד עִיר.

אֵיזֶהוּ עָשִׁיר? הַשָּׂמֵחַ בְּחֶלְקוֹ, שֶׁנֶּאֱמַר: יְגִיעַ כַּפֶּיךָ כִּי תֹאכֵל אַשְׁרֶיךָ וְטוֹב לָךְ — אַשְׁרֶיךָ בָּעוֹלָם הַזֶּה, וְטוֹב לָךְ לָעוֹלָם הַבָּא.

אֵיזֶהוּ מְכֻבָּד? הַמְכַבֵּד אֶת הַבְּרִיּוֹת, שֶׁנֶּאֱמַר: כִּי מְכַבְּדַי אֲכַבֵּד וּבֹזַי יֵקָלּוּ.

ב בֶּן עַזַּאי אוֹמֵר: הֱוֵי רָץ לְמִצְוָה קַלָּה כְּבַחֲמוּרָה, וּבוֹרֵחַ מִן הָעֲבֵרָה; שֶׁמִּצְוָה גּוֹרֶרֶת מִצְוָה, וַעֲבֵרָה גּוֹרֶרֶת עֲבֵרָה; שֶׁשְּׂכַר מִצְוָה מִצְוָה, וּשְׂכַר עֲבֵרָה עֲבֵרָה.

ג הוּא הָיָה אוֹמֵר: אַל תְּהִי בָז לְכָל אָדָם, וְאַל תְּהִי מַפְלִיג לְכָל דָּבָר, שֶׁאֵין לְךָ אָדָם שֶׁאֵין לוֹ שָׁעָה, וְאֵין לְךָ דָּבָר שֶׁאֵין לוֹ מָקוֹם.

ד רַבִּי לְוִיטַס אִישׁ יַבְנֶה אוֹמֵר: מְאֹד מְאֹד הֱוֵי שְׁפַל רוּחַ, שֶׁתִּקְוַת אֱנוֹשׁ רִמָּה.

three cities in the Land of Canaan. For the three cities in Transjordan would not serve as a refuge [for a killer] until three were separated in the Land of Canaan, as [implied by] the verse:[7] "There shall be six cities of refuge." Nevertheless, [Moses] set aside these three solely because [of the following rationale]:[8] "If the opportunity to perform a mitzvah presents itself, I will fulfill it."

If Moses our teacher, he who grasped the truth, the most perfect [of men], endeavored to add the fulfillment of half a mitzvah to his attainments and his perfection, needless to say this course of action should be followed by those who have tainted their souls and allowed this taint to spread.

[There is no man who does not have his hour... -] Surely every person has the potential to cause damage or to promote good, even with regard to things of minor concern and little value. If you have disgraced a person, he may cause you harm.[9]

[Be of an exceedingly humble spirit -] In the [fourth] introductory chapter, we have

appended to the conclusion of the third chapter. The authoritative manuscripts of that text place the statement here. (This also appears correct from a reading of the introductory chapters.)
6. Deuteronomy 4:41.
7. Numbers 35:13. As *Makkot* 9b states, this verse implies that until there are six cities designated for this purpose, the laws of a city of refuge do not apply to any of them.
8. *Makkot* 10a.
9. The latter sentence is lacking in the standard published texts of the Rambam's Commentary on the Mishnah.
10. See Chapter 3, *Mishnah* 13.

already explained that humility is the mean between pride and lowliness. ענוה is the sole word used to denote this quality in [Biblical] Hebrew. There are, by contrast, several terms used [by the Bible] to denote the quality of pride: גבה לב עינים רמות גאה and רם. Similarly, our Sages referred to pride with the terms רוח נבוהה גסות הרוח and מתגאה. And they referred to the opposite quality, humility, with the term שפלות הרוח.

As we explained in the fourth [introductory] chapter, it is preferable for a person to lean toward one of the extremes [of character] as a safeguard, so that he can always find the mean. This applies with regard to all other emotional qualities, with the exception of pride. Since the Sages appreciated the severity of the shortcomings of this trait and knew the damage it could cause, they eschewed it entirely, tending toward the other extreme. [They sought to be utterly lowly in spirit,] so that there would be no trace of pride whatsoever within their souls.[11]

In one of the texts [dedicated to] ethical [development], I saw [the following narrative]: One of the pious was asked: "What was the happiest day of your life?" He answered [as follows]:

Once I was traveling on a ship; my place was among the lowly and I was wearing rags and tatters. On the ship were also merchants and men of substance.

While I was lying in my berth, one of the company had to urinate. My low status and demeaning appearance affected him to the extent that he revealed himself and urinated on me.

I was amazed at the extent of his brashness, but in truth I did not feel any disgrace because of his deed. [Indeed,] I was not aroused to any feeling at all. [When I appreciated this,] I rejoiced with great joy that I had reached the level that I was not bothered at all by the degrading conduct of that base person, and was able to pay him no attention whatsoever.

There is no doubt that this utter extreme of lowliness [was employed] to eschew pride [entirely].

I will continue to cite several of our Sages' statements in praise of humility and in disparagement of pride. This is the spirit of this [Sage], who instructed us to seek lowliness, saying: "Be of an exceedingly humble spirit." He suspected that if a person remained within the [narrow] borders of humility, he might possess some dimension of pride, for he would be close to [this quality], since humility is the mean, as explained.

In praise of humility, our Sages said:[12] [The same quality] that serves as a crown for the head of wisdom serves as a sole for the sandal of humility. For it is written:[13] "The acme of wisdom is the fear of God," implying that the fear of God is more venerable than wisdom; indeed, it is the purpose for the existence of [wisdom]. With regard to humility, by contrast, it is said,[14] "At the heel of humility is the fear of God" - i.e., the fear of God is found at the base of humility. And thus humility is far greater than wisdom.

[Our Sages] also said:[15]

This point is explicit in the Torah, reiterated by the prophets, and mentioned a

11. See similar statements in *Hilchot De'ot* 2:3.
12. Jerusalem Talmud (*Shabbat* 1:3); *Shir HaShirim Rabbah*, Chapter 1.
13. Psalms 111:10.
14. Proverbs 22:4.
15. *Megillah* 31a.

third time in the Holy Writings. Wherever you find the greatness of the Holy One, blessed be He, you find His humility. It is written in the Torah,[16] "God, great, mighty,..." and the following verse continues: "Who performs the judgment of the orphan and the widow."

It is reiterated in the prophets, as it is written:[17] "Thus says the high and lofty One, He who dwells for eternity, holy is His name, 'I dwell on high....'" [And the verse continues,] "but also with he who is broken and of a contrite spirit." And it is mentioned a third time in the Holy Writings, as it is written:[18] "Extol Him who rides the clouds, י‏ is His name." And the following verse continues: "The Father of orphans, the Judge of widows."

One may learn [the virtue of humility] from Moses our teacher, who was perfect in all the intellectual and ethical virtues - this in addition to his status as a prophet. He was a father of wisdom, a father of prophecy, a father of Torah, and yet the Torah praised him with regard to the quality of humility alone, as it is written:[19] "And the man Moses was very humble." And the modifier "very" was added, indicating that he tended to the extreme. This is also indicated by his response:[20] "And we, what are we?"

Similarly, with regard to David, "the anointed of the House of Jacob, and the sweet singer of Israel."[21] He was a king whose orders were obeyed, and whose sovereignty was upraised by God who granted him victories. As our Sages explain,[22] Moses our teacher prophesied about his existence, as it is written:[23] "A star shall shoot forth from Jacob." He was a prophet and the head of the court of seventy elders,[24] as implied by the phrase,[25] "He sat in the seat of the wise men." Nevertheless, he said about himself,[26] "A broken and contrite heart, [O Lord, You will not despise,"] and many other expressions that indicate that he was utterly humble.

Conversely, they have made [disparaging] statements with regard to pride, [among them:][27] Every person who has a haughty spirit is considered as if he served alien gods. For it is written,[28] "All haughty hearts are an abomination to God." And it is written [with regard to alien worship]:[29] "Do not bring an abomination...." Similarly, [a proud person] is considered as if he denied God's existence, as it is written:[30] "And you will lift up your heart and forget God your Lord."

16. Deuteronomy 10:17.
17. Isaiah 57:15.
18. Psalms 68:5.
19. Numbers 12:3.
20. Exodus 16:7.
21. II Samuel 23:1.
22. The source for this interpretation in the works of our Sages is not known to this writer. The Rambam quotes this interpretation himself in *Hilchot Melachim* 11:1.
23. Numbers 24:17.
24. See *Mo'ed Katan* 16b.
25. II Samuel, *loc. cit.*:8. We have translated the verse as it is interpreted in *Mo'ed Katan* (and Rav David Kimchi). Other interpretations are also offered.
26. Psalms 51:19.
27. *Sotah* 4b.
28. Proverbs 16:5.
29. Deuteronomy 7:26.
30. *Ibid.* 8:14.

5. Rabbi Yochanan ben Berokah said: Whenever one desecrates the Heavenly Name in secret, punishment will be meted out to him in public; unwittingly or intentionally, it is all the same with regard to the desecration of [God's] Name.

6. Rabbi Yishmael his son[43] said: He who studies Torah in order to teach, is given the opportunity to study and to teach; and he who studies in order to practice, is given the opportunity to study and to teach, to observe and to practice.

Similarly, the sin of pride is considered equivalent to having sexual relations with all the women with whom relations are forbidden. For it is written, "All haughty hearts are an abomination to God." And with regard to forbidden relations it is written:[31] "For they performed all these abominations."

And our Sages said that pride itself is considered as the worship of alien gods before God. This is derived from the verse,[32] "Separate yourselves from the person whose soul is in his nose" - i.e., who is haughty - "for of what is he to be accounted for." They said: [Do not read *bameh* "for what," but] *bamah*, "an altar."

They said that it would be correct to kill a proud person. And they said,[33] "Everyone with a haughty spirit should be hewed down like an *asherah*.[34] For it is written,[35] "Those of lofty stature will be hewed down," and it is also written,[36] "And you shall cut down their *asherah* trees."

And our Sages said that at the time of the Resurrection of the Dead, God will not resurrect the proud. They said: The dust of all those of a haughty spirit will not be stirred. For it is written,[37] "Those who rest in the dust, arise and rejoice." "It does not say "who lie in the dust," but rather "who rest in the dust" - i.e., one who was close to the dust during his life. This means that it is the humble who will be resurrected.

They stressed this concept to an extreme degree, saying: Whenever a person is haughty, the Divine Presence wails over him, as implied by the verse,[38] "the haughty devastate[39] Him from afar." And there are many similar statements. Also, on the phrase[40] "for the white blotch (שאת) and the leprous discoloration," they commented: שאת indicates elevation, as reflected in the verse:[41] "The lofty (הנשאות) hills." Thus, the

31. Leviticus 18:27.
32. Isaiah 2:22.
33. *Sotah* 5a.
34. A tree that is worshiped.
35. Isaiah 10:33.
36. Deuteronomy 7:5.
37. Isaiah 26:19.
38. Psalms 138:6.
39. Our translation of the verse follows Rashi's commentary on *Sotah, loc. cit.* See a similar interpretation of the word ידע in Ezekiel 19:7.
40. Leviticus 14:56.
41. Isaiah 2:14.

ה רַבִּי יוֹחָנָן בֶּן בְּרוֹקָא אוֹמֵר: כָּל הַמְחַלֵּל שֵׁם שָׁמַיִם בַּסֵּתֶר, נִפְרָעִין מִמֶּנּוּ בַּגָּלוּי. אֶחָד שׁוֹגֵג וְאֶחָד מֵזִיד בְּחִלּוּל הַשֵּׁם.

ו רַבִּי יִשְׁמָעֵאל אוֹמֵר: הַלּוֹמֵד עַל מְנָת לְלַמֵּד, מַסְפִּיקִין בְּיָדוֹ לִלְמֹד וּלְלַמֵּד ; וְהַלּוֹמֵד עַל מְנָת לַעֲשׂוֹת, מַסְפִּיקִין בְּיָדוֹ לִלְמֹד וּלְלַמֵּד, לִשְׁמֹר וְלַעֲשׂוֹת.

previous verse can be interpreted to mean, "Those who are lofty are like a leprous discoloration."

It was also said: Ravva stated: "One who has [pride] should be placed under a ban of ostracism, and he who lacks [pride] should be placed under a similar ban." His intent was that it is not proper to turn entirely to the extreme of lowliness, because it is not one of man's virtues. [The Sages stated that] one should have one sixty-fourth of a measure of pride; i.e., if there are sixty-four measures between a person and an objective, he should stand at the sixty-third measure. In this instance, they counseled that one should deviate from the mean in order to eschew pride. For if one reduced this measure and came closer to pride, one would be worthy of ostracism. This is Ravva's view with regard to humility.

Rav Nachman differs and maintains that it is not proper for a person to possess any measure of pride - neither a small measure nor a large measure - for it involves a great sin. The quality that causes a person to become an abomination for God should not be approached at all. This is implied by their words:

Because of the loss caused by this sin, [our *mishnah*] teaches: "Be of an exceedingly humble spirit, for the expectation of mortal man is but worms" - i.e., you should teach yourself ethical truth until you remove pride by contemplating the ultimate fate of the body, that it will be [consumed by] worms.

[**Unwittingly or intentionally, it is all the same... -**] As you know, the Torah considers an unwitting transgression a sin, and for that reason requires atonement through a sacrifice. As it is written:[42] "God will forgive him for the sin that he committed." Nevertheless, [a person who commits a sin unwittingly] is surely not the same as one who commits [a sin] intentionally. Heaven forbid that God would equate a person who sins unwittingly to one who sins intentionally in any matter.

The intent is that with regard to the desecration of God's name, a person will receive public retribution regardless of whether his deed is committed intentionally or unwittingly. If his sin is intentional, [the retribution will be fitting,] and if his sin is committed unwittingly [the retribution will be fitting]. In both instances, the retribution will be given in an open manner.

42. Leviticus 19:22. See *Keritot* 9a.
Although this is the version in all the texts of the Rambam's Commentary on the Mishnah, it must be noted that this verse refers to a guilt offering sacrificed to atone for relations with a slave betrothed to another person. This offering must be brought regardless of whether the sin is committed willingly or unwittingly. Therefore, some suggest that the Rambam's intent is Leviticus 5:10, which speaks of God's granting pardon for a sin committed unwittingly.
43. I.e., the son of Rabbi Yochanan. The Rambam mentions this Sage's name in his Introduction

7. Rabbi Tzadok said:[44] Do not make [the Torah] a crown for self-aggrandizement, nor an axe with which to cut. So, too, Hillel used to say:[45] He who exploits the crown [of the Torah for his own ends] shall perish. From this you can conclude: anyone who derives personal gain from the words of Torah removes his life from the World [to Come].

[Do not make [the Torah]... an axe with which to cut -] I thought not to comment with regard to this instruction, because [its meaning] is obvious. And also because I know that what I have to say about this will not find favor in the eyes of most of the Torah scholars, and perhaps not in the eyes of any of them. Nevertheless, I will make my statement without paying attention or showing concern for those who preceded me, or [the sages of] the present day.

The meaning of the statement: "Do not make [the Torah]... an axe with which to cut" is not to consider it as a means to earn one's livelihood.[46] [The *mishnah*] explains that everyone who derives benefit from the honor of the Torah in this world will have his soul cut off from the World to Come. People ignore this clear and obvious message and refuse to pay attention to it. Instead, they choose to follow the superficial meaning of certain statements, without comprehending them. I will explain [the true meaning of those statements].

[On the basis of their interpretations,] they imposed assessments on individuals and on communities, and made the positions of status in Torah a collector's enterprise. They [purposely] deceived people with a blatant misconception, [saying] that it is an obligation and a necessity to help the scholars, their students and those people who are involved in the Torah and for whom the Torah is their occupation.

This is an error that has no foundation in the Torah and no support whatsoever. When we observe the conduct of our Sages of blessed memory, we see that they did not impose levies on the people, nor gathered alms for their magnificent and honorable *yeshivot,* nor for the exilarchs, nor for judges, nor for those who spread Torah knowledge, not for the leaders and not for any person.

There were some Sages who lived in indigent poverty, and some were very wealthy. Heaven forbid to say that the wealthy were not generous and did not give charity. If those who were poor had extended their hand [in search of alms], [the wealthy] would have filled their homes with gold and pearls. [The poor] did not do this. Instead, they labored, working to derive their livelihood, whether amply or with difficulty. As you know, Hillel was a hewer of wood and would study before Shemayah and Avtalion.

to the Commentary on the Mishnah. Others attribute this *mishnah* to Rabbi Yishmael ben Rabbi Yosse.
44. Other texts of this *mishnah* add the teaching: "Do not separate yourself from the community, and do not act as a counselor [when sitting as a judge]."
45. See Chapter 1, *Mishnah* 12.
46. See also similar statements by the Rambam in the *Mishneh Torah (Hilchot Talmud Torah* 3:10; *Hilchot Matnot Aniyim* 10:18). It must be mentioned that although the emphasis on work that the Rambam places is appreciated, other Rabbinic authorities have differed, maintaining that working to earn one's livelihood may prevent a person from reaching excellence in Torah scholarship.

ז רַבִּי צָדוֹק אוֹמֵר: אַל תַּעֲשֵׂם עֲטָרָה לְהִתְגַּדֵּל בָּהֶם, וְלֹא קַרְדֹּם לַחְפֹּר בָּהֶם. וְכָךְ הָיָה הִלֵּל אוֹמֵר: וּדְאִשְׁתַּמֵּשׁ בְּתָגָא, חָלָף. הָא לָמַדְתָּ, כָּל הַנֶּהֱנֶה מִדִּבְרֵי תוֹרָה, נוֹטֵל חַיָּיו מִן הָעוֹלָם.

He lived in utter poverty.[47] [Now] his stature was well known, [for] his students were compared to Moses, Aharon, Joshua; the least of them was Rabban Yochanan ben Zakkai.[48] No thinking person would doubt that if he had allowed people to assist him, they would not have let him continue hewing wood.

Similarly, with regard to Chanina ben Dosa: About him it was proclaimed:[49] "The entire world derives its sustenance solely by virtue of My son Chanina. And My son Chanina makes do with a *kav* of carobs from Friday to Friday." He did not seek [assistance] from other men.

And Karna was a judge of renown throughout the diaspora;[50] and he was a water carrier. When litigants would appear before him, he would tell them: "Give me someone who will draw water instead of me while I am busy with you, or pay me what I will forfeit from being involved in my occupation, and I will judge for you."[51]

The Jews of their era or of eras like theirs were not callous, nor did they fail to perform acts of kindness. Indeed, we do not find that a poor sage would criticize the people of his generation for not assisting them. It is only that [the sages] themselves were pious men, who believed in the truth for the sake of the truth, and believed in God and the Torah of Moses, through which a person derives a share of the eternal world. [For this reason,] they did not allow themselves to [ask for assistance].

They considered that as desecrating God's name in the eyes of the public, for they would think that the Torah is a profession like other professions, from which people derive their livelihood. This would cause them to lose respect for it, and to the person who [brought them to such thought would be applied the verse,][52] "He brought scorn upon the word of God."

Nevertheless, those who deny the truth and [ignore] these clear statements take money from people willingly or unwillingly, based on stories from the Talmud about people whose bodies were impaired or who were of extreme old age and for these reasons could not do any work [and support themselves in any other way], except

Therefore, they allow a stipend to be paid to Torah scholars for study. See the gloss of the *Kessef Mishneh* on *Hilchot Talmud Torah, loc. cit.* and the rulings of the *Shulchan Aruch* (*Yoreh De'ah* 246:5) and the Ramah (*loc. cit:*21).

47. See *Yoma* 35b, which states that Hillel received a meager wage for his work. It does not - nor does any source known to this writer - state that he was a hewer of wood.

48. See *Sukkah* 28a, *Bava Batra* 134a.

49. *Berachot* 17b; *Ta'anit* 24b.

50. Our translation follows *Sanhedrin* 17b, which states that Karna would judge the legal matters of the diaspora. Other versions of the Commentary on the Mishnah state "Karna was a judge [of renown] throughout *Eretz Yisrael.*"

51. *Ketubot* 105a, the apparent source for the Rambam's statements, relates that Karna would charge a minimal fee to compensate for his lost wages when judging a case. The narrative regarding drawing water, however, is mentioned with regard to Rav Huna. Perhaps the Rambam had a different version of that text.

52. Numbers 15:31.

by receiving [alms]. What should these people have done? Left themselves to die? The Torah does not obligate that.

[To explain:] One of the sources on which these people depend is the narrative [in the Talmud][53] based on the verse,[54] "She [the Torah] is like a merchant ship, bringing sustenance from afar." This narrative was told about a person whose health was impaired and who was unable to work. But if a person is able to work, he should not employ the Torah for such a purpose.

Rav Yosef would haul wooden beams and declared, "Great is work, for it warms those who perform it."[55] His intent was that through strenuous physical labor one surely warms one's body. He was satisfied with this and rejoiced in it. And he had peace of mind and was happy with his portion, expressing the quality of self-content.

I have heard those fools [who take payment for Torah study] try to support their position with the statement:[56] "One who wishes to derive benefit may derive benefit as Elisha did, and one who does not desire to derive benefit should not, [following the example of] Samuel of Ramah."

There is, however, no comparison between these matters at all. I am certain that this is merely [an attempt at] deception on the part of a person who cites such a proof. For Elisha did not receive money from people. Surely he did not impose levies on others, heaven forbid. [To what were our Sages referring? That] he would accept hospitality. When a person would host him when he was traveling, he would spend the night at his home and eat [the food he was served] that night and/or the following day, and continue with his affairs. Samuel, by contrast, would accept neither lodging nor food from anyone.

It is with regard to such a situation that our Sages said that a Torah scholar may choose whichever example he desires to emulate. Should he not desire to accept hospitality at all, he has the privilege. Conversely, he is also entitled to choose to accept the hospitality a person might offer him in his time of need when he is on a journey. [It is necessary to clarify that such license is granted] for we have been warned against accepting the hospitality of others when it is unnecessary, as our Sages state:[57] "Whenever a Torah scholar eats in many places, it will destroy his home and widow his wife...." And they said,[58] "It is forbidden for a Torah scholar to partake of any feast except a feast associated with a mitzvah."

53. *Bava Metzia* 84b relates that Rabbi Eliezer ben Rabbi Shimeon suffered from severe ailments. His family spent huge amounts on feeding and clothing him, and were distraught because of the expense. At that time a fleet of merchant ships was caught in a storm. Their captain prayed to be saved in Rabbi Eliezer's merit. When his prayers were answered, he brought Rabbi Eliezer many gifts.
54. Proverbs 31:14.
55. See *Gittin* 67b, which quotes such a statement. That text, however, describes Rav Yosef as working in a mill, and mentions that Rav Sheshet would haul beams.
56. *Berachot* 10b.
57. *Pesachim* 49a. The passage continues, citing other misfortunes caused by such conduct. The full text of this passage is quoted in the standard published texts of the Commentary on the Mishnah.
58. *Op. cit.*.

Why should I elaborate further on this matter? [It is sufficient to] cite an instance recorded and explained in the Talmud,[59] and those who wish to differ or deny may do as they desire.

The incident was like this: A man owned a vineyard that was plagued by thieves. Every day, he would inspect it and see that the number of grapes was being reduced, and he was sure that one of the thieves had set his eye on his [holding].

He was distressed throughout the entire grape season until he made his harvest and spread out the grapes to dry and become raisins. When he began to gather the raisins, some fell, as is common. It is permitted for anyone to eat these raisins, because they are considered ownerless, since their owner has abandoned them because of their insignificant number.

By chance, one day Rabbi Tarfon passed by that vineyard and sat down to eat those raisins that had fallen. The owner of the vineyard came, and thinking that this was the person who had stolen from him throughout the year, hurried, pounced on him, and overcame him. He placed him in a sack and was running to throw him in the river to drown.

Now [the owner] had heard of Rabbi Tarfon, but did not recognize him. When Rabbi Tarfon realized [what was happening, he thought] he was doomed, and cried out: "Woe unto you Tarfon, for this man is going to kill you." When the owner heard [the Sage's name], he let him go and fled, recognizing that he had committed a grievous sin.

For the remainder of his life, Rabbi Tarfon was distressed and pained because of [his conduct on] that day, that he saved his life by employing the honor of the Torah. For he was a wealthy man, and he could have offered money in lieu of his life, instead of informing [his captor] that he was [Rabbi] Tarfon. In this way, he could have used his money to save himself, and not the Torah.

Our Sages relate that throughout his entire life, this righteous man was distressed because of this and would grieve: "Woe is me, that I made use of the crown of the Torah. For whoever makes use of the crown of the Torah will be removed from this world." The Sages said that since Rabbi Tarfon was wealthy, he should have appeased [his captor] with money.

[A similar point is obvious from the following narrative:][60] Similarly, once in a year of famine, our holy teacher (Rabbi Yehudah HaNasi) opened his storehouses of grain and declared: Whoever desires to receive his livelihood let him come, provided he is a Torah scholar.

Rabbi Yonatan ben Amram stood before him, [and Rabbi Yehudah] did not recognize him. "Grant me sustenance," Rabbi Yonatan asked.

"What are you studying?" asked Rabbi Yehudah in response.

[Rabbi Yonatan] replied, "Grant me sustenance like a dog or a raven." [His intent being,] as if he had not studied - i.e., just as God grants sustenance to an impure animal and an impure fowl, you should grant me sustenance, for an unlearned person is no worse than they.

59. *Nedarim* 62a.
60. *Bava Batra* 8a. Our translation follows the authoritative manuscripts and editions of the Commentary on the Mishnah. The standard printed text follows our text of the Talmud and thus differs slightly.

8. Rabbi Yosse said: Whoever honors the Torah is himself given honor by men, and whoever dishonors the Torah is himself dishonored by men.

9. Rabbi Yishmael his son said: [A judge] who refrains from handing down legal judgments [but instead seeks compromise between the litigants] removes from himself enmity, theft and [the responsibility for] an unnecessary oath; but one who aggrandizes himself by [eagerly] issuing legal decisions is a fool, wicked and arrogant.

10. He used to say: Do not judge alone, for none may judge alone except One. And do not say [to your fellow judges], "Accept my view," for they [the majority] have that prerogative, but not you.

Rabbi Yehudah gave him. Afterwards, he regretted that [Rabbi Yonatan] had lured him on with his words. "Woe is me," he said; "an unlearned person has derived benefit from my possessions."

His listeners told him: "Perhaps it was Yonatan ben Amram, your student, who did not desire to benefit from the honor of the Torah. [He will avoid this] in whatever way possible, even through subterfuge." They checked and discovered that this was indeed so. These two narratives will surely silence anyone who desires to argue about this matter.

The opportunity that has been given to Torah scholars is to give money to a person to invest for them, if he desires to do so, with the profit going to the scholars.[61] A person who does this will receive reward for his conduct.[62] This is the meaning of [our Sages' phrase for] "one who gives merchandise to a scholar."[63]

Similarly, it is permitted to enable them to sell their merchandise before all the other merchandise offered for sale, and give them the first opportunity to make purchases. It has been transmitted by the Oral tradition that God granted them these two privileges just as He granted the priestly gifts[64] to the priests and the tithes to the Levites. [And there is a rationale for this:] there are times when businessmen will grant these two privileges to a colleague as an expression of respect, even though he is not wise. [And so, these privileges are granted to a Torah scholar, for] it is fitting that a Torah scholar be given the same degree of respect given to an unlearned person.

Similarly, the Torah freed all students of the Torah from the levies of the government

---

61. The latter phrase is found in the standard published texts, but lacking in some of the authoritative editions and manuscripts.
62. See *Berachot* 34b.
63. *Pesachim* 53b.
64. I.e., *terumah, challah* and the like.

ח רַבִּי יוֹסֵי אוֹמֵר: כָּל הַמְכַבֵּד אֶת הַתּוֹרָה, גּוּפוֹ מְכֻבָּד עַל הַבְּרִיּוֹת; וְכָל הַמְחַלֵּל אֶת הַתּוֹרָה, גּוּפוֹ מְחֻלָּל עַל הַבְּרִיּוֹת.

ט רַבִּי יִשְׁמָעֵאל בְּנוֹ אוֹמֵר: הַחוֹשֵׂךְ עַצְמוֹ מִן הַדִּין, פּוֹרֵק מִמֶּנּוּ אֵיבָה וְגָזֵל וְגֵס שְׁבוּעַ שָׁוְא; וְהַגַּס לִבּוֹ בְּהוֹרָאָה — שׁוֹטֶה, רָשָׁע וְגַס רוּחַ.

י הוּא הָיָה אוֹמֵר: אַל תְּהִי דָן יְחִידִי, שֶׁאֵין דָּן יְחִידִי אֶלָּא אֶחָד. וְאַל תֹּאמַר: קַבֵּל דַּעְתִּי, שֶׁהֵן רַשָּׁאִין וְלֹא אָתָּה.

e.g., assessments, property taxes and head taxes. The community should bear this financial responsibility for them. Similarly, they need not participate in the building of the city's walls and the like.

Even if a student of Torah is a very wealthy man, he is freed of these duties. This was the decision that the master, Rav Yosef HaLevi o.b.m.[65] rendered with regard to a man in Spain who owned gardens and orchards worth thousands of *dinarim*. [Rav Yosef] freed him from a levy because he was a Torah scholar, although his levy was paid by all of Israel, [even] the poor. This is a Torah law, just as freeing the priests from the obligation of a half-*shekel* is a Torah law, as explained in its place.[66] The same applies in all similar situations.

Honors the Torah - I.e., honors its commandments by showing an eagerness to fulfill them, honors its scholars who support it, and [honors] the texts composed about it.
Dishonors the Torah - This also concerns the same three matters.

Aggrandizes himself by [eagerly] issuing legal decisions - I.e., he has no hesitation about issuing decisions, and approaches a decision without the fear [of God] and without taking a composed, earnest approach.

[Do not judge alone -] As explained in [the tractate] *Sanhedrin*,[67] the Torah allows a person who is qualified as an expert for the public to act as a judge alone. Although this is the Torah law, as a point of ethics and not of law, [our *mishnah*] warns against this.

[And do not say -] [Our *mishnah* also teaches that if] a person's colleagues disagree based on a different point of logic, he should not obligate them to accept his thinking. The choice is theirs to accept your words; you do not have the choice to compel them to do so.

---

65. Rav Yosef is also known as the *Ri Migash* and was one of the Rambam's teachers.
66. See the Commentary on the Mishnah (*Shekalim* 1:4). Note also the *Mishneh Torah, Hilchot Shekalim* 1:7,10, where the Rambam reverses his ruling and obligates the priests to pay the half-*shekel* as other Jews.
67. *Sanhedrin* 1:1.

11. Rabbi Yonatan said: Whoever fulfills the Torah in poverty will ultimately fulfill it in wealth; but whoever neglects the Torah in wealth will ultimately neglect it in poverty.

12. Rabbi Meir said: Minimize your business activities and occupy yourself with the Torah. Be of humble spirit before every person.

If you should neglect the [study of] Torah, you will have many causes for neglecting [it] confronting you, but if you toil much in the Torah, there is ample reward to be given you.

13. Rabbi Eliezer ben Ya'akov said: He who fulfills one mitzvah acquires for himself one advocate, and he who commits one transgression acquires against himself one accuser. Repentance and good deeds are as a shield against [Divine] retribution.

14. Rabbi Yochanan HaSandlar said: Every assembly [whose purpose is] for the sake of Heaven will be perpetuated, but that which is not for the sake of Heaven will not be perpetuated.

15. Rabbi Eleazar ben Shamua said: Let the honor of your student be as dear to you as your own, the honor of your colleague as the reverence for your teacher, and the reverence for your teacher as the fear of Heaven.

16. Rabbi Yehudah said: Be cautious in study, for an unwitting error in [observance due to insufficient] study is accounted as intentional transgression.

17. Rabbi Shimon said: There are three crowns - the crown of Torah,

[**Whoever fulfills the Torah in poverty -**] [Our *mishnah* teaches that when] a person studies the Torah in a state of poverty and difficulty, compelling himself to study despite [these hardships], he will ultimately study the Torah amid prosperity, without having any factors that disturb him from his study.

Conversely, a person who neglects his study because of his wealth, because he indulges in eating, drinking and pleasure, will ultimately become poverty stricken. The reason for his neglect will be his preoccupation in seeking bread for his meals.

[**Minimize your business activities -**] [The *mishnah*] teaches one to reduce his commercial activities and devote his time to the Torah.

[**Be of humble spirit before every person. -**] I.e., do not be humble only before people

יא רַבִּי יוֹנָתָן אוֹמֵר: כָּל הַמְקַיֵּם אֶת הַתּוֹרָה מֵעֹנִי, סוֹפוֹ לְקַיְּמָהּ מֵעֹשֶׁר; וְכָל הַמְבַטֵּל אֶת הַתּוֹרָה מֵעֹשֶׁר, סוֹפוֹ לְבַטְּלָהּ מֵעֹנִי.

יב רַבִּי מֵאִיר אוֹמֵר: הֱוֵי מְמַעֵט בָּעֵסֶק, וַעֲסֹק בַּתּוֹרָה. וֶהֱוֵי שְׁפַל רוּחַ בִּפְנֵי כָל אָדָם. וְאִם בָּטַלְתָּ מִן הַתּוֹרָה, יֶשׁ לְךָ בְטֵלִים הַרְבֵּה כְּנֶגְדֶּךָ; וְאִם עָמַלְתָּ בַּתּוֹרָה, יֶשׁ שָׂכָר הַרְבֵּה לִתֶּן לָךְ.

יג רַבִּי אֱלִיעֶזֶר בֶּן יַעֲקֹב אוֹמֵר: הָעוֹשֶׂה מִצְוָה אַחַת, קוֹנֶה לוֹ פְּרַקְלִיט אֶחָד; וְהָעוֹבֵר עֲבֵרָה אַחַת, קוֹנֶה לוֹ קַטֵּגוֹר אֶחָד. תְּשׁוּבָה וּמַעֲשִׂים טוֹבִים כִּתְרִיס בִּפְנֵי הַפֻּרְעָנוּת.

יד רַבִּי יוֹחָנָן הַסַּנְדְּלָר אוֹמֵר: כָּל כְּנֵסִיָּה שֶׁהִיא לְשֵׁם שָׁמַיִם, סוֹפָהּ לְהִתְקַיֵּם; וְשֶׁאֵינָהּ לְשֵׁם שָׁמַיִם, אֵין סוֹפָהּ לְהִתְקַיֵּם.

טו רַבִּי אֶלְעָזָר בֶּן שַׁמּוּעַ אוֹמֵר: יְהִי כְבוֹד תַּלְמִידְךָ חָבִיב עָלֶיךָ כְּשֶׁלָּךְ, וּכְבוֹד חֲבֵרְךָ כְּמוֹרָא רַבָּךְ, וּמוֹרָא רַבָּךְ כְּמוֹרָא שָׁמַיִם.

טז רַבִּי יְהוּדָה אוֹמֵר: הֱוֵי זָהִיר בְּתַלְמוּד, שֶׁשִּׁגְגַת תַּלְמוּד עוֹלָה זָדוֹן.

יז רַבִּי שִׁמְעוֹן אוֹמֵר: שְׁלֹשָׁה כְתָרִים הֵם: כֶּתֶר תּוֹרָה, וְכֶתֶר כְּהֻנָּה, וְכֶתֶר מַלְכוּת; וְכֶתֶר שֵׁם טוֹב עוֹלֶה עַל גַּבֵּיהֶן.

of stature, but before all men. Whenever sitting with a person, regardless of who he is, the way you talk and the way you relate should [convey that] his level is greater than yours. This is in order to eschew pride, as explained above.[68]

Many causes for neglecting [it] confronting you - I.e., there are many matters that take up time and require people to involve themselves with them. If you do not devote yourself to Torah study, you will be inconvenienced by one of these matters.

Advocate - i.e., one speaks positively on behalf of a person before the king and makes petitions on his behalf.

Accuser - the opposite of the former; one who maligns a person to the king and endeavors to destroy him.

[Repentance and good deeds... -]I.e., repentance after having committed evil deeds, or doing good deeds at the outset. Either of these two [courses of action] will prevent [Divine] retribution and harm from reaching a person.

[There are three crowns... -] These three great attributes: priesthood, kingship and

68. See the commentary on *Mishnah* 4.

the crown of priesthood and the crown of kingship; but the crown o
a good name surpasses them all.

18. Rabbi Nehorai said: Exile yourself to a place of Torah - and do
not assume that it will come after you - for it is your colleagues who
will cause it to be clearly established in your grasp. Do not rely or
your own understanding.[71]

19. Rabbi Yannai said: We are unable to understand either the well-
being of the wicked or the tribulations of the righteous.

20. Rabbi Matya ben Cheresh said: Be the first to extend greetings to
anyone you meet; and rather be a tail to lions than a head to foxes.

21. Rabbi Ya'akov said: This world is like an anteroom before the
World to Come; prepare yourself in the anteroom so that you may
enter the palace.

22. He used to say: One hour of repentance and good deeds is better
than all the life of the World to Come. And one hour of bliss in the
World to Come is better than all the life of this world.

Torah, were granted to the nation at the very beginning of [God's] commands to it.
The priesthood was acquired by Aharon. The kingship was acquired by David. The
crown of the Torah, by contrast, is left free for whoever desires to crown himself with
it.

Our Sages said:[69] Do not think the crown [of the Torah] is less than the other two.
It is greater than them and they are dependent on it, as it is written:[70] "By me, kings
reign... By me, princes rule."

The crown of a good name - is acquired through the Torah, i.e., through studying
it and observing its mitzvot. For this will bring a person a truly good name.

[Exile yourself to a place of Torah -] [The *mishnah*] teaches that one should seek
a place of study, because others will clarify the subject matter for you, allowing
it to be retained. Do not rely on your own understanding and say, "I do not
need partners in study or students to motivate me."

[Rather be a tail...-] [The *mishnah*] teaches that it is more fitting and better for
a person to be a student of a person who is wiser than he, than a teacher of

69. *Yoma* 72b.
70. Proverbs 8:15-16.
71. Proverbs 3:5.

יח רַבִּי נְהוֹרַאי אוֹמֵר: הֱוֵי גוֹלֶה לִמְקוֹם תּוֹרָה, וְאַל תֹּאמַר שֶׁהִיא תָבוֹא אַחֲרֶיךָ שֶׁחֲבֵרֶיךָ יְקַיְּמוּהָ בְיָדֶךָ. וְאֶל בִּינָתְךָ אַל תִּשָּׁעֵן.

יט רַבִּי יַנַּאי אוֹמֵר: אֵין בְּיָדֵינוּ, לֹא מִשַּׁלְוַת הָרְשָׁעִים, וְאַף לֹא מִיִּסּוּרֵי הַצַּדִּיקִים.

כ רַבִּי מַתְיָא בֶן חָרָשׁ אוֹמֵר: הֱוֵי מַקְדִּים בִּשְׁלוֹם כָּל אָדָם; וֶהֱוֵי זָנָב לָאֲרָיוֹת, וְאַל תְּהִי רֹאשׁ לַשּׁוּעָלִים.

כא רַבִּי יַעֲקֹב אוֹמֵר: הָעוֹלָם הַזֶּה דוֹמֶה לִפְרוֹזְדוֹר בִּפְנֵי הָעוֹלָם הַבָּא; הַתְקֵן עַצְמְךָ בַּפְּרוֹזְדוֹר, כְּדֵי שֶׁתִּכָּנֵס לַטְּרַקְלִין.

כב הוּא הָיָה אוֹמֵר: יָפָה שָׁעָה אַחַת בִּתְשׁוּבָה וּמַעֲשִׂים טוֹבִים בָּעוֹלָם הַזֶּה מִכָּל חַיֵּי הָעוֹלָם הַבָּא, וְיָפָה שָׁעָה אַחַת שֶׁל קֹרַת רוּחַ בָּעוֹלָם הַבָּא מִכָּל חַיֵּי הָעוֹלָם הַזֶּה.

one on a lower level. For in the first instance, he will increase [his wisdom], and in the second instance, he will decrease [it].

As we explained in [the tractate] *Sanhedrin,*[72] they followed the principle of "advance further in holy matters"[73] and would make the head of a [lesser court] of 23 judges, the least member of the [High Court] of 71. [By doing so,] they increased [the new appointee's] level.

Palace - This is the meaning of the Hebrew טרקלין.

Anteroom - or gatehouse. This is the meaning of the Hebrew פרוזדור. The analogy for this is obvious and the intent is well known. It is in this world that we acquire the virtues that enable one to attain the life of the World to Come. This [world] is merely a path and a passageway to there.

[One hour... is better... -] We have already explained in the tenth chapter of *Sanhedrin* that after death there is no [possibility of reaching] perfection or increasing [one's virtues]. To this, Solomon alluded by saying,[74] "There is no deed, nor knowledge, nor accounting, nor wisdom in the grave to which you are going." Instead, the person remains on the same spiritual level at which he enters.

Therefore, it is fitting to endeavor [to use] the short and limited time [we are granted in this world], and not to apply it for anything except study. For its loss is awesome, and there is no substitute for it, nor possibility of compensation. Since the Sages knew this, they sought to use their time only for study and for the increase

72. The Rambam appears to be referring to *Sanhedrin* 4:4, which states how a person was appointed to the *Sanhedrin*. In his commentary there, however, no mention is made of this. The Rambam's statements here are based on *Sanhedrin* 37a.
73. *Berachot* 28a *et al.*
74. Ecclesiastes 9:10. Note similar comments by the Rambam in *Hilchot Teshuvah* 9:1.

23. Rabbi Shimon ben Eleazar said: Do not placate your fellow in the moment of his anger; do not comfort him while his dead lies before him. Do not question him [about the details] of his vow at the moment he makes it; and do not seek to see him at the time of his degradation.

24. Samuel the humble said: When your enemy falls do not rejoice, and when he stumbles let your heart not be glad [lest God see, and regard it with displeasure, and divert His wrath from him].[78] [The verse does not state "His fierce wrath," but "His wrath." This indicates that (the person's) sins are forgiven.][79]

25. Elisha ben Avuyah said: He who studies Torah as a child, to what can he be compared? To ink written on fresh paper; and he who studies Torah as an old man, to what can he be compared? To ink written on paper that has been erased.

26. Rabbi Yosse bar Yehudah of Kefar HaBavli said: He who learns from the young, to what can he be compared? To one who eats unripe grapes or drinks wine from the vat; while he who learns from the old, to what can he be compared? To one who eats ripe grapes or drinks aged wine.

of knowledge. Thus, in truth they used their time to the fullest, without sacrificing anything but the slightest amount for bodily concerns, [involving themselves only with regard] to necessities that they could not do without.

Others wasted all their time with bodily concerns, and they left [the world] as they entered, as it is written:[75] "In all matters, as he comes, so he goes." [And in this manner,] they incur an eternal loss.

All the masses reverse the truth regarding this matter, and say that the first group lost [their chance of success in] this world, and they say that the second group, profited [from] this world. The very opposite is true. They are calling the light darkness, and the darkness light.[76] Woe to those who are truly forfeiting [their opportunity].

This concept is the foundation on which King Solomon based Ecclesiastes, in which he praises those who make good use of [their time in] this world, and reproaches those who waste it, saying explicitly[77] that after death there is no opportunity to achieve what you forfeited in this plane. All this is true. If you contemplate that book according to this perspective, the truth will become clear to you.

75. Ecclesiastes 5:15.
76. Cf. Isaiah 5:20.

כג רַבִּי שִׁמְעוֹן בֶּן אֶלְעָזָר אוֹמֵר: אַל תְּרַצֶּה אֶת חֲבֵרָךְ בִּשְׁעַת כַּעֲסוֹ, וְאַל תְּנַחֲמֵהוּ בְּשָׁעָה שֶׁמֵּתוֹ מוּטָל לְפָנָיו, וְאַל תִּשְׁאַל לוֹ בִּשְׁעַת נִדְרוֹ, וְאַל תִּשְׁתַּדֵּל לִרְאוֹתוֹ בִּשְׁעַת קַלְקָלָתוֹ.

כד שְׁמוּאֵל הַקָּטָן אוֹמֵר: בִּנְפֹל אוֹיִבְךָ אַל תִּשְׂמָח וּבִכָּשְׁלוֹ אַל יָגֵל לִבֶּךָ, (פֶּן יִרְאֶה ה' וְרַע בְּעֵינָיו וְהֵשִׁיב מֵעָלָיו אַפּוֹ).

כה אֱלִישָׁע בֶּן אֲבוּיָה אוֹמֵר: הַלּוֹמֵד יֶלֶד לְמָה הוּא דּוֹמֶה? לִדְיוֹ כְתוּבָה עַל נִיָר חָדָשׁ; וְהַלּוֹמֵד זָקֵן לְמָה הוּא דּוֹמֶה? לִדְיוֹ כְתוּבָה עַל נִיָר מָחוּק.

כו רַבִּי יוֹסֵי בַר יְהוּדָה אִישׁ כְּפַר הַבַּבְלִי אוֹמֵר: הַלּוֹמֵד מִן הַקְּטַנִּים לְמָה הוּא דּוֹמֶה? לְאוֹכֵל עֲנָבִים קֵהוֹת וְשׁוֹתֶה יַיִן מִגִּתּוֹ; וְהַלּוֹמֵד מִן הַזְּקֵנִים לְמָה הוּא דּוֹמֶה? לְאוֹכֵל עֲנָבִים בְּשׁוּלוֹת וְשׁוֹתֶה יַיִן יָשָׁן.

[Do not placate your fellow... -] These [statements] are obvious. They are ethical [truths] that will abet a friendship. For a person should not make statements except in a situation where they will have an effect.

[When your enemy falls do not rejoice -] Although this instruction was given by King Solomon, [Samuel the humble] would teach this quality [of forbearance] and would warn others [against] this sin.[80]

[To ink written on fresh paper -] [The *mishnah*] is teaching that subject matter studied at a young age is retained and is not forgotten easily. [Conversely,] when one studies at a more advanced age, the opposite is true. This is obvious and well known.

[He who learns from the young -] Rabbi Yosse teaches that the knowledge of the young is replete with doubt and questions that have not been clarified and difficulties that must be elucidated. For they have not reviewed their knowledge and resolved their doubts.

---

77. In the verse (9:10) cited above.
78. Proverbs 24:17-18. The second verse is placed in brackets because it is not included in many texts of the Mishnah.
79. The bracketed comment is included in the *mishnah* in the authoritative manuscripts and editions of the Rambam's Commentary on the Mishnah. It thus reflects Samuel the humble's interpretation of the verse he cited. In the standard published text of the Rambam's Commentary on the Mishnah, this statement is included in the Rambam's commentary.
80. I.e., the Rambam is explaining why this teaching is included in *Pirkei Avot* although it is an explicit verse.

Rabbi[81] said: Do not look at the container, but at its contents; there may be a new container filled with aged wine, or an old container in which there is not even new [wine].

27. Rabbi Eleazar HaKappar said: Envy, desire and honor drive a man from the world.

28. He used to say: Those who are born are destined to die; those who are dead are destined to live again; and those who live [again] are destined to be judged. Know, make known and become aware that He is God, He is the Fashioner, He is the Creator, He is the Discerner, He is the Judge, He is the Witness, He is the Plaintiff, He will hereafter sit in judgment.

Blessed is He, before whom there is no iniquity, nor forgetting, nor partiality, nor bribe-taking; and know that all is according to the reckoning. And let not your evil inclination assure you that the grave will be a place of refuge for you, for against your will you were created, against your will you were born; against your will you

Rabbi stated: Do not judge the quality of the wine from its container. At times a new container will contain aged wine, and at times an old container will be empty without anything in it. Similarly, there are young men whose questioning and knowledge has been refined, and who are not confused. They can be compared to aged wine from which the dregs and dirt have already been separated. Conversely, there are older men who have no knowledge at all, and how much more so does this apply when they have knowledge, but it is confused and muddled.

[**Rabbi Eleazar HaKappar said:... -**] Envy, desire and the love of honor drive a person from the world while lacking [in perfection]. For these attributes - indeed even one of them - cause a person to forfeit his faith and prevent him from attaining intellectual and ethical virtue.

Know, make known and become aware - [The *mishnah* is addressing three categories of people]: those who will be born, those who are being born at present and who will die, and those who after death will live again, [and commanding them to know]. Included in this knowledge is the awareness that...
He is the Fashioner, He is the Creator....
He is the Judge... He will hereafter sit in judgment. - This statement implies that at present, He judges everyone with regard to life and death and other matters of the

81. I.e., Rabbi Yehudah HaNasi. This is the Rambam's version of the text. Most other authorities ascribe this teaching to Rabbi Meir.

רַבִּי אוֹמֵר: אַל תִּסְתַּכֵּל בַּקַּנְקַן, אֶלָּא בְּמַה שֶּׁיֶּשׁ בּוֹ; יֵשׁ קַנְקַן חָדָשׁ מָלֵא יָשָׁן, וְיָשָׁן שֶׁאֲפִלּוּ חָדָשׁ אֵין בּוֹ.

כז רַבִּי אֶלְעָזָר הַקַּפָּר אוֹמֵר: הַקִּנְאָה וְהַתַּאֲוָה וְהַכָּבוֹד מוֹצִיאִין אֶת הָאָדָם מִן הָעוֹלָם.

כח הוּא הָיָה אוֹמֵר: הַיִּלּוֹדִים לָמוּת, וְהַמֵּתִים לְהֵחָיוֹת, וְהַחַיִּים לִדּוֹן. לֵידַע לְהוֹדִיעַ וּלְהִוָּדַע, שֶׁהוּא אֵל, הוּא הַיּוֹצֵר, הוּא הַבּוֹרֵא, הוּא הַמֵּבִין, הוּא הַדַּיָּן, הוּא עֵד, הוּא בַּעַל דִּין, וְהוּא עָתִיד לָדוּן. בָּרוּךְ הוּא, שֶׁאֵין לְפָנָיו לֹא עַוְלָה, וְלֹא שִׁכְחָה, וְלֹא מַשּׂוֹא פָנִים, וְלֹא מִקַּח שֹׁחַד, שֶׁהַכֹּל שֶׁלּוֹ. וְדַע, שֶׁהַכֹּל לְפִי הַחֶשְׁבּוֹן.

וְאַל יַבְטִיחֲךָ יִצְרְךָ שֶׁהַשְּׁאוֹל בֵּית מָנוֹס לָךְ; שֶׁעַל כָּרְחֲךָ אַתָּה נוֹצָר, וְעַל כָּרְחֲךָ

world. And He will also judge them in the future when they will be resurrected with regard to reward and punishment.

Nor bribe-taking - As the Torah states,[82] "He will not show favor or accept a bribe." [Obviously,] the intent is not that He will not take money to sway His judgment. For it is not logical even to negate such a possibility with regard to Him, for this could not be conceived with our imagination. How could a bribe be given Him, and what would be given Him as a bribe?

Instead, the concept is, as explained above,[83] that He will not accept a bribe of good deeds. If a person were to perform one thousand good deeds and one bad deed, God will not overlook the one sin he performed because of all the good he performed. He will not consider that the person performed one thousand less one good deeds, or a lesser number of good deeds. Instead, He will hold him accountable for the bad deed and reward him for the good deeds.

This is the meaning of "He will not accept a bribe"; it parallels "He will not show favor." Instead, He exacts retribution from those on an advanced level, even for minor matters - e.g., He exacted retribution from Moses because of the sin of anger, as we explained in the [fourth] introductory chapter. And He granted Esau a reward for honoring his father and mother,[84] and Nebuchadnezzar [a reward for] honoring God's name, as explained in the Talmud in the [tractate] *Sanhedrin*.[85] This is the concept that He does not show favor.

Contemplate the statement...

Against your will you were created - [The *mishnah*] mentions natural circumstances with regard to which man is not granted free choice. With regard to these matters it is said,[86] "Everything is in the hands of Heaven."

82. Deuteronomy 10:17.
83. In the fourth introductory chapter.
84. See *Bereishit Rabbah*, Chapter 68.
85. *Sanhedrin* 96a.
86. *Berachot* 33b *et al.*

live; against your will you die, and against your will you are destined
to give an account before the supreme King of kings, the Holy One,
blessed be He.

CHAPTER FIVE

1. The world was created by means of ten [Divine] utterances. What
does this teach us - for it could indeed have been created by one
utterance? But [it was done so] to bring retribution upon the wicked who
destroy the world that was created by ten utterances, and to bestow
ample reward upon the righteous who sustain the world that was
created by ten utterances.

2. There were ten generations from Adam to Noah - to indicate how
great is His patience; for all those generations repeatedly angered Him,
until He brought upon them the waters of the flood.

There were ten generations from Noah to Abraham to indicate how
great is His patience, for all those generations repeatedly angered Him,
until Abraham our Patriarch came and received the reward of them all.

3. Our Patriarch Abraham was tested with ten trials, and he withstood
them all - to show how great was our Patriarch Abraham's love [for
God].

[The *mishnah*] does not say "you are compelled to sin," "to transgress," "to walk,"
"to stand" or the like. For all these matters are given over to man's volition; he is
not compelled at all, as explained in the eighth [introductory] chapter.[87]

Chapter 5

[The world was created by means of ten... -] If you contemplate the narrative
of creation, counting the times it says ויאמר ("And He said"), you will find nine,
and *Bereishit* is considered to be the tenth [utterance].[1] For although the latter verse
does not explicitly say ויאמר, the context implies that a statement was made. It is
as if the Torah said, "And God said: Let there be heaven and earth," for they
were not created without an utterance.

He could have included the entire creation in a single utterance and said: "Let there
be heaven and earth, let the waters split,... let the earth give forth,..." Instead, the
Torah specifies an individual utterance for every facet [of creation], to indicate the
great importance of this entity, and the sequence. Thus, when one mars, one creates a

87. The standard printed texts of the Commentary on the Mishnah state "the fifth [introductory]
chapter]," but that is an error.

אַתָּה נוֹלָד, וְעַל כָּרְחֲךָ אַתָּה חַי, וְעַל כָּרְחֲךָ אַתָּה מֵת, וְעַל כָּרְחֲךָ אַתָּה עָתִיד לִתֵּן דִּין וְחֶשְׁבּוֹן לִפְנֵי מֶלֶךְ מַלְכֵי הַמְּלָכִים הַקָּדוֹשׁ בָּרוּךְ הוּא.

פֶּרֶק חֲמִישִׁי

א בַּעֲשָׂרָה מַאֲמָרוֹת נִבְרָא הָעוֹלָם. וּמַה תַּלְמוּד לוֹמַר, וַהֲלֹא בְמַאֲמָר אֶחָד יָכוֹל לְהִבָּרְאוֹת? אֶלָּא לְהִפָּרַע מִן הָרְשָׁעִים, שֶׁמְּאַבְּדִין אֶת הָעוֹלָם שֶׁנִּבְרָא בַּעֲשָׂרָה מַאֲמָרוֹת, וְלִתֵּן שָׂכָר טוֹב לַצַּדִּיקִים, שֶׁמְּקַיְּמִין אֶת הָעוֹלָם שֶׁנִּבְרָא בַּעֲשָׂרָה מַאֲמָרוֹת.

ב עֲשָׂרָה דוֹרוֹת מֵאָדָם וְעַד נֹחַ, לְהוֹדִיעַ כַּמָּה אֶרֶךְ אַפַּיִם לְפָנָיו, שֶׁכָּל הַדּוֹרוֹת הָיוּ מַכְעִיסִין וּבָאִין עַד שֶׁהֵבִיא עֲלֵיהֶם אֶת מֵי הַמַּבּוּל.

עֲשָׂרָה דוֹרוֹת מִנֹּחַ וְעַד אַבְרָהָם, לְהוֹדִיעַ כַּמָּה אֶרֶךְ אַפַּיִם לְפָנָיו, שֶׁכָּל הַדּוֹרוֹת הָיוּ מַכְעִיסִין וּבָאִין, עַד שֶׁבָּא אַבְרָהָם אָבִינוּ וְקִבֵּל שָׂכָר כֻּלָּם.

ג עֲשָׂרָה נִסְיוֹנוֹת נִתְנַסָּה אַבְרָהָם אָבִינוּ וְעָמַד בְּכֻלָּם, לְהוֹדִיעַ כַּמָּה חִבָּתוֹ שֶׁל אַבְרָהָם אָבִינוּ עָלָיו הַשָּׁלוֹם.

great blemish, and conversely, when one makes a correction, one makes a correction of great importance.

By saying "mar," the intent is that one mars one's soul, preventing it from attaining perfection. Similarly, the intent of "correction" is that one corrects one's soul. For it is in one's power to correct it or to mar it. It is as if [each individual's soul] were the ultimate purpose of the entire creation, which was brought into being by ten utterances, as we explained in the introduction to this text.[2]

[**There were ten generations from Adam to Noah -**] These generations are explicitly mentioned in the Torah,[3] "so and so bore so and so" in order. [The *mishnah*] mentions these and those mentioned in the following set,[4] because it mentioned the ten utterances of creation. [And so by association, it also mentions these two sets of ten generations,] because there is an ethical message for man [which can be derived from them] that will encourage him to correct his soul, [refining] his ethical and intellectual qualities. [As mentioned, the encouragement of such refinement] is the purpose of this tractate.

[**Ten trials -**] The ten trials with which our Patriarch Abraham was tested are

1. *Rosh HaShanah* 32a. (See also *Bereishit Rabbah* 17:1.)
2. The intent is the Introduction to the Commentary on the Mishnah. There, the Rambam writes that the ultimate purpose of all existence is for there to be people who are perfect in deed and in wisdom.
3. Genesis, Chapter 5.
4. See Genesis, Chapter 10.

Ten miracles were performed for our ancestors in Egypt and ten a'
the Sea. The Holy One, blessed be He, brought ten plagues upon the
Egyptians in Egypt and ten at the sea.

Our ancestors subjected the Holy One, blessed be He, to ten trials
in the desert, as it is stated:[5] "They have tested Me ten times, and they
have not heeded My voice."

explicitly mentioned in the Torah.[6] The first is the departure into exile, [following]
God's command,[7] "Go out from your land and your birthplace." The second is
the famine that came upon the land of Canaan when he dwelled there, despite the
fact that he had been promised:[8] "I will make you [a great nation], I will bless you,
and make you great." This was a great challenge and [about this,] it is written,[9]
"there was a famine in the land."

The third trial was the wrong wrought to him by the Egyptians who took Sarah
for Pharaoh.[10] The fourth trial was his conflict with the four kings.[11] The fifth trial
was his marriage to Hagar after despairing of having progeny through Sarah.[12] The
sixth trial was performing the circumcision that he was commanded at an advanced
age.[13]

The seventh trial was the wrong done him by the King of Gerar in taking Sarah.[14] The
eighth trial was banishing Hagar after she bore him a son. The ninth trial was banishing
Ishmael. This is implied by the verse:[15] "Do not be troubled over the youth and
over your handmaiden." Although the Torah has told us that it was very difficult
for him, as it is written,[16] "And Abraham was very troubled [because of his son],"
he accepted God's command and banished them. The tenth trial was the binding
of Isaac.

The ten miracles wrought for our ancestors in Egypt refer to saving them from the
ten plagues. For each of the plagues was directed against the Egyptians alone, without
affecting the Jews. This is without a doubt a miracle. The Torah explicitly states that
every plague affected the Egyptians alone, with the exception of the lice, in which
instance this was not mentioned explicitly. But it is a well known matter that the Jews
were not punished. Instead, there were [lice] among them, but they were not bothered
by them. This was explained by our Sages.[17]

5. Numbers 14:22.
6. There are other challenges that Abraham faced which are recorded in the Oral Tradition
(e.g., being thrown into a fiery furnace and imprisonment, as related in *Pirkei D'Rabbi Eliezer*,
Chapter 26 ff). Nevertheless, the Rambam chooses to mention only those trials that are explicitly
mentioned in the Torah.
7. Genesis 12:1.
8. *Ibid.*:2.
9. *Ibid.*:10.
10. *Ibid.*:15.
11. *Ibid.* 14:12.
12. *Ibid.* 15:2-3.
13. *Ibid.* 17:24.
14. *Ibid.* 20:2.
15. *Ibid.* 21:12.

עֲשָׂרָה נִסִּים נַעֲשׂוּ לַאֲבוֹתֵינוּ בְמִצְרַיִם וַעֲשָׂרָה עַל הַיָּם.

עֲשָׂרָה נִסְיוֹנוֹת נִסּוּ אֲבוֹתֵינוּ אֶת הַמָּקוֹם בַּמִּדְבָּר, שֶׁנֶּאֱמַר: וַיְנַסּוּ אֹתִי זֶה עֶשֶׂר
פְּעָמִים וְלֹא שָׁמְעוּ בְקוֹלִי.

Concerning the other plagues, however, [the Torah] explicitly states that they did not affect the Jews. With regard to the blood, it is written:[18] "And the Egyptians could not drink water from the river," implying that the affliction affected them alone. With regard to the frogs, it is written:[19] "And they shall enter **your** homes, **your** bedrooms, **your** beds, **your** [bodies], **your** nation and **your** servants." With regard to the swarms [of beasts], it is written:[20] "And I will make a sign on that day concerning the Land of Goshen."

With regard to the cattle plague, it is written:[21] "And of the herds of the Israelites, not one died." With regard to the boils, it is written:[22] "For the boils were upon the wizards and upon all the Egyptians." And it is written with regard to the hail:[23] "Only in the Land of Goshen, where the Israelites were, there was no hail." With regard to the locusts, it is written:[24] "They will fill **your** homes, the homes of **your** servants and the homes of all the Egyptians." And it is written with regard to the darkness:[25] "And for the Israelites, there was light in their dwellings."

The ten wonders performed at the Red Sea are all conveyed by the Oral Tradition.[26] The first is the splitting of the sea, as it is written,[27] "And the sea split." The second miracle is that the waters formed a domed roof, it being neither flat nor sloped. The path was a tunnel through the water, with the water being on the right, on the left and on top. This is alluded to in Chabbakuk's statement,[28] "You have pierced with a shaft the head of his settlement."

The third is that the bed of the sea became firm and solid for them, as it is written:[29] "They walked on dry land" - i.e., it did not remain like a river bed, which is

16. *Ibid.*:11. (Note also the commentary of the Rambam on *Mishnah* 17.)
17. The commentaries have not been able to find the source for the Rambam's statements. It must, however, be noted that both the *Meiri* and the *Rashbatz* also attribute this same concept to our Sages.
18. Exodus 7:21.
19. *Ibid.* 7:28-29.
20. *Ibid.* 8:18.
21. *Ibid.* 9:6.
22. *Ibid.* 9:11.
23. *Ibid.* 9:26.
24. *Ibid.* 10:6. The standard printed texts cite the verse (Exodus 10:14): "And there were locusts throughout the land of Egypt."
25. *Ibid.* 10:23.
26. See the *Midrash Tanchumah, Parashat Beshalach; Avot D'Rabbi Natan*, Chapter 23; *Yalkut Shimoni*, Vol. I, Section 233.
27. Exodus 14:21.
28. Chabbakuk 3:14.
29. Exodus 14:29.

4. Ten miracles were wrought for our ancestors in the Temple:
  a) A woman never miscarried because of the aroma of the meat of the holy sacrifices;
  b) the meat of the holy sacrifices never became putrid;
  c) no fly was ever seen in the slaughter-house;
  d) no bodily impurity ever befell the High Priest on Yom Kippur;
  e) the rains never extinguished the fire on the wood-pile on the altar;
  f) the wind never prevailed over the [vertically rising] column of smoke [from fire of the altar, to dissipate it];

muddy and filled with sediment. The fourth miracle is that when the Egyptians crossed it became like sticky mud, as it is written:[30] ". . . the mortar of great waters." The fifth is that it split into [twelve] paths, one for each of the tribes, semi-circles within semi-circles, as in the accompanying drawing. This is alluded to in the verse:[31] "He split the sea into sections."

The sixth is that the water hardened and became rigid like stone. This is alluded to in the verse,[32] "You broke the heads of the sea monsters on the water" - i.e., the water became so hard that [the sea monsters] broke their heads against it. The seventh was that [the sea] did not harden like ice, [solidifying] into a single mass, but was rather separated and segmented, like stones piled one on top of another. With regard to this, it is said:[33] "You fragmented the sea with Your strength."

The eighth was that it solidified like glass or like sapphire - i.e., it was transparent, allowing them to see each other when they passed through. This is implied by the phrase:[34] "The mounds of water were like the density of the skies" - i.e., the collection of the waters was shiny and transparent, as the skies are. The ninth is that fresh water fit for drinking flowed from the sea. And the tenth miracle was that, after

30. Chabbakuk 3:15.
31. Psalms 136:10.
32. *Ibid.* 74:13.
33. *Ibid.*
34. II Samuel 22:12. The standard printed version of the Commentary on the Mishnah cites Psalms 18:12 as the proof-text.
35. Exodus 15:18.

ד עֲשָׂרָה נִסִּים נַעֲשׂוּ לַאֲבוֹתֵינוּ בְּבֵית הַמִּקְדָּשׁ: לֹא הִפִּילָה אִשָּׁה מֵרֵיחַ בְּשַׂר הַקֹּדֶשׁ, וְלֹא הִסְרִיחַ בְּשַׂר הַקֹּדֶשׁ מֵעוֹלָם, וְלֹא נִרְאָה זְבוּב בְּבֵית הַמִּטְבָּחַיִם, וְלֹא אֵרַע קֶרִי לְכֹהֵן גָּדוֹל בְּיוֹם הַכִּפּוּרִים, וְלֹא כִבּוּ גְשָׁמִים אֵשׁ שֶׁל עֲצֵי הַמַּעֲרָכָה, וְלֹא נִצְּחָה הָרוּחַ אֶת עַמּוּד הֶעָשָׁן, וְלֹא נִמְצָא פְסוּל בָּעֹמֶר וּבִשְׁתֵּי הַלֶּחֶם וּבְלֶחֶם הַפָּנִים;

flowing, so that the people could have water to drink, the waters would again harden, so that they would not descend to the ground [and muddy it]. This is implied by the verse:[35] "They stood up like a wall; the flowing streams congealed;" i.e., that which was flowing became congealed in the depths of the sea.

The Oral Tradition states[36] that greater plagues descended upon the Egyptians at the Red Sea than the plagues of Egypt. These, however, were of the same ten types that descended in Egypt; they merely sub-divided into different categories at the sea. This is alluded to in the verse:[37] "These are the gods who smote Egypt with all the plagues in the wilderness" - i.e., in the desert of the Red Sea.

The ten trials with which our ancestors tried the Omnipresent are all mentioned in the Torah. The first was at the Red Sea, when they said,[38] "Are there no graves in Egypt?" The second was at Marah, as it is written:[39] "And the people complained to Moses saying, 'What shall we drink?'" The third was in the desert of Sin when they requested the manna, as they said:[40] "Would that we had died by the hand of God." The fourth was their rebellion in leaving the manna to remain until the next day, as it is written:[41] "And they did not heed Moses... ."

The fifth was seeking [the manna] on the Sabbath, as it is written:[42] "Some of the people went out to gather, but they did not find it." The sixth was at Refidim with regard to the water.[43] The seventh was at Chorev by making the [Golden] Calf.[44] The eighth was at Tav'erah; at this place they expressed their doubts and rebelled, as it is written:[45] "And the people complained... ." The ninth was at *Kivrot HaTa'avah* when they requested meat, as it is written:[46] "And the mixed multitude in their midst lusted...."

And the tenth was in the desert of Paran with regard to the spies. There it is said:[47] "And they have tried Me these ten times."

[The rains never extinguished the fire... on the altar -] As you know, the altar is in the

---

36. *Mechilta, Parashat Beshalach.*
37. I Samuel 4:8.
38. Exodus 14:11.
39. *Ibid.* 15:24.
40. *Ibid.* 16:3.
41. *Ibid.*:20.
42. *Ibid.*:27.
43. *Ibid.* 17:2.
44. *Ibid.*, Chapter 32.
45. Numbers 11:1.
46. *Ibid.*:4.
47. *Ibid.* 14:22.

g) no disqualifying defect was ever found in the omer,[48] or in the Two [Shavuot] Loaves,[49] or in the Showbread;[50]
h) when the people stood they were crowded together, yet when they prostrated themselves they had ample space;
i) no snake or scorpion ever caused harm in Jerusalem;
j) nor did any man ever say to his fellow, "The place is too crowded for me to lodge overnight in Jerusalem."

5. Ten entities were created on the eve of the [first] Sabbath at twilight. They are:
a) The opening of the earth [to swallow Korach];[52]
b) the mouth of the well [in the wilderness];[53]
c) the mouth of the donkey [of Bil'am];[54]
d) the rainbow;[55]
e) the mannah;[56]
f) the staff [of Moses];[57]
g) the *shamir*;[58]
h) the writing [of the Torah];
i) the inscription [on the Tablets];[59]
j) and the Tablets.[60]

Some say also the spirits of destruction,[61] the burial place of Moses[62] and the ram of Abraham our Patriarch.[63] And some say the [original] tongs as well, for tongs must be made with tongs.

center of the Temple Courtyard; this matter will be explained in its place.[51] Although it was open to the heavens, the rain would never extinguish its fire, nor would the wind dissipate the pillar of smoke that would rise from the sacrifices. Instead, at the time the sacrifices were offered, the wind was still.

[**When the people stood, they were crowded together... -**] [In the Temple Courtyard,] they would stand one person next to his colleague. Nevertheless, when they bowed down, they were not crowded, nor would they press each other, because of their tremendous feelings of honor for the [holy] place.

[**Ten entities were created on the eve of the Sabbath at twilight. -**] In the eighth [introductory] chapter, I have already mentioned that the [Sages] do not maintain that there is a change in the [Divine] will at any time. Instead, at the very beginning of the creation of all the entities, [the potential] for everything that they would do was invested in their nature. This applies whether the matter concerned is a natural event that repeats itself frequently, or it is a wonder that happens only on one occasion.

48. Leviticus 23:9-14.
49. *Ibid.* 23:16-17.
50. See Exodus 25:30; Leviticus 24:5-8.
51. *Middot*, Chapter 3.
52. Numbers 16:32.
53. *Ibid.* 21:16-18; Exodus 17:6.
54. Numbers 22:28.
55. Genesis 9:13.
56. Exodus 16:11-15, 31-36.
57. *Ibid.* 4:2,17.

עוֹמְדִים צְפוּפִים וּמִשְׁתַּחֲוִים רְוָחִים, וְלֹא הִזִּיק נָחָשׁ וְעַקְרָב בִּירוּשָׁלַיִם מֵעוֹלָם, וְלֹא אָמַר אָדָם לַחֲבֵרוֹ: צַר לִי הַמָּקוֹם שֶׁאָלִין בִּירוּשָׁלָיִם.

ה. עֲשָׂרָה דְבָרִים נִבְרְאוּ בְעֶרֶב שַׁבָּת בֵּין הַשְּׁמָשׁוֹת, וְאֵלּוּ הֵן: פִּי הָאָרֶץ, וּפִי הַבְּאֵר, וּפִי הָאָתוֹן, וְהַקֶּשֶׁת, וְהַמָּן, וְהַמַּטֶּה, וְהַשָּׁמִיר, וְהַכְּתָב, וְהַמִּכְתָּב, וְהַלּוּחוֹת. וְיֵשׁ אוֹמְרִים: אַף הַמַּזִּיקִין, וּקְבוּרָתוֹ שֶׁל מֹשֶׁה, וְאֵילוֹ שֶׁל אַבְרָהָם אָבִינוּ. וְיֵשׁ אוֹמְרִים: אַף צְבָת בִּצְבָת עֲשׂוּיָה.

Therefore, [the *mishnah*] states that on the sixth day [of creation] the earth was granted the potential to swallow Korach and his company, the well to provide water, the donkey to speak. The same applies to the other examples.

the writing [of the Torah -] This refers to the Torah which is written before Him, as He said, in a manner that we cannot comprehend. This is implied by the verse:[64] "And I will give you the tablets of stone, the Torah and the mitzvot that I have written to instruct you."

the inscription [on the Tablets -] This is the meaning of the Hebrew מכתב, as it is written:[65] "The inscription was the writing of God."

Were one to ask: If [the potential for] all the miracles was invested in nature during the six days of creation, why does [the *mishnah*] mention these ten specifically?

Know that these [ten] were not specified to the exclusion of the others, [implying] that [the potential for] other miracles was not invested into nature during the six days of creation. Instead, the intent is that only these were made on twilight on Friday, while the others were invested in nature at the time the article was formed.

To cite an example: On the second day, when the waters were separated, they were granted the potential that the Red Sea would split for Moses,[66] that the Jordan would split for Joshua, for Elijah, and for Elisha. On the fourth day, when the sun was created, it was granted the potential to stand still as Joshua commanded it.[67] The same applies with regard to the other miracles. These ten, by contrast, were given the potential [on Friday] at twilight.

the shamir - This was a small animal that was able to split large stones when passing over them. With this [creature], Solomon [split the stones necessary] to build the Temple.

---

58. See *Gittin* 68a; *Sotah* 48b.
59. *Ibid.* 32:16.
60. *Ibid.*
61. See *Bereishit Rabbah* 7:5; *Midrash Tanchumah* Genesis, Sec. 17; *Yalkut Shimoni,* Genesis, Sec. 12.
62. See Deuteronomy 34:6.
63. See Genesis 22:13.
64. Exodus 24:12.
65. *Ibid.* 32:16.
66. Note *Bereishit Rabbah* 5:4, which states that at the beginning of its creation, God made a stipulation that the sea would split for the Jews. Otherwise, it would return to nothingness. See the Rambam's comments on this issue in the Guide for the Perplexed, Vol. II, Chapter 29.

6. Seven things characterize a crude person, and seven a wise man. A wise man does not speak before one who is greater than he in wisdom;[67] he does not interrupt the words of his fellow; he does not become too bewildered to reply; he asks what is relevant to the subject matter and replies to the point; he speaks of first things

tongs - This refers to the tongs with which blacksmiths hold scorching articles so that they can fashion them into whatever they wish.

[Crude person... wise man -] I will explain the [following] terms for they frequently appear in the words of our Sages: *boor, am ha'aretz, golem, chacham,* and *chassid. Boor* [translated in English using the same term] refers to a person who possesses neither intellectual nor moral virtues, neither Torah [knowledge] nor ethics. But also such a person does not have bad tendencies; it is as if he is empty of both good and bad qualities. This is the meaning of the term *boor.* Indeed, we find the same term used with regard to a field that is left fallow, as mentioned in the Order of *Zera'im.*[68]

Am ha'aretz [translated as "common person"] - This refers to a person who possesses ethical virtues, but does not possess intellectual virtues - i.e., he possesses moral refinement, but not Torah [knowledge]. This is why such a person is called an *am ha'aretz,* literally "people of the earth." For he is fit to settle the earth and establish [society within] a city, since he possesses qualities that will bring benefit to his association with others, as we explained in the introduction to this text.[69]

Golem [translated as "crude person"] - refers to a person who has ethical and intellectual virtues, but they are not perfected, nor are they structured as they should be. Instead, they are confused and mixed up, and are somewhat lacking. Therefore, they are called crude, like a utensil made by a craftsman, which already has the desired form, but is lacking completion and perfection - e.g., a knife or a sword that a smith has beaten out and given form, but has not been straightened, sharpened, polished, or engraved in the usual manner. Since they have not been completed, they are called *golmei klei matechet,* "crude iron utensils," as explained in the Order of *Keilim.*[70]

Golem is a Hebrew word, as in the verse,[71] גלמי ראו עיניך "Your eyes saw my crude form," i.e., my body before it received a human form. Since it did not receive a complete form, it was called *golem,* similar to crude matter that is prepared to be molded into a more perfect form.

Chacham [translated as "wise man"] - refers to a person who has acquired both [intellectual and ethical] virtues in a consummate and proper degree. *Chassid* [translated as pious] - refers to a person who is wise, but increases his piety - i.e., with regard to his ethical virtues, he tends slightly to one extreme, as we explained in the fourth [introductory] chapter. His deeds exceed his knowledge; he is called pious because

67. See Joshua 3:16.
68. *Pe'ah* 2:1.
69. I.e., the introduction to the Commentary on the Mishnah.
70. *Keilim* 12:6.
71. Psalms 139:16.

ו שִׁבְעָה דְבָרִים בְּגֹלֶם וְשִׁבְעָה בְּחָכָם. חָכָם אֵינוֹ מְדַבֵּר בִּפְנֵי מִי שֶׁהוּא גָדוֹל
מִמֶּנּוּ בְּחָכְמָה וּבְמִנְיָן, וְאֵינוֹ נִכְנָס לְתוֹךְ דִּבְרֵי חֲבֵרוֹ, וְאֵינוֹ נִבְהָל לְהָשִׁיב; שׁוֹאֵל

of this addition. For a person who is extreme in either direction, good or bad,
is called *chassid*.[72]

[The *mishnah*] states that a wise man will possess these seven qualities. They are
fundamental principles [of ethics] of enormous [importance]; therefore, it elaborates
upon them. For through them, one's Torah [knowledge], study and deed will be
maintained.

They include four ethical virtues:

**[He] does not speak before one who is greater than he in wisdom; he does not
interrupt the words of his fellow** - but instead, waits until he concludes his words. He
does not speak about subjects that he does not know, as it says...

concerning that which he has not heard, he says, "I have not heard" - Nor is
he stubborn. Instead, when he hears the truth, he acknowledges it. Even if he has
the possibility to put off the matter, to argue, or to deceive others, he does not
do so. This is what is meant by...

he acknowledges the truth.

He also possesses three intellectual virtues. When someone tries to lead him astray
in a point of sophistry, he does not become excited or bewildered, and does not
remain in a state of genuine doubt. Instead, he quickly senses the fault [in the
other's reasoning] and reveals it. This is what is meant by...

he does not become too bewildered to reply - This is possible because of the speed
of his understanding, his correct analysis of the sophist's words, and his distinction of
the conceptual differences.

The second virtue is the ability to ask proper questions about subject matter;
he will not seek to understand a point of logic when studying natural science, nor
a principle of nature when studying logic. Similarly, if questions are directed to
him, he will give pertinent answers. If he is asked about matters for which he can bring
proofs, he will bring proofs. If he is asked about other matters, he will give an answer
appropriate to the subject at hand. If he is asked about the material dimensions
of a subject, he will not reply about its abstracts. And if he is asked about the abstracts,
he will not reply about the material dimensions. Instead, he will go to the crux of the
matter. This is what is meant by...

he asks what is relevant to the subject matter and replies to the point - This ability
comes only after much study.

The third virtue is the ability to maintain a conceptual structure, to give priority to
matters that should be given priority, and to delay matters that should not be given
priority. This is what is meant by...

he speaks of first things first and of last things last.

A crude person is characterized by the opposite of these traits. Since, as explained,
he has not perfected himself, he has not reached this [refined] level [of conduct].

---

72. We generally think of the term *chassid* as used in a positive context. The use of the term in a
negative context is reflected in Rav Sa'adiah Gaon's interpretation of the term *chesed* in Leviticus
20:17.

first and of last things last; concerning that which he has not heard, he says, "I have not heard"; and he acknowledges the truth.

And the reverse of these characterize a crude person.

7. Seven kinds of punishment come to the world for seven kinds of transgressions. If some tithe and some do not, a famine of drought ensues: some suffer hunger and some have plenty. If all decide not to tithe, a famine of panic and drought ensues, and if they also decided not to separate *challah*,[73] a famine of destruction ensues.

Plague comes to the world as retribution for the transgressions which the Torah mentions that are punishable by death, but which the Court of Justice was not empowered to carry out; and for making forbidden use of the fruits of the Sabbatical year.[74]

War comes to the world for the delay of justice, for the perversion of justice and for rendering a Torah decision not in accordance with halachah.

Wild beasts come upon the world for swearing falsely and for profaning the Divine name. Exile comes to the world for idolatry, for prohibited sexual relations, for murder, and for not leaving the earth at rest during the Sabbatical year.

8. At four periods [within the seven-year agricultural cycle] pestilence increases - in the fourth year, in the seventh year, in the year following the Sabbatical year, and annually at the conclusion of the festival of Sukkot.

In the fourth year - for not having given the tithe for the poor in the third; in the seventh year - for not having given the tithe for the poor in the sixth; in the year following the Sabbatical year - for [not observing

---

A famine of drought - It will be a year in which only a small amount of rain descends. In some places it will rain, and in others it will not rain. Even in the places where it does rain, the rain will be less [than usual].

A famine of panic - That people will be embroiled in wars, battles, and problems that confront them and cause them to desert their fields and not sow them when they should because of these difficulties.

---

73. See Numbers 15:20; Ezekiel 44:30.
74. See Exodus 23:11; Leviticus 25:1-7.

כָּעִנְיָן וּמֵשִׁיב כַּהֲלָכָה; וְאוֹמֵר עַל רִאשׁוֹן רִאשׁוֹן וְעַל אַחֲרוֹן אַחֲרוֹן, וְעַל מַה שֶּׁלֹּא שָׁמַע אוֹמֵר: לֹא שָׁמָעְתִּי; וּמוֹדֶה עַל הָאֱמֶת. וְחִלּוּפֵיהֶם בַּגֹּלֶם.

ז שִׁבְעָה מִינֵי פֻרְעָנִיּוֹת בָּאִין לָעוֹלָם עַל שִׁבְעָה גּוּפֵי עֲבֵרָה:

מִקְצָתָן מְעַשְּׂרִין וּמִקְצָתָן אֵינָן מְעַשְּׂרִין, רָעָב שֶׁל בַּצֹּרֶת בָּאָה; מִקְצָתָן רְעֵבִים וּמִקְצָתָן שְׂבֵעִים.

גָּמְרוּ שֶׁלֹּא לְעַשֵּׂר, רָעָב שֶׁל מְהוּמָה וְשֶׁל בַּצֹּרֶת בָּאָה.

וְשֶׁלֹּא לִטֹּל אֶת הַחַלָּה, רָעָב שֶׁל כְּלָיָה בָּאָה.

דֶּבֶר בָּא לָעוֹלָם — עַל מִיתוֹת הָאֲמוּרוֹת בַּתּוֹרָה שֶׁלֹּא נִמְסְרוּ לְבֵית דִּין, וְעַל פֵּרוֹת שְׁבִיעִית.

חֶרֶב בָּא לָעוֹלָם — עַל עִנּוּי הַדִּין, וְעַל עִוּוּת הַדִּין, וְעַל הַמּוֹרִים בַּתּוֹרָה שֶׁלֹּא כַהֲלָכָה.

חַיָּה רָעָה בָּאָה לָעוֹלָם — עַל שְׁבוּעַת שָׁוְא, וְעַל חִלּוּל הַשֵּׁם.

גָּלוּת בָּא לָעוֹלָם — עַל עֲבוֹדַת כּוֹכָבִים, וְעַל גִּלּוּי עֲרָיוֹת, וְעַל שְׁפִיכַת דָּמִים, וְעַל שְׁמִטַּת הָאָרֶץ.

ח בְּאַרְבָּעָה פְרָקִים הַדֶּבֶר מִתְרַבֶּה: בָּרְבִיעִית, וּבַשְּׁבִיעִית, וּבְמוֹצָאֵי שְׁבִיעִית, וּבְמוֹצָאֵי הֶחָג שֶׁבְּכָל שָׁנָה וְשָׁנָה.

בָּרְבִיעִית, מִפְּנֵי מַעְשַׂר עָנִי שֶׁבַּשְּׁלִישִׁית; בַּשְּׁבִיעִית, מִפְּנֵי מַעְשַׂר עָנִי שֶׁבַּשִּׁשִּׁית;

A famine of destruction - I.e., that no rain descends at all, and the rivers and streams dry out, as alluded to in the verse,[75] "And your heavens will be like iron."

the delay of justice, - spending many days [ruminating] over a simple matter. This is the meaning of the phrase עיכוב הדין.

the perversion of justice - Judging [matters] improperly.

[The seven-year agricultural cycle -] On several occasions in the Order of *Zera'im*, the cycle of the separation of agricultural gifts was explained. In the third and sixth year [of the cycle], the first tithe should be separated and given to the Levites, as it is every year. Afterwards, another tithe is separated and given to the poor. This is called the "tithe of the poor"; it replaces the second tithe, which is separated in the other years of the cycle.

75. Deuteronomy 28:23.

the laws pertaining to] the produce of the Sabbatical year; annually, at the conclusion of the festival of Sukkot - for stealing the [harvest] gifts for the poor.

9. There are four [character] types among men: He who says, "What is mine is mine, and what is yours is yours" - this is a median characteristic; some say this is the characteristic of [the people of] Sodom. "What is mine is yours, and what is yours is mine," is an ignoramus. [He who says,] "What is mine is yours, and what is yours is yours," is pious. And [he who says,] "What is yours is mine, and what is mine is mine," is wicked.

10. There are four types of temperaments: Easily angered and easily pacified - his loss is outweighed by his merit; hard to anger and hard to pacify - his merit is outweighed by his loss; hard to anger and easy to pacify is pious; easily angered and hard to pacify is wicked.

11. There are four types of students: Quick to grasp and quick to forget - his gain is overridden by his loss; slow to grasp and slow to forget - his loss is overridden by his gain; quick to grasp and slow to forget - this is a good portion; slow to grasp and quick to forget - this is a bad portion.

12. There are four types among those who give charity: One who wishes to give but that others should not - he begrudges others; that others should give and he should not - he begrudges himself; that he should give and others should too - is pious; that he should not give nor should others - is wicked.

The [harvest] gifts for the poor - Fallen stalks,[76] forgotten sheaves,[77] *pe'ah*,[78] individual fallen grapes,[79] and incompletely formed grape clusters.[80]

The wording of this teaching emphasizes that the term...
pious - refers to a person who increases his positive activity. [In doing so,] he leans slightly to one of the extremes.
wicked - refers to someone who possesses personal shortcomings - i.e., who conducts himself to an extreme, increasing [his indulgence], as explained in the fourth [introductory] chapter. Since this person desires to possess both his own money and that of his colleagues, he is craving and is [therefore] termed "wicked."

76. Which may not be collected and must be left for the poor (Leviticus 19:9).

וּבְמוֹצָאֵי שְׁבִיעִית, מִפְּנֵי פֵּרוֹת שְׁבִיעִית; וּבְמוֹצָאֵי הֶחָג שֶׁבְּכָל שָׁנָה וְשָׁנָה, מִפְּנֵי גֶזֶל מַתְּנוֹת עֲנִיִּים.

ט אַרְבַּע מִדּוֹת בָּאָדָם: הָאוֹמֵר שֶׁלִּי שֶׁלִּי וְשֶׁלְּךָ שֶׁלָּךְ — זוֹ מִדָּה בֵּינוֹנִית; וְיֵשׁ אוֹמְרִים: זוֹ מִדַּת סְדֹם. שֶׁלִּי שֶׁלְּךָ וְשֶׁלְּךָ שֶׁלִּי — עַם הָאָרֶץ. שֶׁלִּי שֶׁלְּךָ וְשֶׁלְּךָ שֶׁלָּךְ — חָסִיד. שֶׁלִּי שֶׁלִּי וְשֶׁלְּךָ שֶׁלִּי — רָשָׁע.

י אַרְבַּע מִדּוֹת בְּדֵעוֹת: נוֹחַ לִכְעֹס וְנוֹחַ לִרְצוֹת — יָצָא שְׂכָרוֹ בְהֶפְסֵדוֹ; קָשֶׁה לִכְעֹס וְקָשֶׁה לִרְצוֹת — יָצָא הֶפְסֵדוֹ בִשְׂכָרוֹ. קָשֶׁה לִכְעֹס וְנוֹחַ לִרְצוֹת — חָסִיד; נוֹחַ לִכְעֹס וְקָשֶׁה לִרְצוֹת — רָשָׁע.

יא אַרְבַּע מִדּוֹת בְּתַלְמִידִים: מַהֵר לִשְׁמֹעַ וּמַהֵר לְאַבֵּד — יָצָא שְׂכָרוֹ בְהֶפְסֵדוֹ; קָשֶׁה לִשְׁמֹעַ וְקָשֶׁה לְאַבֵּד — יָצָא הֶפְסֵדוֹ בִשְׂכָרוֹ. מַהֵר לִשְׁמֹעַ וְקָשֶׁה לְאַבֵּד — חָכָם; קָשֶׁה לִשְׁמֹעַ וּמַהֵר לְאַבֵּד — זֶה חֵלֶק רָע.

יב אַרְבַּע מִדּוֹת בְּנוֹתְנֵי צְדָקָה: הָרוֹצֶה שֶׁיִּתֵּן וְלֹא יִתְּנוּ אֲחֵרִים — עֵינוֹ רָעָה בְּשֶׁל אֲחֵרִים; יִתְּנוּ אֲחֵרִים וְהוּא לֹא יִתֵּן — עֵינוֹ רָעָה בְּשֶׁלּוֹ. יִתֵּן וְיִתְּנוּ אֲחֵרִים — חָסִיד; לֹא יִתֵּן וְלֹא יִתְּנוּ אֲחֵרִים — רָשָׁע.

Contemplate that [the *mishnah*] is calling a person whose patience is such that his forbearance comes close to a lack of sensitivity...
pious. - And it calls one who possesses the shortcoming of [being easily] angered...
wicked.

[**Quick to grasp and slow to forget** -] Note that [the *mishnah*] does not refer to a person with a good memory and quick perception as "pious," for [this person's] virtues are intellectual. He may be termed a *chacham*, "wise." Conversely, a person who is slow to grasp and who forgets easily is not termed "wicked," for this is not within his potential to change. These are not qualities that a person can acquire for himself, as explained in the second [introductory] chapter.

Pious - Contemplate how [the *mishnah*] refers to a person who is exceedingly merciful, so much so that not only does he show mercy himself, he desires that others do so as well. [In contrast,] a hard-hearted person is called...
wicked.

77. Which one may not return to collect and which must instead be left for the poor (Deuteronomy 24:19-22).
78. The ends of the field that must be left unharvested for the poor to take (Leviticus, *loc. cit.*).
79. Which may not be gathered and must be left for the poor (*op. cit.*:10).
80. Which may not be reaped and must be left for the poor (*Ibid.*).

13. There are four types among those who attend the House of Study: One who attends, but does not engage [in study] earns the reward for going. One who engages [in study], but does not attend earns the reward for the act [of studying]. One who attends and engages [in study] is pious. One who does not attend, nor does he engage [in study] is wicked.

14. There are four types among those who sit before the Sages. [They are likened to] a sponge, a funnel, a strainer and a sifter. A sponge,

---

Those who attend the House of Study - There are four different approaches to attending the House of Study. Contemplate how [the *mishnah*] refers to a person who strains to increase his virtues as...

pious - and one who is lazy and does not seek to acquire them as...

wicked.

You should be aware of the intellectual and ethical virtues and know their particulars. And if you desire to know both deed and wisdom, you should know that the middle path in conduct is called "good." Making a slight deviation from the mean reflects the conduct of the renowned men of piety. You should also know that excess and restriction are both undesirable. [In every particular instance,] one of the extremes is more aptly termed "evil," and the other "sin" or "improper conduct."

For example, restraint is definitely a positive quality. Indulgence of desire is definitely an undesirable quality. A lack of sensitivity to pleasure is bad; it is not, however, as bad as the indulgence of desire. One can call it sin or improper conduct. It is proper for people who seek perfection to deviate slightly from [the mean of] restraint toward a lack of sensitivity to pleasure.

Thus, a person who deviates slightly from the quality of restraint is called pious, while one who is lacking in the sensitivity for pleasure is called a sinner. Therefore, a nazirite is described[81] as "one who sinned against his soul," as we explained in the fourth [introductory] chapter.

Based on all the above, you can appreciate which people are fit to be described with the term *boor, am ha'aretz, golem, chacham, chassid, rasha* (wicked) and *chotea* (sinner). These seven terms are used to describe seven types of people according to their different levels of intellectual and ethical virtue, as explained in our commentary.

Sometimes these terms are combined, as befits the nature of a person. For example, if a person who has ethical shortcomings and is therefore described as wicked, also possesses intellectual virtues, but he uses them for undesirable purposes, he is called a רשע ערום, a clever wicked person.

And if a wicked person would harm others - i.e., among his ethical shortcomings would also be qualities that hurt others - e.g., rashness, cruelty, or the like - he is called a רשע רע, an evil wicked person.

---

81. Numbers 6:11.
82. Jeremiah 4:22.
83. Deuteronomy 33:1; I Samuel 2:27; Psalms 90:1.

יג אַרְבַּע מִדּוֹת בְּהוֹלְכֵי לְבֵית הַמִּדְרָשׁ: הוֹלֵךְ וְאֵינוֹ עוֹשֶׂה — שְׂכַר הֲלִיכָה בְּיָדוֹ;
עוֹשֶׂה וְאֵינוֹ הוֹלֵךְ — שְׂכַר מַעֲשֶׂה בְּיָדוֹ. הוֹלֵךְ וְעוֹשֶׂה — חָסִיד; לֹא הוֹלֵךְ וְלֹא
עוֹשֶׂה — רָשָׁע.

יד אַרְבַּע מִדּוֹת בַּיּוֹשְׁבִים לִפְנֵי חֲכָמִים: סְפוֹג, וּמַשְׁפֵּךְ, מְשַׁמֶּרֶת, וְנָפָה.

Similarly, if he possesses intellectual virtues and ethical shortcomings that cause harm, he is called a חכם לרע, a wise man with evil tendencies, as mentioned in the verse:[82] "They are wise, [but] oriented to evil; they do not know to precipitate good" - i.e., they use their intellectual virtues for evil purposes, rather than positive ones.

For a person to possess all the intellectual virtues and all the ethical virtues to the extent that there is neither an intellectual nor an ethical virtue that he does not possess, is indeed a rare occurrence. The philosophers say that it is highly improbable to find such a person, but it is not impossible. If such a person were found, they would call him a Godly man. Similarly, in [the Bible],[83] we find the expression "the man of God." Moreover, I say that a man of this type is fit to be called "angel of God," as it is written:[84] "And the angel of God ascended."

The philosophers also say that it is impossible for there to be a person who possesses all the shortcomings - both intellectual and ethical - that exist. If such a person be found, however improbable this would be, they refer to him as "a wild beast" or "a poisonous snake," and the like, using the names of predatory beasts. In this vein, Solomon used the term,[85] "a bereft bear."

Thus, there are five terms that combine different qualities: four of them disparaging: "a clever wicked person," "an evil wicked person," "a wise man with evil tendencies," and "a bereft bear." There is one term that refers to the most praiseworthy of qualities: "a man of God" or "an angel of God." For the Bible has already termed a person who possesses all of both the intellectual and ethical virtues as angel of God, as it is written:[86] "For the priest's lips will keep knowledge, [others] will seek Torah from his mouth, for he is an angel of the God of Hosts." "Knowledge" includes all the intellectual virtues, for a person cannot develop himself without it. The phrase "seek Torah from his mouth" indicates perfection in ethics, as explained in the fourth [introductory] chapter, for this is the goal of the Torah, as it is written,[87] "And all its paths are peace." As explained in the fourth [introductory] chapter, "peace" refers to the ethical qualities. [And concerning such a person, the prophet uses the appellation,] "he is an angel of God."

[**A sponge -**] [The *mishnah*] likens a person who remembers everything he hears, without differentiating between what is true and false, to a sponge that absorbs

84. Judges 2:1. Note *VaYikra Rabbah*, Chapter 1, which interprets this phrase as referring to Pinchas. See also the Rambam's comments in this regard in the Guide for the Perplexed, Vol. I, Chapter 15; Vol. II, Chapter 6.
85. Proverbs 17:12.
86. Malachi 2:7.
87. Proverbs 3:17.

which absorbs everything; a funnel, which takes in from one end and spills out from the other; a strainer, which allows the wine to flow out and retains the dregs; and a sifter, which allows the flour to pass through and retains the fine flour.

15. Whenever love is dependent upon a specific consideration - when that consideration vanishes, the love ceases. If, by contrast, it is not dependent upon a specific consideration - it will never cease.

Which is a love that is dependent upon a specific thing? The love of Amnon and Tamar.[88] And one which is not dependent upon a specific thing? The love of David and Jonathan.[89]

16. Any controversy that is for the sake of Heaven will be perpetuated; and that which is not for the sake of Heaven will not be perpetuated.

Which is a controversy for the sake of Heaven? The controversy between Hillel and Shammai.[91] And which is not for the sake of Heaven? The controversy of Korach and all his faction.[92]

Whenever a person causes the many to have merit, no sin shall come through him; but one who causes the many to sin shall not be granted the opportunity to repent.

Moses was himself meritorious and caused the many to attain merit; [therefore] the merits of the many are attributed to him, as it is stated: "He (Moses) performed the righteousness of the Lord and His ordinances together with Israel."[93]

everything. It likens the person who has a quick power of comprehension, but retains nothing, neither the true nor the false, to a funnel. It also likens a person who retains erroneous information and faulty reasoning, but who forgets true matters - [i.e.,] Torah law - actually to a strainer that retains the dregs and allows the pure [wine] to flow out. And it likens a person with opposite tendencies to a sifter that discharges the earth and dust through its holes and retains the fine flour. This is done by using a sifter for fine flour, which discharges the light flour which is of no value, and retains the heavy flour.

[Whenever love is dependent upon a specific consideration... -] The explanation of the matter is as follows: Whenever love is dependent on a matter of no significance, when that matter vanishes the love will cease. If the love is not dependent on an insignificant matter, it will never cease.[90]

You know that all physical matters are all meaningless and transient, and thus as the cause for the effect [the relationship] passes, the effect [the relationship] will also cease.

88. II Samuel 13:1ff.
89. I Samuel 18:1; 20:17; II Samuel 1:26.

סְפוֹג, שֶׁהוּא סוֹפֵג אֶת הַכֹּל; מַשְׁפֵּךְ, שֶׁמַּכְנִיס בָּזוֹ וּמוֹצִיא בָזוֹ; מְשַׁמֶּרֶת, שֶׁמּוֹצִיאָה אֶת הַיַּיִן וְקוֹלֶטֶת אֶת הַשְּׁמָרִים; וְנָפָה, שֶׁמּוֹצִיאָה אֶת הַקֶּמַח וְקוֹלֶטֶת אֶת הַסֹּלֶת.

טו כָּל אַהֲבָה שֶׁהִיא תְלוּיָה בְדָבָר — בָּטֵל דָּבָר, בְּטֵלָה אַהֲבָה; וְשֶׁאֵינָהּ תְּלוּיָה בְדָבָר, אֵינָהּ בְּטֵלָה לְעוֹלָם.

אֵיזוֹ הִיא אַהֲבָה הַתְּלוּיָה בְדָבָר? זוֹ אַהֲבַת אַמְנוֹן וְתָמָר; וְשֶׁאֵינָהּ תְּלוּיָה בְדָבָר? זוֹ אַהֲבַת דָּוִד וִיהוֹנָתָן.

טז כָּל מַחֲלֹקֶת שֶׁהִיא לְשֵׁם שָׁמַיִם, סוֹפָהּ לְהִתְקַיֵּם; וְשֶׁאֵינָהּ לְשֵׁם שָׁמַיִם, אֵין סוֹפָהּ לְהִתְקַיֵּם.

אֵיזוֹ מַחֲלֹקֶת שֶׁהִיא לְשֵׁם שָׁמַיִם? זוֹ מַחֲלֹקֶת הִלֵּל וְשַׁמַּאי; וְשֶׁאֵינָהּ לְשֵׁם שָׁמַיִם? זוֹ מַחֲלֹקֶת קֹרַח וְכָל עֲדָתוֹ.

כָּל הַמְזַכֶּה אֶת הָרַבִּים, אֵין חֵטְא בָּא עַל יָדוֹ; וְכָל הַמַּחֲטִיא אֶת הָרַבִּים, אֵין מַסְפִּיקִין בְּיָדוֹ לַעֲשׂוֹת תְּשׁוּבָה.

מֹשֶׁה זָכָה וְזִכָּה אֶת הָרַבִּים — זְכוּת הָרַבִּים תָּלוּי בּוֹ, שֶׁנֶּאֱמַר: צִדְקַת ה׳ עָשָׂה וּמִשְׁפָּטָיו עִם יִשְׂרָאֵל.

If [by contrast] the cause of the love is a Godly matter, true knowledge, it is impossible that this love will ever be nullified, for its cause exists eternally.

[Any controversy that is for the sake of Heaven -] All these concepts are clear. They are relevant to [the concepts of] reward and punishment, for the words of a person who dissents for no petty, selfish purpose, nor solely because he seeks truth, will continue to prevail; they will not falter. Similarly, when a person directs other men in the path of good, he will be rewarded by God, who will prevent him from sinning.

Conversely, a person who leads others astray will be punished by God by having the potential for repentance withdrawn from him. This is clear and does not present a conceptual difficulty, provided one understands the concepts explained in the eighth [introductory] chapter.

---

90. The Rambam's commentary is based on a double entendre of the word בטל, which means both "cease" and "insignificant." The Rambam is stating that love between two people will always be dependent on an external factor. If the external factor is ephemeral and petty in nature, the relationship will be short lived. If, however, the source for the relationship is matters of genuine and lasting value, the relationship will have an ongoing, proactive quality.

Significantly, these few lines are lacking in the standard published text of the Commentary on the Mishnah, but are found in early editions and authoritative manuscripts.

91. *Eruvin* 13b.
92. Numbers, Chapter 16.
93. Deuteronomy 33:21.

Yorov'am the son of Nevat himself sinned and caused the many to sin; [therefore] the sins of the many are attributed to him, as it is stated: "For the sins of Yorov'am that he transgressed and caused Israel to sin."[94]

17. Whoever possesses the following three characteristics is of the disciples of Abraham our Patriarch. Anyone who does not possess these characteristics is of the disciples of the wicked Bil'am.

The disciples of our Patriarch Abraham possess a good eye, a humble spirit and a meek soul. The disciples of the wicked Bil'am possess an evil eye, an arrogant spirit and a greedy soul.

What is the difference between the disciples of Abraham our Patriarch and the disciples of the wicked Bil'am? The disciples of the wicked Bil'am inherit Hell and descend into the nethermost pit, as it is stated: "And You, O God, will bring them down to the nethermost pit; bloodthirsty and treacherous men shall not live out half their days; and I will trust in You."[95]

But the disciples of Abraham our Patriarch enjoy [the fruits of their good qualities] in this world and inherit the World to Come, as it is stated: "To cause those who love Me to inherit an everlasting possession [the World to Come], and I will fill their storehouses [in this world]."[96]

A good eye - As we explained several times previously,[97] this term refers to the quality of contentment.

a humble spirit - i.e., the restraint of desire

and a meek soul - an extreme dimension of humility, as explained in the previous chapter.[98] The three traits that run contrary to these are:

An evil eye - the burning desire for money

an arrogant spirit - sexual desire

and a greedy soul - pride.

All of the three virtues [mentioned above] were given expression by Abraham our patriarch. Therefore, anyone who possesses these virtues is considered to be a disciple of Abraham, for he emulates his qualities. Conversely, anyone who practices the three opposite qualities is considered to be a disciple of Bil'am, because he emulates his qualities.

I will now mention the sources that show that Abraham displayed these [three] virtues, and show that Bil'am displayed these three shortcomings. They are all explicitly mentioned in the Torah.

94. I Kings 15:30.
95. Psalms 55:24.
96. Proverbs 8:21. Cf. *Uktzin* 3:12.

יָרָבְעָם חָטָא וְהֶחֱטִיא אֶת הָרַבִּים — חֵטְא הָרַבִּים תָּלוּי בּוֹ, שֶׁנֶּאֱמַר : עַל חַטֹּאות
יָרָבְעָם (בֶּן נְבָט) אֲשֶׁר חָטָא וַאֲשֶׁר הֶחֱטִיא אֶת יִשְׂרָאֵל.

יז כָּל מִי שֶׁיֵּשׁ בְּיָדוֹ שְׁלֹשָׁה דְבָרִים הַלָּלוּ, מִתַּלְמִידָיו שֶׁל אַבְרָהָם אָבִינוּ; וּשְׁלֹשָׁה
דְבָרִים אֲחֵרִים, מִתַּלְמִידָיו שֶׁל בִּלְעָם הָרָשָׁע.

עַיִן טוֹבָה, וְרוּחַ נְמוּכָה, וְנֶפֶשׁ שְׁפָלָה — מִתַּלְמִידָיו שֶׁל אַבְרָהָם אָבִינוּ.

עַיִן רָעָה, וְרוּחַ גְּבוֹהָה, וְנֶפֶשׁ רְחָבָה — מִתַּלְמִידָיו שֶׁל בִּלְעָם הָרָשָׁע.

מַה בֵּין תַּלְמִידָיו שֶׁל אַבְרָהָם אָבִינוּ לְתַלְמִידָיו שֶׁל בִּלְעָם הָרָשָׁע? תַּלְמִידָיו שֶׁל
בִּלְעָם הָרָשָׁע יוֹרְשִׁין גֵּיהִנֹּם וְיוֹרְדִין לִבְאֵר שַׁחַת, שֶׁנֶּאֱמַר: וְאַתָּה אֱלֹהִים תּוֹרִדֵם
לִבְאֵר שַׁחַת, אַנְשֵׁי דָמִים וּמִרְמָה לֹא יֶחֱצוּ יְמֵיהֶם, וַאֲנִי אֶבְטַח בָּךְ. תַּלְמִידָיו
שֶׁל אַבְרָהָם אָבִינוּ אוֹכְלִין בָּעוֹלָם הַזֶּה וְנוֹחֲלִין לָעוֹלָם הַבָּא, שֶׁנֶּאֱמַר: לְהַנְחִיל
אֹהֲבַי יֵשׁ וְאֹצְרֹתֵיהֶם אֲמַלֵּא.

Abraham's contentment is obvious from his statement to the King of Sodom:[99] "Not a thread, nor a shoelace; I will not take anything that is yours." This reflected the ultimate of contentment, that he forgo [an offer of] a large sum of property and not derive any benefit at all, not even a slight amount.

His virtue of restraint is reflected in his statement to Sarah when they approached Egypt:[100] "Now I know that you are an attractive woman." This indicates that he had not looked at her physical form intently until that very day. This shows the ultimate of restraint.

This quality is evidenced by his statement concerning Hagar:[101] "Behold, your maidservant is in your hand...." This indicates that he was not at all concerned with deriving pleasure from her. When Sarah asked him to banish her together with Ishmael, the Torah states:[102] "And the matter was very bitter for Abraham, because of his son," showing that it was merely the sending away of Ishmael that was difficult for him. The verse indicates that he had no inclination towards Hagar, despite the intimacy he shared with her. These are all signs of [his mastery of the quality of] restraint. And his humility is evident from the verse,[103] "I am dust and ashes."

Bil'am's desire for money was made known, because of his [long] journey from Aram Naharayim to earn a wage for cursing the Jews. This is reflected by the Torah's statement:[104] "Who hired Bil'am from Petor of Aram Naharayim, to curse you."

97. See Chapter 2, *Mishnayot* 11-13.
98. Chapter 4, *Mishnah* 4.
99. Genesis 14:23.
100. *Ibid.* 12:11. The interpretation offered by the Rambam is based on *Bava Batra* 16a.
101. Genesis 16:6.
102. *Ibid.* 21:11.
103. *Ibid.* 18:27.
104. Deuteronomy 23:5.

18. Yehudah ben Tema said: Be bold as a leopard, light as an eagle, swift as a deer and brave as a lion, to carry out the will of your Father in heaven.

He used to say: The brazen is headed for Hell, but the shamefaced for heaven.

May it be Your will, God our Lord and Lord of our fathers, that the Temple[109] be rebuilt speedily in our days, and grant us our portion in Your Torah.

19. Ben Bag Bag said: Learn it and learn it [the Torah], for everything is in it. With it, you will see [truly]. Grow old and gray over it and do not stir from it, for there is nothing more edifying for you than it.

Ben Hey Hey said: Commensurate with the painstaking effort is the reward.

His [immoderate] tendency to [sexual] desire is reflected in his advice to Balak to send his women to the Jews to seduce them, making prostitutes of them. Had he not had an [immoderate] tendency towards [sexual] desire within his soul, and had the matter not been attractive and appealing to him, he would not have given such instructions. For a person's instructions reflect his character, and good people do not instruct people to do bad things; on the contrary, they warn against them. This matter is alluded to in the verse:[105] "These are exactly the ones who consorted with the children of Israel at Bil'am's instigation. Our Sages state[106] that Bil'am would sodomize his donkey. There is no doubt that someone who thinks like this would perform such deeds. [Bil'am's] pride is reflected by his [description of himself, saying:[107] "[This is] the discourse of he who hears the word of God."

The proof-text cited concerning Bil'am: "And You, O God, will bring them down to the nethermost pit...," applies to him, for he was bloodthirsty and treacherous, as reflected in his instigation of the death of the Jews through the plague. He was also treacherous, as reflected in his crafty thoughts to do harm, as explained. The proof-text cited concerning Abraham's disciples, "To cause those who love Me to inherit...," [is appropriate], as reflected in another verse[108] [which describes the righteous as]: "the descendants of Abraham who loved Me."

[Yehudah ben Tema said: Be bold as a leopard -] Although he also taught...

The brazen is headed for Hell - He instructed us to apply boldness in rebuking non-believers. It is as if he said, employ emotional faults in the proper place for the sake of heaven. In a similar way, the prophet states,[110] "With the perverse, act subtly." This applies solely when your intent is for the sake of heaven. This is indicated by the phrase:

105. Numbers 31:16.
106. *Sanhedrin* 105a.
107. Numbers 24:16.

יח יְהוּדָה בֶן תֵּימָא אוֹמֵר: הֱוֵי עַז כַּנָּמֵר, וְקַל כַּנֶּשֶׁר, רָץ כַּצְּבִי, וְגִבּוֹר כָּאֲרִי לַעֲשׂוֹת רְצוֹן אָבִיךָ שֶׁבַּשָּׁמָיִם. הוּא הָיָה אוֹמֵר: עַז פָּנִים לְגֵיהִנָּם, וּבֹשֶׁת פָּנִים לְגַן עֵדֶן.

יְהִי רָצוֹן מִלְּפָנֶיךָ ה׳ אֱלֹהֵינוּ וֵאלֹהֵי אֲבוֹתֵינוּ, שֶׁתִּבָּנֶה עִירְךָ בִּמְהֵרָה בְיָמֵינוּ וְתֵן חֶלְקֵנוּ בְּתוֹרָתֶךָ.

יט בֶּן בַּג בַּג אוֹמֵר: הֲפָךְ בָּהּ וַהֲפָךְ בָּהּ, דְּכֹלָּא בָהּ; וּבָהּ תֶּחֱזֵי, וְסִיב וּבְלֵה בָהּ, וּמִנָּהּ לָא תְזוּעַ, שֶׁאֵין לְךָ מִדָּה טוֹבָה הֵימֶנָּה.

בֶּן הֵא הֵא אוֹמֵר: לְפוּם צַעֲרָא אַגְרָא.

To carry out the will of your Father in heaven.
God has been generous with our nation, the Jews, in endowing them with the quality of shame. Our Sages said[111] that the signs of the descendants of Abraham are that they are shamefaced and merciful, and perform deeds of kindness. And on the verse,[112] "So that the fear of Him shall be upon your faces," our Sages commented:[113] "This refers to shame." [The conclusion of the *mishnah*...]
[**May it be Your will, God...** -] is as if to say: Just as You graciously granted us this attribute, so may You graciously build Your city in our days.

[The *mishnah*] refers to the Torah and instructs us to learn it over and over again and to contemplate it, for it contains everything.
With it, you will see [truly]. - [The Torah] will enable you to see the truth and to look at things with open eyes. [תחזי means "see," as reflected] in the Aramaic translation וירא as וחזא.
Grow old and gray over it - I.e., involve yourself with it until you grow old and reach advanced age; do not shift from it to other matters.
Ben Hey Hey said - Commensurate with the effort you apply to Torah study will be your reward. Our Sages said that the only knowledge that will endure is that which is gained through wearisome effort and fear of one's teacher. [Knowledge gained] through reading amid pleasure and repose will not endure, nor will it bring benefit. On the verse:[114] "And yet, my wisdom endured for me," our Sages commented:[115] "The

---

108. Isaiah 41:8.
109. Some texts state "Your city" - i.e., Jerusalem - instead of "the Temple."
110. II Samuel 22:27.
111. *Yevamot* 79a.
112. Exodus 20:17.
113. *Nedarim* 20a.
114. Ecclesiastes 2:9.
115. *Kohelet Rabbah* 2:12. The interpretation depends on the double entendre of the word אף, translated in the verse as "And yet," but which also means "anger."

כ הוּא הָיָה אוֹמֵר: בֶּן חָמֵשׁ שָׁנִים לְמִקְרָא; בֶּן עֶשֶׂר לְמִשְׁנָה; בֶּן שְׁלֹשׁ עֶשְׂרֵה
לְמִצְוֹת; בֶּן חָמֵשׁ עֶשְׂרֵה לִגְמָרָא; בֶּן שְׁמוֹנֶה עֶשְׂרֵה לְחֻפָּה; בֶּן עֶשְׂרִים לִרְדֹּף;
בֶּן שְׁלֹשִׁים לְכֹחַ; בֶּן אַרְבָּעִים לְבִינָה; בֶּן חֲמִשִּׁים לְעֵצָה; בֶּן שִׁשִּׁים לְזִקְנָה;
בֶּן שִׁבְעִים לְשֵׂיבָה; בֶּן שְׁמוֹנִים לִגְבוּרָה; בֶּן תִּשְׁעִים לָשׁוּחַ; בֶּן מֵאָה — כְּאִלּוּ מֵת
וְעָבַר וּבָטַל מִן הָעוֹלָם.

נשלמה מסכת אבות

20.[117] He used to say: At five years of age, [one should approach] the study of Scripture; at ten - the study of Mishnah; at thirteen - the mitzvot; at fifteen - the study of Gemara; at eighteen - marriage; at twenty - pursuit [of a livelihood]; at thirty - [one attains] full strength; at forty - understanding; at fifty - [the potential to give] counsel; at sixty - old age; at seventy - ripe old age; at eighty - [special] strength; at ninety - [the body] is stooped; at one hundred - it is as if one were dead and had departed and ceased connection with the world.

wisdom that I gained in [the face of] anger endured for me." Therefore, [our Sages] commanded a teacher to project awe to his students, as they said:[116] "Cast fear into the students."

116. *Ketuvot* 103b.
117. This *mishnah* is not included in many authoritative manuscripts and editions of the Commentary on the Mishnah. According to these versions, it is a baraita that was not accepted as binding. Significantly, when discussing the phases of a child's study in *Hilchot Talmud Torah*, Chapter 2, the Rambam makes no reference to the different ages mentioned in this teaching.

Appendix A

CHAPTER SIX

פֶּרֶק שִׁשִּׁי

פֶּרֶק קִנְיַן תּוֹרָה

1. Our Sages taught [this chapter][1] in he language of the Mishnah; blessed is He who chose them and their teaching. Rabbi Meir said: Whoever occupies himself with [the study of] the Torah for its own sake merits many things. Furthermore, he is worthy that the whole world shall have been created because of him. He is called friend, beloved; he loves God, he loves the created beings; he brings joy to God, he brings joy to the created beings. [The Torah] garbs him with humility and fear [of God]. It makes him fit to be righteous, pious, upright and faithful; it keeps him far from sin and brings him near to meritorious deeds.

Others derive from him the benefit of counsel and wisdom, insight and strength, as it is stated:[2] "Counsel and wisdom are mine; I am understanding; strength is mine." [The Torah] bestows upon him royalty, authority, and discerning judgment; the secrets of the Torah are revealed to him, and he becomes like a fountain that flows with ever-increasing strength, and like a never-ceasing stream. He becomes modest, patient and forgiving of insult to himself; and [the Torah] makes him great and exalts him above all things.

שָׁנוּ חֲכָמִים בִּלְשׁוֹן הַמִּשְׁנָה.
בָּרוּךְ שֶׁבָּחַר בָּהֶם וּבְמִשְׁנָתָם.

א רַבִּי מֵאִיר אוֹמֵר: כָּל הָעוֹסֵק
בַּתּוֹרָה לִשְׁמָהּ, זוֹכֶה לִדְבָרִים
הַרְבֵּה. וְלֹא עוֹד, אֶלָּא שֶׁכָּל
הָעוֹלָם כֻּלּוֹ כְּדַאי הוּא לוֹ. נִקְרָא
רֵעַ, אָהוּב, אוֹהֵב אֶת הַמָּקוֹם,
אוֹהֵב אֶת הַבְּרִיוֹת, מְשַׂמֵּחַ אֶת
הַמָּקוֹם, מְשַׂמֵּחַ אֶת הַבְּרִיוֹת.
וּמַלְבַּשְׁתּוֹ עֲנָוָה וְיִרְאָה, וּמַכְשַׁרְתּוֹ
לִהְיוֹת צַדִּיק, וְחָסִיד, יָשָׁר וְנֶאֱמָן,
וּמְרַחַקְתּוֹ מִן הַחֵטְא, וּמְקָרַבְתּוֹ
לִידֵי זְכוּת; וְנֶהֱנִין מִמֶּנּוּ עֵצָה
וְתוּשִׁיָּה, בִּינָה וּגְבוּרָה, שֶׁנֶּאֱמַר:
לִי עֵצָה וְתוּשִׁיָּה, אֲנִי בִינָה לִי גְבוּרָה.
וְנוֹתֶנֶת לוֹ מַלְכוּת וּמֶמְשָׁלָה וְחִקּוּר
דִּין. וּמְגַלִּים לוֹ רָזֵי תוֹרָה,
וְנַעֲשֶׂה כְּמַעְיָן שֶׁאֵינוֹ פוֹסֵק וּכְנָהָר
שֶׁמִּתְגַּבֵּר וְהוֹלֵךְ, וְהֱוֵי צָנוּעַ וְאֶרֶךְ
רוּחַ וּמוֹחֵל עַל עֶלְבּוֹנוֹ, וּמְגַדַּלְתּוֹ
וּמְרוֹמַמְתּוֹ עַל כָּל הַמַּעֲשִׂים.

---

1. As mentioned in the introduction, this chapter is not part of the Talmudic tractate of *Avot*. As such, the Rambam does not include this in his text of the Mishnah, nor does he comment on these teachings.

Instead, the chapter is a collection of *baraitot* ("teachings not included in the Mishnah") which appear in the text *Kallah Rabati,* Chapter 8, and which were appended to this tractate, because of the custom of studying *Pirkei Avot* between Pesach and Shavuot. There are six Sabbaths between these holidays, and with this addition, a

2. Rabbi Yehoshua ben Levi said: Each and every day a Heavenly Voice goes forth from Mount Chorev, proclaiming and saying, "Woe to the created beings because of [their] affront to the Torah!" For whoever does not occupy himself with the Torah is called censured, as it is stated:[3] "[Like] a golden ring in a swine's snout is a beautiful woman who lacks discretion."

And it is further stated:[4] "The Tablets were the work of God, and the writing was the writing of God, engraved (*charut*) on the Tablets." Do not read *charut*, but *cherut* (freedom), for there is no free man except one who occupies himself with the study of the Torah.

And anyone who occupies himself with the study of the Torah becomes elevated, as it is stated:[5] "From Matanah ['the gift'] to Nachliel ['the heritage of God'], and from Nachliel to Bamot ['high places']."

3. He who learns from a colleague a single chapter, a single Torah law, a single verse, a single statement, or even a single letter, must show him honor.

For so we find concerning David, King of Israel, who learned from Achitofel only two things - yet he called him his teacher, his guide, his mentor -

ב אָמַר רַבִּי יְהוֹשֻׁעַ בֶּן לֵוִי: בְּכָל יוֹם וָיוֹם בַּת קוֹל יוֹצֵאת מֵהַר חוֹרֵב וּמַכְרֶזֶת וְאוֹמֶרֶת: אוֹי לָהֶם לַבְּרִיּוֹת מֵעֶלְבּוֹנָהּ שֶׁל תּוֹרָה! שֶׁכָּל מִי שֶׁאֵינוֹ עוֹסֵק בַּתּוֹרָה נִקְרָא נָזוּף, שֶׁנֶּאֱמַר: נֶזֶם זָהָב בְּאַף חֲזִיר, אִשָּׁה יָפָה וְסָרַת טָעַם. וְאוֹמֵר: וְהַלֻּחֹת מַעֲשֵׂה אֱלֹהִים הֵמָּה, וְהַמִּכְתָּב מִכְתַּב אֱלֹהִים הוּא חָרוּת עַל הַלֻּחֹת — אַל תִּקְרָא חָרוּת אֶלָּא חֵרוּת, שֶׁאֵין לְךָ בֶּן חֹרִין אֶלָּא מִי שֶׁעוֹסֵק בְּתַלְמוּד תּוֹרָה. שֶׁכָּל מִי שֶׁעוֹסֵק בַּתּוֹרָה, הֲרֵי זֶה מִתְעַלֶּה, שֶׁנֶּאֱמַר: וּמִמַּתָּנָה נַחֲלִיאֵל, וּמִנַּחֲלִיאֵל בָּמוֹת.

ג הַלּוֹמֵד מֵחֲבֵרוֹ פֶּרֶק אֶחָד, אוֹ הֲלָכָה אַחַת, אוֹ פָּסוּק אֶחָד, אוֹ דִבּוּר אֶחָד, אוֹ אֲפִלּוּ אוֹת אַחַת, צָרִיךְ לִנְהֹג בּוֹ כָּבוֹד; שֶׁכֵּן מָצִינוּ בְדָוִד מֶלֶךְ יִשְׂרָאֵל, שֶׁלֹּא לָמַד מֵאֲחִיתֹפֶל אֶלָּא שְׁנֵי דְבָרִים בִּלְבָד, קְרָאוֹ רַבּוֹ אַלּוּפוֹ וּמְיֻדָּעוֹ,

different chapter could be studied on each Sabbath. This particular chapter, called *Kinyan Torah* ("On the Acquisition of the Torah") is particularly appropriate to be studied on the Sabbath before Shavuot, because it is devoted entirely to the praise of the Torah and its study.

2. Proverbs 8:14.

3. Proverbs 11:22.

4. Exodus 32:16.

5. Numbers 21:19. The *baraita* is offering a homiletic interpretation of the Hebrew names of these places.

as it is stated:[6] "You are a man equal to me; you are my guide and my mentor."

Surely an obvious inference can be drawn: If David, King of Israel, who learned from Achitofel only two things, called him his teacher, his guide, his mentor, one who learns from his peer a single chapter, a single Torah law, a single verse, a single statement, or even a single letter, how much more ought he to treat him with honor.

And honor is due only for the Torah, as it is stated:[7] "The wise shall inherit honor" [and it is stated]:[8] "and the perfect shall inherit good." And the [true] good is only Torah, as it is stated:[9] "I have given you a good Teaching; do not forsake My Torah."

4. This is the way [to acquire] the Torah: Eat bread with salt, drink water in small measure, sleep on the ground, live a life of deprivation and toil in the Torah. If you do this, "you shall be happy, and it shall be well with you."[10] "You shall be happy" - in this world; "and it shall be well with you" - in the World to Come.

5. Do not seek greatness for yourself, and do not desire honor; let your deeds exceed your learning. Do not yearn for the table of kings, for your table is greater than theirs, and your crown is greater than theirs; and your Employer is trustworthy to pay you remuneration for your deeds.

שֶׁנֶּאֱמַר: וְאַתָּה אֱנוֹשׁ כְּעֶרְכִּי אַלּוּפִי וּמְיֻדָּעִי. וַהֲלֹא דְבָרִים קַל וָחֹמֶר: וּמַה דָּוִד מֶלֶךְ יִשְׂרָאֵל, שֶׁלֹּא לָמַד מֵאֲחִיתֹפֶל אֶלָּא שְׁנֵי דְבָרִים בִּלְבַד, קְרָאוֹ רַבּוֹ, אַלּוּפוֹ וּמְיֻדָּעוֹ — הַלּוֹמֵד מֵחֲבֵרוֹ פֶּרֶק אֶחָד, אוֹ הֲלָכָה אַחַת, אוֹ פָסוּק אֶחָד, אוֹ אֲפִלּוּ אוֹת אַחַת, עַל אַחַת כַּמָּה וְכַמָּה שֶׁצָּרִיךְ לִנְהֹג בּוֹ כָבוֹד! וְאֵין כָּבוֹד אֶלָּא תוֹרָה, שֶׁנֶּאֱמַר: כָּבוֹד חֲכָמִים יִנְחָלוּ, וּתְמִימִים יִנְחֲלוּ טוֹב; וְאֵין טוֹב אֶלָּא תוֹרָה, שֶׁנֶּאֱמַר: כִּי לֶקַח טוֹב נָתַתִּי לָכֶם, תּוֹרָתִי אַל תַּעֲזֹבוּ.

ד כָּךְ הִיא דַרְכָּהּ שֶׁל תּוֹרָה: פַּת בַּמֶּלַח תֹּאכַל, וּמַיִם בַּמְּשׂוּרָה תִשְׁתֶּה, וְעַל הָאָרֶץ תִּישַׁן, וְחַיֵּי צַעַר תִּחְיֶה, וּבַתּוֹרָה אַתָּה עָמֵל. וְאִם אַתָּה עוֹשֶׂה כֵּן, אַשְׁרֶיךָ וְטוֹב לָךְ; אַשְׁרֶיךָ בָּעוֹלָם הַזֶּה, וְטוֹב לָךְ לָעוֹלָם הַבָּא.

ה אַל תְּבַקֵּשׁ גְּדֻלָּה לְעַצְמְךָ וְאַל תַּחְמֹד כָּבוֹד. יוֹתֵר מִלִּמּוּדְךָ עֲשֵׂה; וְאַל תִּתְאַוֶּה לְשֻׁלְחָנָם שֶׁל שָׂרִים, שֶׁשֻּׁלְחָנְךָ גָדוֹל מִשֻּׁלְחָנָם וְכִתְרְךָ גָדוֹל מִכִּתְרָם. וְנֶאֱמָן הוּא בַּעַל מְלַאכְתְּךָ שֶׁיְּשַׁלֶּם לְךָ שְׂכַר פְּעֻלָּתֶךָ.

6. Psalms 55:14.   7. Proverbs 3:35.   8. *Ibid.* 28:10.   9. *Ibid.* 4:2.   10. Psalms 128:2.

6. The Torah is greater than priesthood or royalty. For royalty is acquired [together] with thirty virtues, and the priesthood with twenty-four, but for one to acquire the Torah, he must have the following forty-eight virtues:

1) Study, 2) attentive listening, 3) verbal articulation, 4) an understanding heart, 5) dread, 6) awe, 7) humility, 8) joy, 9) purity, 10) serving the sages, 11) close association with colleagues, 12) sharp discussion with students, 13) sobriety, 14) [knowledge of] Scripture [and of] Mishnah, 15) a minimum of business activity, 16) a minimum of preoccupation with worldly matters, 17) a minimum of indulgence in [worldly] pleasure, 18) a minimum of sleep, 19) a minimum of conversation, 20) a minimum of laughter, 21) patience, 22) a good heart, 23) faith in the sages, 24) acceptance of suffering, 25) knowing his place, 26) being happy with his lot, 27) making a fence around his words, 28) remaining modest despite his achievements, 29) being loved [by others], 30) loving God, 31) loving [His] created beings, 32) loving the ways of righteousness, and loving justice, 33) loving reproof, 34) keeping far from honor, 35) not being arrogant while studying, 36) not taking pleasure in handing down [halachic] decisions, 37) bearing the burden with his fellow, 38) judging him favorably [and giving him the benefit of the doubt], 39) establishing him in [the path of] truth, 40) establishing him in [the way of] peace, 41) deliberating in his study, 42) intellectual "give and take", 43) listening and adding [to his

גְּדוֹלָה תוֹרָה מִן הַכְּהֻנָּה
מִן הַמַּלְכוּת; שֶׁהַמַּלְכוּת נִקְנֵית
בִּשְׁלֹשִׁים מַעֲלוֹת, וְהַכְּהֻנָּה
בְּעֶשְׂרִים וְאַרְבַּע, וְהַתּוֹרָה נִקְנֵית
בְּאַרְבָּעִים וּשְׁמוֹנָה דְבָרִים.
אֵלוּ הֵן: בְּתַלְמוּד, בִּשְׁמִיעַת
הָאֹזֶן, בַּעֲרִיכַת שְׂפָתַיִם, בְּבִינַת
הַלֵּב, בְּשִׂכְלוּת הַלֵּב, בְּאֵימָה,
בְּיִרְאָה, בַּעֲנָוָה, בְּשִׂמְחָה,
בְּשִׁמּוּשׁ חֲכָמִים, בְּדִקְדּוּק חֲבֵרִים,
בְּפִלְפּוּל הַתַּלְמִידִים, בְּיִשּׁוּב,
בְּמִקְרָא, בְּמִשְׁנָה, בְּמִעוּט סְחוֹרָה,
בְּמִעוּט שֵׁנָה, בְּמִעוּט תַּעֲנוּג,
בְּמִעוּט שְׂחוֹק, בְּמִעוּט דֶּרֶךְ אֶרֶץ,
בְּאֹרֶךְ אַפַּיִם, בְּלֵב טוֹב, בֶּאֱמוּנַת
חֲכָמִים, בְּקַבָּלַת הַיִּסּוּרִין.
הַמַּכִּיר אֶת מְקוֹמוֹ, וְהַשָּׂמֵחַ
בְּחֶלְקוֹ, וְהָעוֹשֶׂה סְיָג לִדְבָרָיו,
וְאֵינוֹ מַחֲזִיק טוֹבָה לְעַצְמוֹ, אָהוּב,
אוֹהֵב אֶת הַמָּקוֹם, אוֹהֵב אֶת
הַבְּרִיּוֹת, אוֹהֵב אֶת הַצְּדָקוֹת,
אוֹהֵב אֶת הַתּוֹכָחוֹת, אוֹהֵב אֶת
הַמֵּישָׁרִים, מִתְרַחֵק מִן הַכָּבוֹד,
וְלֹא מֵגִיס לִבּוֹ בְּתַלְמוּדוֹ, וְאֵינוֹ
שָׂמֵחַ בְּהוֹרָאָה, נוֹשֵׂא בְעֹל עִם
חֲבֵרוֹ, מַכְרִיעוֹ לְכַף זְכוּת, מַעֲמִידוֹ
עַל הָאֱמֶת, מַעֲמִידוֹ עַל הַשָּׁלוֹם,
מִתְיַשֵּׁב לִבּוֹ בְּתַלְמוּדוֹ, שׁוֹאֵל
וּמֵשִׁיב, שׁוֹמֵעַ וּמוֹסִיף, הַלּוֹמֵד
עַל מְנָת לְלַמֵּד, וְהַלּוֹמֵד עַל

acquired knowledge], 44) studying in order to teach, 45) studying in order to practice, 46) increasing the wisdom of his teacher, 47) properly understanding the intent of what he learns, and 48) quoting a concept in the name of its author.

Indeed, we have learned: Whoever quotes a concept in the name of its author brings redemption to the world, as it is stated:[11] "And Esther told the king in the name of Mordechai."

7. Great is the Torah, for it gives life to those who practice it - both in this world and in the World to Come, as it is stated:[12] "For they [the teachings of the Torah] are life to the one who finds them, and a healing to all his flesh." And it says:[13] "It shall be a remedy to your body and marrow to your bones;" and it is stated:[14] "It is a tree of life to those who hold fast to it, and those who support it are fortunate."

And it [also] says:[15] "They are a garland of grace for your head and a necklace for your neck;" and also:[16] "It will give to your head a garland of grace, a crown of glory will it bestow on you;" and further:[17] "Indeed, through me [the Torah] your days shall be increased, and years of life shall be added to you;" and again:[18] "Long life is at its right, riches and honor at its left;" and also:[19] "Length of days, years of life, and peace shall they add to you."

מְנָת לַעֲשׂוֹת, הַמַּחְכִּים אֶת רַבּוֹ, וְהַמְכַוֵּן אֶת שְׁמוּעָתוֹ, וְהָאוֹמֵר דָּבָר בְּשֵׁם אוֹמְרוֹ. הָא לָמַדְתָּ, שֶׁכָּל הָאוֹמֵר דָּבָר בְּשֵׁם אוֹמְרוֹ מֵבִיא גְאֻלָּה לָעוֹלָם, שֶׁנֶּאֱמַר: וַתֹּאמֶר אֶסְתֵּר לַמֶּלֶךְ בְּשֵׁם מָרְדְּכָי.

ז גְּדוֹלָה תוֹרָה, שֶׁהִיא נוֹתֶנֶת חַיִּים לְעוֹשֶׂיהָ בָּעוֹלָם הַזֶּה וּבָעוֹלָם הַבָּא, שֶׁנֶּאֱמַר: כִּי חַיִּים הֵם לְמֹצְאֵיהֶם וּלְכָל בְּשָׂרוֹ מַרְפֵּא. וְאוֹמֵר: רִפְאוּת תְּהִי לְשָׁרֶךָ וְשִׁקּוּי לְעַצְמוֹתֶיךָ. וְאוֹמֵר: עֵץ חַיִּים הִיא לַמַּחֲזִיקִים בָּהּ וְתֹמְכֶיהָ מְאֻשָּׁר. וְאוֹמֵר: כִּי לִוְיַת חֵן הֵם לְרֹאשֶׁךָ וַעֲנָקִים לְגַרְגְּרֹתֶיךָ. וְאוֹמֵר תִּתֵּן לְרֹאשְׁךָ לִוְיַת חֵן, עֲטֶרֶת תִּפְאֶרֶת תְּמַגְּנֶךָּ. וְאוֹמֵר: אֹרֶךְ יָמִים בִּימִינָהּ, בִּשְׂמֹאולָהּ עֹשֶׁר וְכָבוֹד. וְאוֹמֵר: כִּי אֹרֶךְ יָמִים וּשְׁנוֹת חַיִּים וְשָׁלוֹם יוֹסִיפוּ לָךְ.

ח רַבִּי שִׁמְעוֹן בֶּן מְנַסְיָא אוֹמֵר מִשּׁוּם רַבִּי שִׁמְעוֹן בֶּן יוֹחַאי: הַנּוֹי, וְהַכֹּחַ, וְהָעֹשֶׁר, וְהַכָּבוֹד, וְהַחָכְמָה, וְהַזִּקְנָה, וְהַשֵּׂיבָה, וְהַבָּנִים — נָאֶה לַצַּדִּיקִים וְנָאֶה

8. Rabbi Shimon ben Yehudah said in the name of Rabbi Shimon ben Yochai: Beauty, strength, wealth, honor, wisdom, old age, the grace of white hair, and children, are pleasing for the righteous

---

11. Esther 2:22.   12. Proverbs 4:22.   13. *Ibid.* 3:8.   14. *Ibid.* 3:18.   15. *Ibid.* 1:9.
16. *Ibid.* 4:9.   17. *Ibid.* 9:11.   18. *Ibid.* 3:16.   19. *Ibid.* 3:2.

and pleasing for the world, as it is stated:[20] "The grace of white hair is a crown of glory; it is to be found in the path of righteousness;" and it says:[21] "The glory of young men is their strength, and the beauty of the elderly is the grace of white hair." And it [also] says:[22] "Grandchildren are the crown of the aged, and the glory of children are their fathers;" and also:[23] "The moon shall be abashed and the sun put to shame when the Lord of hosts will reign on Mount Zion and in Jerusalem, and honor shall be before His elders."

Rabbi Shimon ben Menasya said: "These seven qualities that the Sages enumerated [as pleasing for] the righteous were all realized in Rabbi [Rabbi Yehudah Hanasi] and in his sons."

9. Rabbi Yosse ben Kisma said: Once I was walking on the road, when a certain man met me. He greeted me, "Shalom," and I returned his greeting, "Shalom."

He said to me, "Rabbi, from what place are you?"

I said to him, "I am from a great city of scholars and sages."

He said to me, "Rabbi, if you would be willing to live with us in our place, I would give you a million golden *dinarim*, precious stones and pearls."

I replied, "Even if you were to give me all the silver and gold, precious stones and pearls in the world, I would dwell nowhere but in a place of Torah."

לָעוֹלָם, שֶׁנֶּאֱמַר: עֲטֶרֶת תִּפְאֶרֶת שֵׂיבָה, בְּדֶרֶךְ צְדָקָה תִּמָּצֵא. וְאוֹמֵר: עֲטֶרֶת זְקֵנִים בְּנֵי בָנִים, וְתִפְאֶרֶת בָּנִים אֲבוֹתָם. וְאוֹמֵר: תִּפְאֶרֶת בַּחוּרִים כֹּחָם, וַהֲדַר זְקֵנִים שֵׂיבָה. וְאוֹמֵר: וְחָפְרָה הַלְּבָנָה וּבוֹשָׁה הַחַמָּה, כִּי מָלַךְ ה' צְבָאוֹת בְּהַר צִיּוֹן וּבִירוּשָׁלַיִם וְנֶגֶד זְקֵנָיו כָּבוֹד.

רַבִּי שִׁמְעוֹן בֶּן מְנַסְיָא אוֹמֵר: אֵלּוּ שֶׁבַע מִדּוֹת שֶׁמָּנוּ חֲכָמִים לַצַּדִּיקִים, כֻּלָּם נִתְקַיְּמוּ בְרַבִּי וּבְבָנָיו.

ט אָמַר רַבִּי יוֹסֵי בֶן קִסְמָא: פַּעַם אַחַת הָיִיתִי מְהַלֵּךְ בַּדֶּרֶךְ, וּפָגַע בִּי אָדָם אֶחָד וְנָתַן לִי שָׁלוֹם, וְהֶחֱזַרְתִּי לוֹ שָׁלוֹם. אָמַר לִי: רַבִּי, מֵאֵיזֶה מָקוֹם אָתָּה? אָמַרְתִּי לוֹ: מֵעִיר גְּדוֹלָה שֶׁל חֲכָמִים וְשֶׁל סוֹפְרִים אָנִי. אָמַר לִי: רַבִּי, רְצוֹנְךָ שֶׁתָּדוּר עִמָּנוּ בִמְקוֹמֵנוּ, וַאֲנִי אֶתֵּן לְךָ אֶלֶף אֲלָפִים דִּינָרֵי זָהָב וַאֲבָנִים טוֹבוֹת וּמַרְגָּלִיּוֹת? אָמַרְתִּי לוֹ: בְּנִי, אִם אַתָּה נוֹתֵן לִי כָל כֶּסֶף וְזָהָב וַאֲבָנִים טוֹבוֹת וּמַרְגָּלִיּוֹת שֶׁבָּעוֹלָם, אֵינִי דָר אֶלָּא בִמְקוֹם תּוֹרָה, וְכֵן כָּתוּב בְּסֵפֶר תְּהִלִּים

And so it is written in the Book of Psalms by David, King of Israel:[24] "The Torah of Your mouth is more precious to me than thousands of gold and silver [pieces]." Furthermore, at a time of a man's passing from this world, neither silver nor gold nor precious stones nor pearls accompany him, but only Torah [knowledge] and good deeds, as it is stated:[25] "When you walk, it [the Torah] shall guide you; when you lie down, it shall watch over you; and when you awake, it shall speak for you." [This can be interpreted to mean:] "When you walk, it shall guide you - in this world;" "when you lie down, it shall watch over you - in the grave;" "and when you awake, it shall speak for you - in the World to Come."

And it [also] says:[26] "Mine is the silver and Mine is the gold, says the Lord of hosts."

10. Five possessions did the Holy One, blessed be He, make His very own in His world. They are: the Torah is one possession; heaven and earth are one possession; Abraham is one possession; the people Israel is one possession; the Temple is one possession.

From where do we know this concerning the Torah? Since it is written:[27] "God made me [the Torah] His possession prior to Creation, before His works in time of yore."

From where do we know this concerning heaven and earth? Since it is written:[28] "Thus speaks God: The heaven is My throne, and the earth is My footstool; what house [then] can you

עַל יְדֵי דָוִד מֶלֶךְ יִשְׂרָאֵל: טוֹב לִי תוֹרַת פִּיךָ מֵאַלְפֵי זָהָב וָכֶסֶף; שֶׁבִּשְׁעַת פְּטִירָתוֹ שֶׁל אָדָם אֵין מְלַוִּין אוֹתוֹ, לֹא כֶסֶף וְלֹא זָהָב וְלֹא אֲבָנִים טוֹבוֹת וּמַרְגָּלִיּוֹת, אֶלָּא תוֹרָה וּמַעֲשִׂים טוֹבִים בִּלְבַד, שֶׁנֶּאֱמַר: בְּהִתְהַלֶּכְךָ תַּנְחֶה אֹתָךְ, בְּשָׁכְבְּךָ תִּשְׁמֹר עָלֶיךָ, וַהֲקִיצוֹתָ הִיא תְשִׂיחֶךָ. בְּהִתְהַלֶּכְךָ תַּנְחֶה אֹתָךְ — בָּעוֹלָם הַזֶּה, וּבְשָׁכְבְּךָ תִּשְׁמֹר עָלֶיךָ — בַּקֶּבֶר, וַהֲקִיצוֹתָ הִיא תְשִׂיחֶךָ — לָעוֹלָם הַבָּא. וְאוֹמֵר: לִי הַכֶּסֶף וְלִי הַזָּהָב נְאֻם ה' צְבָאוֹת.

י חֲמִשָּׁה קִנְיָנִים קָנָה לוֹ הַקָּדוֹשׁ בָּרוּךְ הוּא בְּעוֹלָמוֹ, וְאֵלּוּ הֵן: תּוֹרָה קִנְיָן אֶחָד, שָׁמַיִם וָאָרֶץ קִנְיָן אֶחָד, אַבְרָהָם קִנְיָן אֶחָד, יִשְׂרָאֵל קִנְיָן אֶחָד, בֵּית הַמִּקְדָּשׁ קִנְיָן אֶחָד.

תּוֹרָה קִנְיָן אֶחָד, מִנַּיִן? דִּכְתִיב: ה' קָנָנִי רֵאשִׁית דַּרְכּוֹ, קֶדֶם מִפְעָלָיו מֵאָז.

שָׁמַיִם וָאָרֶץ קִנְיָן אֶחָד, מִנַּיִן? שֶׁנֶּאֱמַר: כֹּה אָמַר ה' הַשָּׁמַיִם כִּסְאִי וְהָאָרֶץ הֲדֹם רַגְלָי, אֵי זֶה

24. Psalms 119:72.   25. Proverbs 6:22. See Rashi, *loc. cit.*   26. Chaggai 2:8.
27. Proverbs 8:22.   28. Isaiah 66:1.

build for Me and where is the place of
My rest?" And it [also] says:29 "How
manifold are Your works, O Lord! You
have made them all with wisdom; the
earth is full of Your possessions."

From where do we know this
concerning Abraham? Since it is
written:30 "And he blessed him and said:
'Blessed be Abraham by God Most High,
possessor of heaven and earth.'"

From where do we know this
concerning the people Israel? Since it
is written:31 "Until Your people pass
over, O God, until this people You
have acquired pass over;" and it [also]
says:32 "To the holy people who are in
the land and the noble ones - in them is
all My desire."

From where do we know this
concerning the Temple? Since it is
written:33 "The place which You, O
God, have made for Your abode;
the Sanctuary which Your hands, O
God, have established;" and it [also]
says:34 "And He brought them to the
place of His holiness, the mountain that
His right hand has acquired."

11. All that the Holy One, blessed be He,
created in His world, He created solely
for His glory, as it is stated:35 "All that
is called by My Name, indeed, it is for
My glory that I have created it, formed
it and made it"; and it says:36 "God shall
reign forever and ever."

בֵּית אֲשֶׁר תִּבְנוּ לִי וְאֵיזֶה מָקוֹם
מְנוּחָתִי; וְאוֹמֵר: מָה רַבּוּ מַעֲשֶׂיךָ
ה' כֻּלָּם בְּחָכְמָה עָשִׂיתָ מָלְאָה
הָאָרֶץ קִנְיָנֶךָ.

אַבְרָהָם קִנְיָן אֶחָד, מִנַּיִן? דִּכְתִיב:
וַיְבָרְכֵהוּ וַיֹּאמַר, בָּרוּךְ אַבְרָם לְאֵל
עֶלְיוֹן קֹנֵה שָׁמַיִם וָאָרֶץ.

יִשְׂרָאֵל קִנְיָן אֶחָד, מִנַּיִן? דִּכְתִיב:
עַד יַעֲבֹר עַמְּךָ ה' עַד יַעֲבֹר עַם
זוּ קָנִיתָ; וְאוֹמֵר: לִקְדוֹשִׁים אֲשֶׁר
בָּאָרֶץ הֵמָּה וְאַדִּירֵי כָּל חֶפְצִי בָם.
בֵּית הַמִּקְדָּשׁ קִנְיָן אֶחָד, מִנַּיִן?
שֶׁנֶּאֱמַר: מְקֹדָשׁ אֲדֹנָי כּוֹנְנוּ יָדֶיךָ;
וְאוֹמֵר: וַיְבִיאֵם אֶל גְּבוּל קָדְשׁוֹ,
הַר זֶה קָנְתָה יְמִינוֹ.

יא כָּל מַה שֶׁבָּרָא הַקָּדוֹשׁ בָּרוּךְ
הוּא בְּעוֹלָמוֹ לֹא בְרָאוֹ אֶלָּא
לִכְבוֹדוֹ, שֶׁנֶּאֱמַר: כֹּל הַנִּקְרָא
בִשְׁמִי וְלִכְבוֹדִי בְּרָאתִיו יְצַרְתִּיו
אַף עֲשִׂיתִיו; וְאוֹמֵר: ה' יִמְלֹךְ
לְעוֹלָם וָעֶד.

אָמַר רַבִּי חֲנַנְיָא בֶן עֲקַשְׁיָא:
רָצָה הַמָּקוֹם לְזַכּוֹת אֶת יִשְׂרָאֵל,
לְפִיכָךְ הִרְבָּה לָהֶם תּוֹרָה וּמִצְוֹת,
שֶׁנֶּאֱמַר: ה' חָפֵץ לְמַעַן צִדְקוֹ,
יַגְדִּיל תּוֹרָה וְיַאְדִּיר.

29. Psalms 104:24.   30. Genesis 14:19.   31. Exodus 15:16   32. Psalms 16:3.
33. Exodus 15:17.   34. Psalms 78:54.   35. Isaiah 43:7.   36. Exodus 15:18.

Appendix B

The Rambam's Introduction to the tenth chapter of the tractate of *Sanhedrin, Perek Chelek* which contains his Thirteen Principles of Faith

כָּל יִשְׂרָאֵל יֵשׁ לָהֶם חֵלֶק לָעוֹלָם הַבָּא, שֶׁנֶּאֱמַר: וְעַמֵּךְ כֻּלָּם צַדִּיקִים, לְעוֹלָם יִירְשׁוּ אָרֶץ, נֵצֶר מַטָּעַי, מַעֲשֵׂה יָדַי לְהִתְפָּאֵר.

All Israel have a share in the World to Come, as it is stated:[1] "And Your people are all righteous; they shall inherit the land forever. They are the branch of My planting, the work of My hands, in which to take pride."

I find it necessary to take this opportunity to elaborate on many principles of faith that are of great importance. Know that the Torah Sages have differences of opinion about the happiness that a person will attain through the fulfillment of the mitzvot that God commanded us through Moses, and the retribution that will come because of transgressing them. There are many different opinions, depending on their differences in understanding.

This has led to great confusion, to the extent that it is possible that one will not find a person who has clarified this matter for himself. Similarly, one may not find an organized presentation of the concept at all; instead a confusion [of ideas].

There is one approach that maintains that the [ultimate] happiness is the Garden of Eden, and that this is a place where people will eat and drink without any physical exertion or difficulty. There they will have houses built of precious stones, spreads of silk, rivers flowing with wine and spices, and much more of these types [of comforts].

[According to this conception,] retribution refers to Gehinnom. This will be a place of fiery flames where people's bodies are burned, and

1. Isaiah 60:21.

people will be made to suffer many different forms of affliction, as these writers elaborate in their texts. Those who share this approach find many sources in the works of our Sages that appear to support this approach, or at least do so partially.

A second approach believes that the ultimate happiness is the era of the *Mashiach*, may he be revealed speedily. In that era, they maintain, all people will be like kings. Their bodies will wax great and they will live in this world in an eternal manner. According to their conception, the *Mashiach* will live forever, as does the Creator, blessed be He. In that era, the earth will produce clothes that have already been woven, and bread that has already been baked.

They conceive of retribution as being the inability to live in that era, and not meriting to see it. They also cite verses from Scripture and statements of our Sages, which, at least superficially, appear to support their position, or at least do so partially.

A third approach believes that the ultimate happiness is the resurrection of the dead - that after a person's death, he will return and live together with his family and relatives, and eat and drink and never die again. [According to this conception,] the meaning of retribution is not to be resurrected. They also quote certain statements of our Sages and some verses from Scripture to support this position.

The fourth approach imagines that the ultimate happiness to be attained through the observance of the mitzvot is the pleasure of the body and the achievement of worldly attainments in this material setting - i.e., to gain the bounty of the earth, many possessions, large buildings, long years, physical health and security: that we should have sovereignty and reign over our enemies.

[According to this approach, the ultimate] retribution that will come for our disobedience is the opposite of these situations, as is manifest at present in our condition of exile. And they, too, bring support for their position from Scripture, from the blessings and curses and from the stories told in Scripture.

The fifth approach - and this is shared by the multitude of people - combines all these differing views and maintains that [the reward that is] expected is that the *Mashiach* will come, he will resurrect the dead, and then we will enter the Garden of Eden, where we will eat and drink in health forever.

But with regard to the wondrous concept - the World to Come - there are few who think about it, consider it or contemplate this fundamental issue. [By and large, people] do not ask what is meant by this name. Is it the ultimate of good, or is one of the approaches mentioned previously [correct in its appreciation of] the ultimate good? [No] differentiation is made between the ultimate purpose and something that leads to that purpose. There is no one who inquires about this issue or who talks about it.

Instead, people - both individuals and groups - ask questions such as: Will the dead be resurrected naked or clothed? Will they be resurrected in the clothes in which they were buried - with all their embroidery, ornaments and attractive needlework - or with a garment that merely covers their bodies alone? Will the *Mashiach* create equality between the rich and the poor, or will the distinctions between the strong and the weak apply in that era as well? These are the types of questions that are frequently raised.

With you, my reader, I would like to share an analogy, and afterwards pay attention to my words concerning the concept as a whole.[2] Let us assume that a young child were brought to an educator with the intent that he teach the child Torah [knowledge]. This is the ultimate good and will lead the child to perfect his [character]. Nevertheless, because he is young and immature, he will not appreciate that this is good, nor will he see how it will bring him to perfection.

Therefore, it is necessary for the educator, who is himself a more developed personality, to encourage the child by offering something he will appreciate according to his childish conception of things. And so, the educator will tell him: Study and I will give you nuts, figs, or a piece of sugar.

This [promise] will make the child study and try. It is not that he is interested in the study itself - he does not comprehend the value of that at all. He wants to gain the food [he has been promised]. Eating that food is more important for him than the study, and undoubtedly more satisfying. Therefore, he will regard the study as work and effort that he must undergo to receive the object of his desire: the nut or the piece of sugar.

When he grows older and develops his mind, he will view lightly the things that he previously thought were important, and instead will consider other things to be valuable. Therefore, to encourage him to study, he will be promised the things that he then thinks are valuable. For example, his teacher will tell him: Study, and I will buy you attractive shoes or clothes that look like this. Then also, he will not

2. I.e., the Rambam's intent is, as he states, to explain the concept of the World to Come, for this is a central point in the *mishnah* concerning which he is commenting. To explain that concept, he feels it necessary to preface his remarks by emphasizing our Sages' stress on the need for selfless divine service.

be studying for the sake of study, but instead to receive the promised garment. The clothes are more important to him than his study. Indeed, they are the object of his study.

When his mind becomes more developed, and he understands enough to regard these things as negligible, he will be encouraged to study [by promises of] things that are more valuable. His teacher will tell him: Study this passage or this chapter and I will give you a *dinar* or two *dinarim*. Even at that stage, he will be studying and applying effort for the sake of obtaining the money, and he will regard obtaining the money as more important than the study itself. For [in his mind], the ultimate purpose of the study is to obtain the money he was promised.

And when he reaches a deeper level of understanding, and knows to appreciate even this matter, [money,] as having little importance, he will be encouraged by something that is of even greater eminence. He will be told: Study so that you will become a Rabbi or a judge, and others will honor you. They will stand before you, endeavor to uphold your words and enhance your reputation, both in your lifetime and afterwards, like so and so, and so and so. And so he will study to reach this position; the ultimate in his mind will be that other people will honor him, elevate him and praise him.

All this is shameful. Nevertheless, it is necessary, because of the capricious nature of man, who makes the ultimate goal of study something else than the study itself, and who says: why am I studying? To gain [something I want - i.e., he takes] a facetious [approach to] truth.

Our Sages called this *shelo lishmah*, "not for the sake [of the Torah] itself" - i.e., the person observes the mitzvot and performs them, studies and tries, not for the sake of [the Torah and mitzvot] themselves, but for another purpose. Our Sages warned against this, saying:[3] "Do not make [the Torah] a crown for self-aggrandizement, nor an axe with which to cut." This means, as I explained above, that the ultimate goal of study should not be to receive honor from people or to acquire wealth. A person should not make God's Torah his livelihood.

Instead, the purpose of study should be knowledge, and the ultimate purpose of truth should be to know that it is true. The mitzvot are true; therefore, their purpose is their performance. It is therefore forbidden for a person who has developed his character to say: I have done these good deeds, and I have abstained from those evil deeds that God has warned against. What then will be my reward?

3. *Avot* 4:7. Note the Rambam's commentary on that teaching.

This is like a child's saying: I have studied. What will you give me? He will be told "such and such" [- i.e., a material reward]. Since we see his lack of intellectual development, that he does not appreciate the value of [study] and instead seeks [to substitute] another purpose for the [ultimate] purpose, we reply to him according to his capriciousness, as it is written:[4] "Answer a fool according to his folly."

Our Sages already advised us about this matter - i.e., not to consider the purpose of one's divine service and fulfillment of the mitzvot to be any particular entity - as reflected in the statement of the perfect pious man who perceived the truth, Antigonus of Socho:[5] "Do not be like servants who serve their master for the sake of receiving a grant, but rather be like servants who serve their master without the intent of receiving a grant." With this, he desired to say: Believe in the truth because it is the truth. Our Sages referred to this as "service out of love."[6] And on the verse,[7] "Desire His commandments very much," Rabbi Eleazar commented:[8] "[Desire] His commandments, and not the reward for His commandments." How great and clear a support for the concepts we mentioned are these quotes.

And there is an even greater support from the *Sifre*[9], which states:

Shall a person say: I will study the Torah so that I will become wealthy,... so that I will be called "Rabbi,"... so that I will receive a reward in the World to Come. Behold, it is written: "to love God your Lord." Everything that you do, do only out of love.

This concept is thus explained, and it has been clarified that this is the fundamental goal of the Torah and the intent of our Sages. The only one who will ignore this is a fool, whose conceptions have already been damaged by inane thoughts and tainted ideas.

The positive expression of this quality was personified by Abraham, who served God out of love, and we are obligated to strive for this ideal. Our Sages knew that this approach is difficult and cannot be achieved by all people. [Moreover,] even one who achieves it will not accept it at the outset, and initially will not regard it to be a true principle. For, by nature, a person will not perform a deed unless it will bring him benefit or prevent harm. Indeed, if this were not true, a person's deeds would be purposeless. How could we possibly say to a person

4. Proverbs 26:5.
5. *Avot* 1:3. Note the Rambam's commentary on that teaching.
6. In this context, see also *Hilchot Teshuvah*, Chapter 10.
7. Psalms 112:1.
8. *Avodah Zarah* 19a.
9. Commenting on Deuteronomy 11:13.

who occupies himself with the Torah: "Perform these deeds," or "Do not perform these deeds" - not out of fear of Divine retribution, nor out of hope of receiving a reward from Him? This is very difficult. For people at large do not perceive the truth to the extent [that their level of service resembles that] of our patriarch Abraham.

Therefore, [the Torah] permits people at large to remain with their [preconceived] opinions, to do good out of a desire for reward, and to eschew evil out of the fear of punishment. Indeed, they are encouraged to believe this, and this conception is strengthened until [they develop their knowledge] and appreciate the nature of the truth and the path to perfection, as is done to a child, as I mentioned in the allegory above.

Indeed, the Sages reproved Antigonus of Socho for communicating his insight to the people at large. In this regard, our Sages said: "Sages, be careful with your words," as we will explain in *Avot*.[10] [In this way,] the people at large do not lose entirely, for they fulfill the mitzvot out of fear of punishment and hope for reward; it is just that they are not developed. It is preferable that they follow this path, so that they sensitize themselves and acquire traits that prepare them to uphold the Torah. [One hopes they will ultimately] appreciate the truth and serve [God] out of love. This is implied by our Sages' statement:[11] "A person should always occupy himself with the Torah, even when his intent is not for the Torah itself. For from service that is not for the Torah itself, is born service that is for the sake of the Torah itself."

[One further preface is necessary.][12] There are three approaches taken concerning statements of our Sages [that appear to contradict the principles of logic]. The first approach is that of most people whom I have met, whose texts I have seen, and about whom I have heard. They understand [our Sages'] statements literally, and do not attempt to explain them [and extend their meanings] at all. They consider all the things that are logically impossible as what must be absolutely true.

10. *Avot* 1:11. Note the Rambam's commentary on that *mishnah*, where he refers to the undesirable effect that the words of Antigonus had on his students, Tzadok and Boethus.
11. *Sanhedrin* 105b.
12. I.e., before speaking about the concept of the World to Come, the Rambam feels it necessary to emphasize the importance of appreciating our Sages' statements as allegories and analogies when necessary, and therefore to understand that they should be accepted in the abstract, rather than literally.

They do this only as a result of their inexperience with wisdom and their distance from science. They have not developed themselves to the point where they feel motivated to seek [a deeper conception] themselves, nor have they found anyone else to motivate them. Therefore, they think that our Sages' intent in their wise statements was only what these people could themselves perceive - i.e., the simple meaning of our Sages' words.

Certain of our Sages' statements may appear strange and farfetched to the extent that if their simple meanings were told to the common people - let alone to the sophisticates - they would be startled and would exclaim: How is it possible that there exists a person who imagines these things and believes them to be true? Needless, to say, such words would not find favor in their eyes.

The people who follow this approach are truly pathetic - may God have mercy on their foolishness. According to their conception, they are elevating the Sages, while in truth they are denigrating them utterly,[13] and yet they are unaware of their effects.

As God lives, this approach destroys the glory of the Torah and dims its radiance. It distorts and perverts God's Torah, causing it to be appreciated in opposition to its intent. For with regard to the wisdom of His Torah, God has said:[14] "When the nations will hear of all these statutes, [and they will say: 'A wise and understanding people...']." But when the people who follow this approach expound on the literal meaning of our Sages' words, those who hear them will say: "A foolish and perverse people is this puny nation."

Many of the preachers do this in their attempts to educate the people about that which they themselves do not understand. Would it be that they would remain silent, for they do not understand. "O that you would all keep silent. It would be [an act of] wisdom."[15] At the very least, they should say: we do not know our Sages' intent in these statements, or what their meaning is.

Instead, they think that they do understand, and place themselves in a position to convey to the people what they understood, but not what the Sages said. They expound upon the homiletic content of the tractate of *Berachot*, that of the chapter of *Chelek*,[16] and the like

---

13. I.e., by ascribing such ideas to the Sages, they are causing people at large to lose respect for them.
14. Deuteronomy 4:6.
15. Job 13:5.
16. The tenth chapter of the tractate of *Sanhedrin* (eleventh as the tractate appears in

literally, word for word [without seeking to understand or interpret the symbolism the Sages employed].

The second approach - and there are also many who follow it - saw or heard the words of our Sages and understood them literally. They also imagined that the Sages had no deeper intent than the literal meaning of their words. As a result, they belittle and malign them, deeming bizarre that which is not at all bizarre. They ridicule the words of the Sages frequently, and consider themselves to be more intelligent and clearer thinkers than they. They deem our Sages to be fools, men with no understanding, and utterly witless, as if they never understood anything at all.

The majority of those who follow this approach are physicians and astrologers, who see themselves as clever men of wisdom and philosophers. How distant from humanity are they when compared to those who are truly wise and philosophical! They are even more foolish and more inane than those who follow the first approach. They are a cursed persuasion who flare out against men of lofty character, whose wisdom was appreciated by the wise.

Had these [misguided individuals] trained themselves in science to the extent that they knew how to explain metaphysical concepts and the like to the common people and to the Sages, and had they trained themselves in the practical application of philosophy, they would understand whether or not our Sages were wise. And they would understand the intent of our Sages' words.

The third approach - and indeed, as God lives, the number of people who follow it are so few, it can hardly be called a persuasion, just as the sun cannot be called a species, for it is unique - is followed by people who have been impressed by the greatness of our Sages and the excellence of their wisdom, from having discovered statements that reflect profound truths within their teachings as a whole.

Although these [truths] are dispersed throughout [our Sages'] texts, they show their personal development and their comprehension of the truth. Similarly, [these people] have appreciated that certain situations are impossible, and that certain rules always prevail. They appreciate that the Sages did not speak empty words, and they understand that their words contain both a simple meaning and deeper secrets. Thus, whenever [our Sages] made a statement mentioning things that could not possibly have occurred, they understood that these were merely allegories and analogies.

the Talmud). In the Rambam's Commentary on the Mishnah, the present text serves as a preface for that chapter.

This is the manner in which great sages speak, and therefore the greatest of the wise men opened his book with the statement:[17] "To understand an analogy and a proverb, the words of the wise and their allegories." And, as is known to the master linguists, the intent of the word חידה, allegory or riddle, is a message whose meaning is hidden and is not revealed in its literal meaning, as reflected in the verse,[18] "Let me propose a riddle (חידה) for you." For when all the masters of wisdom would speak about abstract matters, which are the ultimate [goal of wisdom], they would speak in allegories and analogies.

Why then should one wonder that [our Sages] communicated their wisdom through allegories, despite the fact that some would interpret them to be lowly and common matters? We see that the wisest of all men, Solomon, did so, inspired by the spirit of prophecy in the Book of Proverbs, in the Song of Songs and in portions of Ecclesiastes. Why then should we consider it foreign to interpret our Sages' words in this fashion, understanding them in the abstract, so that they will befit their intellectual content, reflect the truth and be germane to Scripture?

Indeed, we find that [our Sages] would interpret Scripture in this manner, abstracting the content beyond the literal meaning and explaining it as allegories - and this is the true approach. For example, the verse states:[19] "And he smote the two lionhearted men of Moab" - this is all an analogy,[20] as is the continuation of the verse, "and he slew the lion in the cistern on the day of the snowstorm."[21] Similarly, the request,[22] "O that someone would draw water for me from the cistern of Bethlehem," and the remainder of the subsequent narrative is interpreted as an allegory.[23] Similarly, one of the Sages stated[24] that the entire Book of Job is an allegory. The intent of this allegory is not

---

17. Proverbs 1:6.
18. Judges 14:12.
19. II Samuel 23:20; I Chronicles 11:22.
20. See *Berachot* 18b, which interprets this praise of Benayahu as meaning that no person of his caliber arose in either the First or Second Temple era.
21. *Berachot, ibid.*, interprets this to be a reference to the fact that he broke ice to immerse himself in purification after a seminal emission. Alternatively, that he studied the *Sifra*, the most difficult of the texts of Biblical exegesis, on a winter day.
22. II Samuel 23:15; I Chronicles 11:17.
23. *Bava Kama* 60b interprets this to be a reference to clarification on a point of Torah law that David sought from the elders of Bethlehem.
24. *Bava Batra* 15a quotes an opinion stating that the entire story of Job never occurred and that it is only an allegory.

explained.[25] Similarly, [the narrative of the resurrection of] the dead by Ezekiel is interpreted as an allegory by one of the Sages.[26]

If you, my reader, follow one of the first two approaches, do not pay any attention to my words about this matter, for they will not suit your thinking. On the contrary, they will embitter you and cause you to hate them. For how could food that is light in substance, but high in quality, be attractive to a person who has already accustomed himself to eating heavy, bad foods? [Such foods] will cause him only harm and he will hate them. For example, people who were used to eating onions, garlic and fish said[27] of the manna, "We are disgusted by this loathsome bread."

But if you follow the third approach, and thus, whenever you encounter a statement of [our Sages] that reason rejects, contemplate the matter at length, knowing that it is an allegory or an analogy. Concentrate your energies, both emotional and intellectual, on understanding it. Endeavor to find the path of truth and a straightforward conception, as it is written,[28] "To find desirable words and to write the words of truth in a straightforward manner." [With this approach,] consider this text, and it will bring you benefit with God's help.

I will now begin to explain the subject in question. Know that just as a blind man cannot conceive of color, nor a deaf person of sound, nor a eunuch of the desire for sex, so too, the body cannot appreciate the pleasure of the soul. Just as the fish do not know the element of fire - for they live in the midst of its very opposite - so too, it is impossible to appreciate spiritual pleasure in this physical world.

We possess no form of pleasure other than the physical and the sensory satisfaction that is derived from eating, drinking, or sex. Anything other than this is a non-entity; we do not recognize it, nor can we understand it at first glance, but only after substantial exploration. The reason for this is that we live in a physical world, and it is therefore only its pleasures that we can appreciate.

Spiritual pleasures, by contrast, are constant, never to be interrupted. There is no form of comparison between these [spiritual forms of

25. Concerning the interpretation of Job, see the Guide for the Perplexed, Vol. II, Chapters 21-22.
26. *Sanhedrin* 92b.
27. Numbers 21:5.
28. Ecclesiastes 12:10.

pleasure] and [physical] pleasure. Nevertheless, it would be improper for the masters of the Torah and the metaphysical philosophers to say that [spiritual entities,] the angels, the stars and the heavenly orbits29 do not enjoy pleasure. Instead, they do enjoy great pleasure, stemming from their comprehension of the Creator, blessed be He. This generates constant and uninterrupted pleasure for them. They have no sense of physical pleasure and cannot conceive of it, for they do not have [physical] senses to enable them to perceive what we perceive.

Similar concepts apply when a person has refined himself and reaches such a rung [in the spiritual worlds] after his death; he will not comprehend physical pleasure, and will have no desire for it. [To do so could be compared to] a powerful king leaving his kingship and going back to playing ball in the streets of the city. Although surely there was a time when he preferred to play ball rather than deal with the affairs of the kingdom, this was when he was immature and had not learned to distinguish between the nature of the two matters. In the same way, we glorify and give greater regard to the pleasures of the body than to the pleasures of the soul.

If you contemplate these two forms of pleasure, you will appreciate the baseness of the one and the supremacy of the other, even in this [material] world. This is obvious from the fact that most people - and perhaps all people - will expend prodigious psychological and physical energies in order to attain position and honor in the eyes of others. This pleasure is not physical pleasure, such as eating and drinking. Similarly, many people choose to seek revenge on their enemies rather than indulge themselves in physical pleasure. And we find that many people eschew the greatest of physical pleasures out of fear that this will bring them shame and embarrassment in the eyes of people, or because they desire to enhance their reputation.

If this is our situation in the material world, surely this applies in the spiritual world, the World to Come,30 where our souls will be able

29. The Rambam is following the conception, reaffirmed in *Hilchot Yesodei HaTorah* 3:9, that the heavenly bodies are not merely inert objects, but rather conscious beings, each containing a soul that appreciates Godliness in a manner that surpasses the comprehension of humans.
30. At this point, the Rambam explains - as he promised at the outset - the meaning of the term "the World to Come," interpreting it to be referring to the afterlife of the souls in the spiritual realms. It must be emphasized that the term World to Come is used by other authorities to refer to the Era of the Resurrection.

to perceive the Creator in the manner in which the heavenly bodies perceive Him, and in an even more refined manner. The pleasure [that this conception will bring] cannot be parceled or described, nor can an analogy be given to define it, as the prophet exclaims in his amazement over the greatness of this good, as it is written:[31] "How great is the good that You have hidden away for those who fear You." And similarly, our Sages said:[32] "In the World to Come, there is neither eating, nor drinking, nor bathing, nor anointment, nor sex. [All that will be is] the righteous sitting with crowns on their heads, deriving pleasure from the radiance of the Divine Presence."

[The statement is an analogy.] With the expression, "crowns on their heads," they meant the endurance of the soul through the endurance of the subject it conceived,[33] for it and the soul are one, as the finest of the philosophers[34] have mentioned and elaborated in their explanations on this subject.

With the expression, "deriving pleasure from the radiance of the Divine Presence," they meant that these souls derive satisfaction from their conception of the Creator as the holy *chayyot*,[35] and the other levels of angels derive benefit from their comprehension of His existence. The ultimate satisfaction and most consummate purpose is to reach this exalted station and for the soul to exist forever, as the Creator does. He becomes the reason for the soul's endurance, for the soul comprehends His [Being], as explained in the first of the texts of philosophy.[36]

The differences between those authorities and the Rambam in this matter are twofold: a) a difference in terminology, and b) a difference of emphasis. For the Rambam considers the afterlife the ultimate goal of existence, while the other authorities view the Era of the Resurrection as that aspiration. See *Hilchot Teshuvah*, Chapter 8, and *Sha'ar HaG'mul* of the Ramban, which comments on it.

31. Psalms 31:20.

32. *Berachot* 17a. See *Hilchot Teshuvah* 8:2, and the Guide for the Perplexed, Vol. I, Chapter 68, where the Rambam also discusses this quote in a similar fashion.

33. The Rambam explains in the Guide for the Perplexed, *loc. cit.*, that before a person conceives of an idea, he and the idea are two separate entities. After he has comprehended the matter, however, his mind has become fused with the concept and is unified with it. Taking that concept a step further, when the soul leaves the body, the knowledge that it had conceived remains constant and true, existing forever.

34. The commentaries maintain that the Rambam is referring to the Arab philosophers Alfarabi and Ibn Sına.

35. See *Hilchot Yesodei HaTorah* 2:7, which explains that the holy *chayyot* are the most exalted of the angels.

36. I.e., Nicomethean Ethics, Discourse 10, Chapter 7.

This is the ultimate of good to which no good can be compared, nor can any pleasure be likened to it. For how can there be any comparison between that which is eternal and endless, and any temporal matter? This is alluded to in God's promise,[37] "so that good will be granted to you and your days will be prolonged." The Oral Tradition, as recorded by our Sages,[38] explains: "'Good will be granted to you,' in the realm that is all good. 'Your days will be prolonged,' in the realm that is eternally long."

Conversely, the ultimate retribution is that the soul will be cut off and will not endure. This is the meaning of the term כרת used by the Torah.[39] The cutting off of the soul is mentioned in the verse:[40] "That soul will surely be cut off (הכרת תכרת)." Our Sages [noted the repetition of the wording and] commented:[41] "הכרת in this world. תכרת in the World to Come."

Scripture states:[42] "May the soul of my master be bound in the bond of life" [- i.e., bound with God in eternal life]. When, however, a person immerses himself in physical pleasure, ignoring the truth and favoring the false, [his soul] will be cut off from that lofty [state] and will remain merely as severed matter. For, as the prophet explained, the World to Come cannot be appreciated by our physical senses, as it is written,[43] "No eye has seen that a power aside from You will do such things for one who awaits." And in explanation of this verse, our Sages said:[44] All the visions of the prophets apply only to the era of the *Mashiach*. To the World to Come is applied the verse, "No eye has seen...."

[Having established that the true reward is the life of the World to Come,] it is necessary to clarify the promises [of reward] and the opposite found in the Torah. These can be explained as follows: It is as if God said: "If you observe these commandments, I will help you to do so, and thus [enable you to reach] perfection. I will remove from you all hindrances." For it is impossible for a person to serve God when

---

37. Deuteronomy 22:7.
38. *Kiddushin* 39b.
39. *Mo'ed Katan* 28a states that a person liable for *karet* will die before he becomes fifty. Nevertheless, as the Rambam emphasizes, the fundamental dimension of this punishment is not physical death, but the soul's being cut off in the World to Come. (See also *Hilchot Teshuvah*, Chapter 8.)
40. Numbers 15:31.
41. *Sanhedrin* 64b.
42. I Samuel 25:29.
43. Isaiah 64:3.
44. *Berachot* 34b.

he is sick, starving, thirsty or confronted by war. Therefore, the Torah promises that all such factors will be removed, that [its adherents] will be healthy and live in prosperity, so they can perfect their knowledge and merit the life of the World to Come.

Thus, the intent of the Torah is not material prosperity, long life and health. It is only that these factors [will be granted] because they aid in its observance.

Similarly, if people transgress [the Torah's laws], the punishment they will be given is that they will be confronted with all these difficulties, so that they will not be able to do good, as implied by the verse,[45] "Because you did not serve God [with happiness during the abundance of good, you will serve your enemies]."

When you contemplate this wondrous concept, you will appreciate that if you perform some of the mitzvot with love and zeal, God will help you perform the others by removing all the obstructions and hindrances. Conversely, if you neglect the observance of some of them out of contempt, God will bring you obstructions that will prevent you from fulfilling any of them. Thus, you will not attain personal development, nor will your [soul] endure. This is the intent of our Sages' statement,[46] "the reward for a mitzvah is the mitzvah, and the recompense for a transgression is a transgression."

The Garden of Eden[47] is a luscious place in this material world, with a warm climate and many trees. God will reveal this place to men in the future, showing them the way to it. There they will derive pleasure. Perhaps in this place they will discover plants that can bring greater benefit and offer greater pleasure than those known to us at

---

45. Deuteronomy 28:47. The Rambam's intent is that the verse is a statement of causality. Because the Jews did not serve God when they had the opportunity, they were punished by exile, where divine service is more difficult.
46. *Avot* 4:2 - i.e., the performance of one mitzvah will lead to the observance of others.
47. The Rambam continues with the objective he mentioned at the beginning of this section to explain the terms: the World to Come, the Garden of Eden, Hell, the Resurrection and the era of the *Mashiach*.

He interprets the Garden of Eden to be referring to the place in this world in which the narrative of Adam and Eve took place, and to which man will return in the future. It must be emphasized that other Rabbis interpret the term "Garden of Eden" to be referring to the spiritual world of the souls, the realm the Rambam refers to with the term "the World to Come." The differences between these approaches are largely semantic, for both opinions maintain that the Garden of Eden is an actual physical place, and both speak of the afterlife of the soul.

present. All this is by no means impossible or farfetched. On the contrary, the possibility of the existence of such a realm is eminent, even had it not been mentioned by the Torah. Surely [one can believe in it] after it has been mentioned in the Torah, and [its existence] has been publicized.

Gehinnom (Hell) is a term used to refer to the pain that will be visited upon the wicked. The Talmud does not describe the nature of that pain. There are some who say[48] that the sun will approach them and consume them in flames. They draw support from the verse:[49] "Behold the day is coming, burning as an oven." Others interpret[50] it as a strange fever that will begin in their bodies and burn them. As support, they cite the verse:[51] "Your spirit, fire will consume you."

The resurrection of the dead is one of the fundamental principles of the Torah taught by Moses. A person who does not believe in this has no faith, nor does he share any bond with Judaism.

[The resurrection] will be [only] for the righteous. As *Bereishit Rabbah* states:[52] "The mighty rains are for the righteous and for the wicked. The resurrection of the dead is only for the righteous." How could one say that the wicked would be resurrected? They are as dead even during their lifetime, as our Sages said,[53] "The wicked are considered dead during their lifetime, and the righteous are considered alive even after their death." You must know that inevitably [all] men will die and [the elements of their bodies] will separate and return to their uncompounded state.

The era of the *Mashiach*, by contrast, is a time when kingship will return to Israel, and [the Jews] will return to *Eretz Yisrael*. The king who arises will rule from Zion, and his reputation will become great, extending to the ends of the earth, even beyond that of King Solomon. The nations will establish a covenant of peace with him, and all lands will serve him because of his great righteousness. Wonders will be revealed by him. Whoever stands up against him will be cut down by God and given over to his hand. Very many verses in Scripture testify to the success he will find, and the success with which he will endow us.

48. See *Sanhedrin* 110b.
49. Malachi 3:19.
50. *Sanhedrin* 108a.
51. Isaiah 33:11.
52. *Bereishit Rabbah* 13:6. Our text of *Bereishit Rabbah* differs slightly. See the *Yefei To'ar* and *Ta'anit* 7a, which substantiate the Rambam's version.
53. *Berachot* 18b.

[During the era of the *Mashiach,*] the natural order will not change from the present, except that kingship will return to Israel. As our Sages said:[54] "There is no difference between the present era and that of the *Mashiach* except [the end of Israel's] subjugation [to the gentile] kingdoms." In his days, there will still be those who are weak and those who are strong.

[What differences will there be?] In that era, it will be very easy for men to earn their livelihood. A person will perform only a small amount of work and reap great benefit from it. This is what our Sages meant by their statement,[55] "In the future, *Eretz Yisrael* will produce pastry and ready-made garments." [This is an analogy,] as people will say when a person finds an abundant source of readily usable objects, "So and so has found bread already baked and food already cooked."

Proof [that this is an analogy] can be brought from the verse:[56] "The sons of foreigners will be your plowmen and vine dressers," implying that there will be plowing and harvesting [as in the present era]. For this reason, [Rabban Gamliel,] the wise man who made the above statement [concerning pastry], became upset at his student, who did not comprehend his intent, and thought that the concept was to be understood literally. Accordingly, [Rabban Gamliel] answered him according to his [underdeveloped] conception and did not give him the true answer. The proof that the answer he gave him was not the truth is the mention of this concept in the discussion of the verse,[57] "Do not answer a fool according to his folly."

The great benefit that will be achieved in that age is that we will be able to rest from the rule of the wicked nation that prevents us from performing good deeds. [In that era,] knowledge will increase, as it is written,[58] "And the earth will be full with the knowledge of

---

54. *Berachot* 34b; *Sanhedrin* 99a. The Rambam repeats these statements in the *Mishneh Torah, Hilchot Melachim* 12:1-2. Many other commentaries differ and state that the coming of the *Mashiach* will be accompanied by miracles. The Rambam himself admits such a possibility in *Iggeret Teiman.* See the Moznaim edition of *Hilchot Melachim* for a detailed explanation of the subject.
55. *Shabbat* 30b. One cannot help commenting how close the statement is to being fulfilled in actual fact through the breakthroughs of microbiology.
56. Isaiah 61:5.
57. Proverbs 26:4. It appears that the Rambam's intent is the verse that follows: "Answer a fool according to his folly." *Shabbat, loc. cit.,* discusses the interpretation of these two verses, and Rabban Gamliel's statements are explained in this context.
58. Isaiah 11:9.

God." The wars and battles will cease, as it is written:[59] "Nation will not lift up sword against nation." All those who are alive in that era will attain great fulfillment and will attain a portion in the World to Come.

The *Mashiach* will die. Afterwards, his son will rule and then his grandson.[60] God alludes to his death in the verse,[61] "He will not fail nor be discouraged until he establishes judgment in the earth." His rule will continue for an extended period, and the life span of people will be lengthened. For when worries and troubles are removed, life will be extended. It would not be remarkable for his reign to last thousands of years,[62] for, as the wise man said,[63] "When an excellent composite is achieved, it will not dissolve quickly."

We do not desire the era of the *Mashiach* in order to benefit from an abundance of produce or property, nor in order to ride on horses and drink wine abundantly, listening to music as some of the confused people think. Instead, the reasons the prophets desired this era and the pious yearned for it, were for the results that will come about from the synergy of the righteous, and [the outgrowths of] their good and wise conduct, the justice practiced by the King [*Mashiach*], his prodigious wisdom and his closeness to his Creator, as reflected in God's statement to him,[64] "You are My son."

[Then] the totality of Moses' law will be observed without worry, fear or compulsion, as implied by the promises,[65] "A person will no longer teach his friend... for they will all know Me, from the small to the great, and I will place My Torah in your hearts," "I will remove the heart of stone from your flesh," and many similar verses.

In such a situation, a portion of the World to Come will be attained with strength. The ultimate purpose [of everything] is to attain the World to Come, and to this goal our effort should be directed. Therefore the wise man [Rabbi Yehudah HaNasi, the redactor of the

---

59. Michah 4:3.
60. The Rambam appears to be referring to the statement (*Sanhedrin* 99a) that the era of the *Mashiach* will last three generations.
61. Isaiah 42:4. The implication is that after the *Mashiach* succeeds in fulfilling his mission, he will "fail" - i.e., die.
62. See *Sanhedrin* 99a, which mentions one opinion that maintains that the era of the *Mashiach* will last seven thousand years.
63. Nicomethean Ethics, Discourse 8, Chapter 13.
64. Psalms 2:7.
65. Jeremiah 31:33.

Mishnah], who comprehended the truth, focused on the ultimate goal and did not pay attention to any other matters. He stated:

All Israel have a share in the World to Come - Although this is the ultimate goal, it is not fitting for a person who desires to serve God from love to serve Him in order to attain a portion of the World to Come, as explained above. Instead, one should follow the path of divine service to be explained.

For if a person believes that there is knowledge transmitted by God to the prophets, revealing what is virtuous and what is a failing, because he is an earnest person he should feel obligated to seek to attain the virtues and eschew the failings. If he follows this course of action, he will perfect his human potential and distinguish himself from the beasts. And for a developed human, it is natural that there will be no obstructions holding back his soul from enduring together with the intellectual truths [which he perceives]; this being the World to Come, as we explained.

This is implied by the verse,[66] "Be not like the horse or the mule, which have no understanding..." - i.e., for [the animals] what restrains their wildness is an external factor: a bit or a bridle. For a human, the only factor that restrains him should be his soul - i.e., his human qualities. If he is a developed individual, this will prevent him from indulging in the shortcomings that prevent him from reaching perfection, and it will encourage him to attain the virtues that lead him to perfection. This is my conception of these lofty truths that are perilous [and require care lest one err].

I intend to compose a text that will collect all the homilies that are found in the Talmud and the other texts, and explain them in a manner that reflects the truth. I will bring proofs for all these matters, and reveal those that are to be understood literally, those that are analogies, and those that were seen in dreams, but were related as if they happened in actual life.

In this text, I will explain many fundamental points of faith, and there I will explain all the points that I have mentioned here [in brief, citing] examples from which other concepts can be derived.[67] One

66. Psalms 32:9.

67. As he writes in the introduction to the Guide for the Perplexed, the Rambam began writing such a text, explaining the various analogies given by our Sages. In the midst of this work, he terminated the project, for he felt that it would not be right to reveal what the Sages had concealed. And if he had explained through parables and

should not look at my words with exacting meticulousness, comparing them to the words and concepts explained by the men of wisdom. For I purposely was not meticulous in these matters, in order to make my words accessible to a person who was not trained in the study of these lofty matters, which cannot be grasped by everyone.

[The Rambam continues, explaining various concepts pertaining to the second clause of the *mishnah* from *Sanhedrin*. Afterwards, he states:]

It is appropriate to mention here - and this is the most appropriate place [in this text] to mention the following points - the essential [beliefs] of our sacred Torah and its fundamental principles of faith. There are thirteen fundamental principles:

The first fundamental principle[68] is the existence of the Creator - i.e., the existence of a Being who is perfect in all manners of perfection. He is the cause of the existence of all other beings, and from Him they derive their continued existence. If one imagined that His existence would cease, all other existence would be nullified and would no longer continue to be. Conversely, however, if all other existence ceased, He would continue to exist and would not be lacking, for He is not dependent on any being other than Himself. Everything in existence other than Him, [even] the entities whose existence is on the plane of intellect - e.g., the angels and the forms of the orbits - and surely, the lower [forms of existence] depend on Him for their being. This is the first fundamental principle, and it is alluded to in the commandment,[69] "I am God, your Lord."

The second fundamental principle is His oneness,[70] that this Cause of all being is one. [This oneness] cannot be compared to the oneness of a species or of a general category [that includes many different entities], nor is it a oneness that is a composite that can be divided

analogies, what he would have been doing would be exchanging one analogy for another. Nevertheless, certain portions of the work were included in the Guide for the Perplexed.
68. See *Hilchot Yesodei HaTorah* 1:1-6. The foundation of faith in God is that He is the perfection of Being. If He were a power that is merely somewhat - or even very much - greater than we are, it would be incorrect to ascribe divinity to Him. Only because He is perfect - and the nature of His perfection is beyond our conception - it is proper to consider Him God.
69. Exodus 20:2.
70. See *Hilchot Yesodei HaTorah* 1:7. If God were not one, there would be another entity that could somehow be compared to Him, and thus there would be no concept of absolute divinity.

into different elements. Neither is it a oneness of a single entity that is one in number, but can be divided and segmented *ad infinitum.* Instead, it is a [simple] oneness, to which there is no comparison whatsoever. This second fundamental principle is alluded to in the verse:[71] "Hear Israel, God is our Lord; God is one."

The third fundamental principle[72] is the negation of all material properties from His Being; i.e., that this oneness is not a body, nor physical power. Nor may any of the functions of the body. e.g., movement or rest, be ascribed to Him, neither innately nor circumstantially. Therefore, our Sages negated the possibility of joining [anything to] Him or separating anything [from Him]. They said:[73] "[To Him cannot be ascribed] either sitting or standing, either separation or combination." The word עיפוי, which they used, means "combination," as reflected in the verse,[74] ועפו בכתף פלשתים, which means that they will all join shoulders together to displace the Philistines.

[In reflection of God's uniqueness,] the prophet says:[75] "To whom will you liken God," and "'To whom will you compare Me, that I should be his equal,' says the Holy One."[76] If He had a body, He could be compared to other bodies.

All the descriptions of Him in physical terms - e.g., walking, standing, sitting, speaking and the like - found in Scripture are all borrowed terms and analogies. As our Sages said:[77] "The Torah spoke in the language of men." This concept has been spoken about at length. This is the third fundamental principle that is reflected in the verse:[78] "You did

---

71. Deuteronomy 6:4.
72. See *Hilchot Yesodei HaTorah* 1:7-12. (See also *Hilchot Teshuvah* 3:7, where the Rambam states that anyone who considers God in corporeal terms is a heretic, who does not have a portion in the World to Come. If God could be compared in any manner to energy and matter as we know them, He could be neither one nor perfect.)
73. *Chaggigah* 15a.
74. Isaiah 11:14.
75. *Ibid.* 40:18.
76. *Ibid.* 40:25.
77. *Berachot* 31b. The Rambam is employing this expression for a slightly different purpose from that of the Talmud. The Talmud uses this expression as an explanation why the Torah uses certain stylistic techniques - e.g., the repetition of words. The Rambam is saying that not only the style, but also the content of the Torah's words was chosen to fit the terminology man could understand and relate to. See also the Guide for the Perplexed, Vol. I, Chapter 26.
78. Deuteronomy 4:15. This verse refers to the revelation at Sinai.

not see any form" - i.e., you did not see Him as having a form, because - as mentioned above - He possesses neither a body nor physical power. The fourth fundamental principle is [His] primeval existence - i.e., that this unified Being exists above all concepts of time. All other existence, by contrast, cannot be considered to be independent of time. There are many texts that bring proofs to this concept. This fourth principle is indicated by the verse:[79] "The abode of the eternal God."

[Know that one of the great fundamentals of the Torah of Moses is that our world is a new entity, created and formed by God out of absolute nothingness. One of the reasons I put so much emphasis on (the negation of the concept of) the world existing before time, as (some of) the philosophers maintain is because (the creation of the world from nothingness) proves God's existence absolutely, as I explained in the Guide for the Perplexed].[80]

The fifth fundamental principle is that it is fitting to serve and exalt God and publicize His greatness and the obligation to serve Him. This is not true of all the [spiritual] beings on a lower rung than He - the angels, the stars, the heavenly spheres, the elements - or any combination of them. For all of these entities have been given a specific nature according to which they conduct themselves. They have no authority, nor choice; these are the sole province of God, blessed be He.

Nor should these entities be considered as intermediaries through which one can reach God. Instead, we should direct our thoughts to Him alone, disregarding any other entity. This is the fifth fundamental principle, the warning against the worship of false divinities.[81] Throughout the Torah, there are commands forbidding this.

The sixth fundamental principle is prophecy - i.e., to know that among mortals there will be individuals with heightened sensory potentials

79. Deuteronomy 33:27.
80. The bracketed portion is taken from Rav Kapach's text of the Rambam's Commentary on the Mishnah. It is a later addition that the Rambam wrote on the margin of his copy of this work.
81. The negation of the worship of other entities is mentioned in *Hilchot Yesodei HaTorah* 1:6. (See also *Hilchot Avodat Kochavim*, Chapter 1, which explains different conceptions of why other entities should be worshiped, and why these are false approaches.)
   The negation of other gods is considered a principle of faith, not merely a prohibition, because when one has a conception of God as the perfection of being, utterly one and above time, it follows that it is impossible that there be another being comparable to Him in any way.

and highly developed characters. When they concentrate their minds, they are able to receive the pure form of intellect, and fuse mortal intellect with the active potential for intellect, from which they will derive sublime influence. These are the prophets, and these are their attributes.

The explanation of this principle in its entirety would require substantial elaboration [and that is not the purpose of this text]. Its goal is not to explain all the details of each fundamental principle, but rather to mention them in a general manner. [Many] verses in the Torah speak of prophecy.[82]

The seventh fundamental principle is the supremacy of the prophecy of Moses our teacher.[83] This includes the belief that he is the master of all the prophets, those who preceded him and those who followed him; they are all beneath his level. He was the chosen of all mankind, who perceived more about God than any other person who has existed or who will exist. He attained the highest level of greatness above all humanity; he comprehended the level of the angels, and indeed, attained their level.

There remains no veil that he did not rend. Nothing hindered him, no physical impediment, nor did any of the spiritual shortcomings, neither to a small or to a great degree. His powers of imagination and all the aspects of his powers of sensation were negated entirely. The element that governs stimulation[84] was overwhelmed; all that remained was the power of intellect. Concerning this, it is written that he spoke to God without the intercession of the angels.

---

82. The Rambam develops the concept of prophecy in *Hilchot Yesodei HaTorah* 7:1-5. (See also the Introduction to the Commentary on the Mishnah; *Shemonah Perakim*, Chapter 7; and the Guide for the Perplexed, Vol. II, Chapters 36-46, where the Rambam outlines his conception of prophecy.)

The importance of prophecy as a fundamental principle of faith is that prophecy bridges the gap between man and God. Since God is infinite and unbounded, perfect on a level totally above that of man, there is no way that man can establish a connection with Him on his own initiative. The initiative can, however, be taken by God, and this is accomplished through prophecy.

83. The supremacy of Moses' quality of prophecy is described in *Hilchot Yesodei HaTorah* 7:6 and 8:1. (See also *Shemonah Perakim*, Chapter 7; and the Guide for the Perplexed, Vol. II, Chapter 35.)

Singling out the uniqueness of Moses' prophecy as a separate principle of faith is important as a preparation for the next two principles: that the Torah in its entirety is of Divine origin, and that it is immutable in nature. Had Moses not reached the ultimate peak of prophecy, he would not have been fit to convey this revelation.

84. See *Shemonah Perakim*, Chapter 1.

At this point, I would have liked to elaborate upon a marvelous concept, which explains the inner meaning of the Torah's verses, interpreting the phrase:[85] "Mouth to mouth I speak to him," and the other concepts contained in that verse. Nevertheless, I saw that these concepts were very abstract, and they need lengthy explanation and many prefaces and analogies. First, it is necessary to explain the nature of the existence of the angels and their different levels before God. And it is necessary to explain the nature of the soul and its powers. The scope of the discussion would then expand to touch on the forms the prophets have ascribed to the angels and to the Creator, entering the concepts of *Shi'ur Komah*.[86] Even one hundred pages would not suffice to explain the concept, even when writing in a most concise form. Therefore, I will leave it for [a more appropriate] place: the book explaining the Sages' homilies that I intend to write [mentioned previously], or the the Book of Prophecy that I have begun writing,[87] or another text that I will write to explain these fundamental principles.

To return to this seventh fundamental principle: There are four differences between the prophecy of Moses and that of the other prophets:

a) God would speak to all the other prophets by means of an intermediary, but He would speak to Moses without an intermediary, as alluded to in the phrase: "Mouth to mouth I speak to him."

b) All the other prophets would receive visions only when asleep, as reflected in several verses [that mention visions coming]: "in a dream at night,"[88] "[when] he dreamed,"[89] "in a dream, in a vision at night."[90] And there are many similar references.

Alternatively, they would receive their visions by day after the prophet fell into a trance. In this state, his senses ceased to function,

---

85. Numbers 12:8.
86. This refers to an early kabbalistic text that is part of the *Heichalot* literature, and which is regarded with reverence by the kabbalists. In his later days, the Rambam took objection to the anthropomorphic references in the book and maintained that its authorship could not be ascribed to the Sages, and that it was Greek in origin. In the later edition of his Commentary on the Mishnah, he struck out the reference to this text.
87. See the notes concerning this text in *Shemonah Perakim*.
88. Genesis 31:24.
89. *Ibid.* 30:10.
90. Job 33:15.

and his thought became empty, as during sleep. This state is called vision or revelation, as reflected in the verse[91], which describes "the revelations of God."

To Moses, by contrast, prophecy would come during the day, while he was standing between the two *cherubs*, as God promised him:[92] "And I will commune with you there and speak to you." And God said [to Miriam and Aaron, comparing their prophecy with that of Moses]:[93] "If one receives prophecy from God, it is in a vision that I make Myself known to him; I speak to him in a dream. This is not true about Moses."

c) When another prophet will receive prophecy, despite the fact that it is through a vision and through the medium of an angel, his powers will become faint, he will collapse, and he will be overcome with great fear as if he were going to die. As Daniel stated when [the angel] Gabriel spoke to him in a vision:[94] "No strength remained within me; my appearance was ravaged. I could not retain any strength.... I was in a deep sleep, flat on my face, with my face to the ground." And it says,[95] "Because of the vision, it is as if labor pains have come upon me."

This is not true about Moses. God's word would come to him, and he would not be daunted at all. This is alluded to in the verse,[96] "And God spoke to Moses face to face, as a person would speak to his friend" - i.e., just as a person does not feel trembling when speaking to a friend, so Moses was not at all in dread of the Divine word; it was communicated to him "face to face." This is because of his powerful bond with the active intellect, as we explained.

d) None of the other prophets could receive a vision at will, but only when God desired. There were prophets who would remain several years without receiving a vision. And there are times when a prophet would seek a vision, but it would be days or months before it would come. And at times, it did not come at all.

Similarly, we see that the prophets would prepare themselves by making their hearts joyful and by refining their thoughts, as did Elisha, as it is written:[97] "And now, bring a minstrel for me." Through this

91. Ezekiel 8:3.
92. Exodus 25:22.
93. Numbers 12:6-7.
94. Daniel 10:8-9.
95. *Ibid.* 10:16.
96. Exodus 33:11.
97. II Kings 3:15.

he received prophecy. And it is not necessarily true that whenever [a prophet] prepared himself he would receive prophecy. Concerning Moses our teacher, by contrast, [he would prophesy] whenever he desired, as reflected by his statement:98 "Stand and I will let you know what God commands you." And on the verse,99 "Tell Aaron your brother: 'Do not enter the holy chamber at all times,'" our Sages commented: Aaron was enjoined not to enter at all times, but Moses was not so enjoined.

The eighth fundamental principle is that the Torah is from heaven, that we should believe that the entire Torah that we possess today is the Torah that was given to Moses, and that it is of Godly origin in its entirety. [The Torah as a comprehensive whole] was granted [to Moses] by God. The manner in which it was granted to him we call - by analogy - speech.100

The only one who knows the nature of this process of communication is Moses, the one to whom it was granted. Nevertheless, metaphorically he can be compared to a scribe taking dictation, writing down all the events that took place, the stories and the mitzvot. For this reason, he is referred to as101 "the scribe."

And thus, there is no difference between the verses: "And the sons of Cham were Kush, Mitzrayim, Put and Canaan,"102 "And his wife's name was Meheitav'el, the daughter of Matred,"103 and "Timna was a concubine,"104 and "I am God your Lord,"105 and "Hear Israel, God is our Lord, God is one."106 All is from the Almighty; all is His perfect Torah, pure, holy and true.

---

98. Numbers 9:8. This refers to the instance when men who were impure asked whether there was a possibility of them compensating for their inability to offer the Paschal sacrifice. Moses could not answer them, and he brought the question to God, confident that he would receive an immediate reply.
99. Leviticus 16:2. The interpretation mentioned by the Rambam is found in the *Sifre* commenting on that verse.
100. I.e., Moses did not hear God talking as one hears another human being. Nevertheless, the term speech serves as an appropriate metaphor for the communication of the Torah's wisdom to him.
101. Numbers 21:18. The term literally means "the engraving," for at that time letters were engraved with a stylus on clay tablets. See also Deuteronomy 33:21.
102. Genesis 10:6.
103. *Ibid.* 36:39.
104. *Ibid.* 36:12.
105. Exodus 20:2.
106. Deuteronomy 6:4.

Menasheh was considered by our Sages as one who denied God, and a non-believer, worse than any others, only because he thought that the Torah possessed a husk and a core, and that the narratives and stories [it contains] are of no value, being Moses' own statements.[107] This is an example of one who says "the Torah is not from heaven."

Our Sages state:[108] "To anyone who says that the entire Torah originated from God, with the exception of a single verse that Moses himself wrote, is applied the verse,[109] 'He defamed the word of God.'" May God be blessed and uplifted above those who deny Him.

Instead, every letter in the Torah contains wondrous knowledge, as appreciated by one to whom God has granted understanding. The scope of its wisdom cannot be grasped. "Its measure extends beyond the earth and is wider than the seas."[110] A person should pray [for such knowledge] as did David, the anointed of the God of Jacob, who pleaded:[111] "Open my eyes and let me behold the wonders of Your Torah."

Similarly, the interpretation of the Torah transmitted by tradition also stems from the Almighty. The manner in which we make a *sukkah, lulav, shofar, tzitzit, tefillin* and the like is exactly the same as God told Moses, who communicated it to us. He was merely a messenger, carrying out a mission, which he performed faithfully. The verse that reflects this eighth principle is:[112] "With this, you shall see that God sent me; it is not of my own initiative."

The ninth principle is that the Torah of Moses will never be nullified. There will never come another Torah aside from this. There will be no additions to this, nor any deletions from it - neither in its text nor in its explanation.[113] And thus, we are commanded,[114] "Do not add to

107. See *Sanhedrin* 99b.
108. *Ibid.* 99a.
109. Numbers 15:31.
110. Job 11:9.
111. Psalms 119:18.
112. Numbers 16:28. Significantly, the Rambam does not mention this eighth principle in *Hilchot Yesodei HaTorah*. It is, however, reflected in the beginning of the Introduction to the *Mishneh Torah*, and the punishment given a person who impugns this principle is mentioned in *Hilchot Teshuvah* 3:8.
113. The standard published texts of the Commentary on the Mishnah state: "That the Torah of Moses was received from God and from no other being." It is possible that the difference stemmed from a misunderstanding of the Rambam's Arabic, or more probably from censorship. This principle, quoted in *Hilchot Yesodei HaTorah* 9:1 and *Hilchot Melachim* 11:3, was challenged by Christianity and Islam, faiths that accepted

it or detract from it." We have already explained what is necessary regarding this fundamental principle in the introduction to this text.[115] The tenth fundamental principle is that God knows the deeds of men and has not forsaken them.[116] This runs contrary to those who say,[117] "God has abandoned the earth." Instead, [the correct approach is reflected] in the verse:[118] "Great in counsel, mighty in deed, whose eyes are open on the ways of men." And it is written,[119] "And God saw that man had performed great evil in the world," and "the outcry of Sodom and Amorah is great."[120] These all reflect this tenth fundamental principle.

The eleventh fundamental principle is that God grants a generous reward to those who observe the mitzvot of the Torah, and punishes those who transgress its prohibitions. The ultimate reward is the World to Come, and the ultimate punishment is *karet*. We have explained this principle sufficiently [above].

This principle is reflected in [Moses' dialogue with God]:[121] [Moses said:] "Will You bear with their sin? And if not, blot me out of Your book." God replied: "It is the one who sinned against Me [whom I will blot out]." This shows that He knows who serves Him and who sins, and He will grant a generous reward to the one, and punishment to the other.

The twelfth principle is the era of the *Mashiach*[122] - i.e., to believe

the authenticity of Moses' law, but explained that it could be superseded by a new law revealed to later prophets.

The Rambam rejected these claims in his writings and in his letters to Jews throughout the world. The gentile authorities, however, controlled the printing presses and struck the more obvious references to this principle from the Rambam's works.

114. Deuteronomy 13:1.
115. I.e., the Introduction to the Commentary on the Mishnah. There the Rambam states that if a prophet claims to have received a vision from God telling him to alter one of the Torah's mitzvot, one should know that his prophecy is false.
116. Unlike the former principles, which describe God's Being and His communication to man, this and the following principle focus on the manner in which God responds to man's conduct. This is basic to Judaism, for Judaism is not merely a theoretical exposition of God's greatness, but more importantly, a guide for man's conduct, showing him how to express Godliness in his life and in his surroundings.
117. Ezekiel 8:12. See the Guide for the Perplexed, Vol. III, Chapter 17.
118. Jeremiah 32:19.
119. Genesis 6:5.
120. *Ibid.* 18:20.
121. Exodus 32:32-33.
122. See *Hilchot Melachim*, Chapters 11 and 12, which elaborate on the coming of the *Mashiach*.

earnestly that the *Mashiach* will come, and not to say that the time for his coming has passed. Instead, if he tarries, wait for him.[123]

One should not attempt to interpret the verses of Scripture in an attempt to calculate the time of his coming. Indeed, our Sages said,[124] "May the spirit of those who calculate the time [of the Redemption] expire." Instead, one should have faith in his greatness and his love, and pray for his coming, as has been prophesied by all the prophets from Moses until Malachi.

A person who does not believe in the *Mashiach* or who belittles these matters denies the Torah, which promises that he will come - in the passages of Bil'am and in the reading *Attem Nitzavim*.[125]

Included in this fundamental principle is the concept that there is no king in Israel except one who has descended from David and Solomon.[126] Whoever disputes this family's right denies God and the words of His prophets.

The thirteenth fundamental principle is the resurrection of the dead, which we have already explained.

When a person believes in all these fundamental principles and has earnest faith in them, he accepts upon himself his Jewish identity. We are obligated to love him, have mercy upon him, and to conduct ourselves in relation to him in all the paths of love and brotherhood

---

The *Mashiach's* coming and the resurrection are not merely continuations of the previous principle - that God will reward man for his good deeds; there is a deeper intent. It is in the era of the *Mashiach* - and more so, in the era of the resurrection - that the ultimate purpose of the world's existence will be manifest. We will realize the Godly nature of our existence and express it in our lives. The belief in the existence of such an era is fundamental to our faith.

123. Cf. Chabbakuk 2:3.

124. *Sanhedrin* 97b.

125. These are the two proof-texts cited in *Hilchot Melachim* 11:1. There the Rambam interprets Numbers 24:17-18, which include the verse: "A star shall go forth from Jacob, and a staff shall arise in Israel," as a reference to the *Mashiach*. The passage from *Attem Nitzavim* refers to Deuteronomy 30:3-5, which begins "And God your Lord will return your captivity and will have compassion on you."

126. See *Hilchot Melachim* 1:7. The mention of Solomon appears to be directed against

commanded by God.[127] Even if he transgresses several sins because of his desires or because of the overpowering influence of his evil inclination, he still retains a portion in the World to Come. He is considered to be one of the sinners of Israel, and he will be punished according to the severity of his transgressions, [but his share in the World to Come is not forfeited].

When, by contrast, a person will dispute one of these fundamental principles, he steps beyond the circle [of our people], and denies the essence [of our faith]. He is called a heretic, an apostate and one who uproots the saplings [of our belief]. We are obligated to hate such a person, to destroy him; concerning him is applied the verse,[128] "Behold: those who hate You, O God, will I hate."

I have elaborated extensively, going beyond the scope of this text. I did this because I saw that this would bring great benefit, [and strengthen many people's] faith. For I have collected many beneficial concepts that were scattered throughout many great works. Take pleasure in [my words]. Contemplate them thoroughly. If your mind tries to deceive you by telling you that you have understood the matter after a single reading - or even after ten readings - God knows that you have been deceived.

Do not read this text hurriedly. I did not write it casually, but instead did so after much contemplation and reserved thought, concentrating on [differentiating between] correct principles and incorrect ones, with the intent of reaching a conclusion concerning what our beliefs are, and clarifying the supports for each particular matter. I have asked God to guide me in the path of truth.

the Christians, who maintain that Jesus descended from David's family, but not from Solomon.
127. The Rambam is referring to Leviticus 19:18: "Love your neighbor as yourself," which our Sages explain refers to all Jews, but excludes from this obligation to love those individuals who forsake the ways of our people. The Rambam is saying that a person who accepts these fundamental beliefs is included as part of our people even if certain dimensions of his conduct are unworthy.
128. Psalms 139:21.

184

Appendix C

אָמַר רַבִּי חֲנַנְיָא בֶּן עֲקַשְׁיָא: רָצָה הַמָּקוֹם לְזַכּוֹת אֶת יִשְׂרָאֵל, לְפִיכָךְ
הִרְבָּה לָהֶם תּוֹרָה וּמִצְוֹת, שֶׁנֶּאֱמַר: ה' חָפֵץ לְמַעַן צִדְקוֹ, יַגְדִּיל תּוֹרָה
וְיַאְדִּיר.

Rabbi Chanania ben Akashya said:[1] The Holy One, blessed be
He, wished to make the people of Israel meritorious; therefore, He
gave them the Torah and its mitzvot in abundant measure, as it is
written:[2] "God desired, for the sake of his [Israel's] righteousness, to
make the Torah great and glorious."

He gave them Torah and mitzvot in abundant measure - One of the
fundamentals of [our] faith in the Torah is that if a person observes the
613 mitzvot in a proper manner, as is befitting, without intermingling
a [selfish] intention for the matters of this world, but instead performs
[the mitzvot] for their own sake, out of love, as I explained,[3] this will
enable him to acquire the life of the World to Come.

Therefore, Rabbi Chanania said that because there are many mitzvot,
it is impossible that a person will not perform [at least] one each day
in a perfect manner, and thus merit to grant his soul life through that
deed.

This fundamental principle is reflected in the story of Rabbi Chanania
ben Teradion,[4] in which he asked: "What is my status concerning the
World to Come?"

He was answered,[5] "Have any deeds presented themselves to you?"
- i.e., have you had the opportunity of performing a mitzvah in a
befitting manner.

Rabbi Chanania answered that he had been granted the opportunity
to perform the mitzvah of charity in the most complete manner possible.
Through this, he attained [a portion in] the World to Come.

[The *mishnah*] interprets the proof-text as meaning that God desired
to make Israel righteous. For this reason, He made the Torah great
and glorious.

1. *Makkot* 3:16.
2. Isaiah 42:21.
3. See the Rambam's commentary on the beginning of the tenth chapter of *Sanhedrin*.
4. *Avodah Zarah* 18a.
5. By Rabbi Yosse ben Kisma.